Memory Resident Programming on the IBM PC

Memory Resident Programming on the IBM PC

Thomas A. Wadlow

Addison-Wesley Publishing Company, Inc.

Reading, Massachusetts • Menlo Park, California • New York
Don Mills, Ontario • Wokingham, England • Amsterdam • Bonn • Sydney
Singapore • Tokyo • Madrid • Bogotá • Santiago • San Juan

Many of the designations used by manufacturers and sellers to distinguish their products are claimed as trademarks. Where those designations appear in this book, and Addison-Wesley was aware of a trademark claim, the designations have been printed in initial caps or all caps.

Library of Congress Cataloging-in-Publication Data

Wadlow, Thomas A.
     Memory resident programming on the IBM PC.

     Includes index.
     1. IBM Personal Computer–Programming. I. Title.
QA76.8.I2594W334   1987   005.265   87-3571
ISBN 0-201-18595-2

Printed in the United States of America. Published simultaneously in Canada.

Cover design by Doliber Skeffington Design.
Text set in 12 point Almost Computer Modern from TEX files.

ABCDEFGHIJ-HA-8987
First printing, August, 1987

This book is dedicated to all the people
who taught me to look under the hood,
especially my Dad.

I would like to acknowledge the contributions of several people who helped with this book. First, to my family who put up with me sitting in the basement over Christmas, typing like mad. Peggy Watt, who dug up answers when I needed them. Karri Dubbleman and John Bruner, who put up with my sometimes silly questions. Amy Atkinson, Judy Weinstein, and Thia Kellner Hill, who listened to my complaining. And of course, Steve Stansel, Ted Buswick, and the folks at Addison-Wesley, who got me started on this project in the first place.

–Tom Wadlow

Contents

Chapter 1

Looking under the Hood

In a book about programming, it's often a temptation to leap right into the code and hope that the reader will soak up the important points as the programs unfold. That approach does work sometimes, because the best way to learn to program is to actually create programs. Reading code written by other programmers is a good way to pick up new techniques, in exactly the same way that a musician becomes a better composer by reading and playing works by other composers. But musicians, or programmers, studying the works of others in their field, have already developed a great deal of insight into how problems are solved. They know that certain approaches to problems will probably work, and others may not. They know why these techniques are successful or unsuccessful. They may not know everything, but they know enough to get started.

Some people have learned to program, with moderate success, simply by repeating strings of incantations that they have memorized but don't really understand. This is a fine approach, as long as you can be sure every detail you need is written down somewhere or you can find someone who can answer your questions. When you step across the boundary between what is well known and what is not completely understood, memorization does not give you the skills to look around and find the correct path to your destination.

Some people have learned to fix automobiles, with moderate success, simply by tightening bolts, or replacing hoses, or doing other things they have learned without really understanding. You might expect such a person to adjust a carburetor, but you would not expect them to replace that carburetor with a more efficient one of a different design. That step requires another level of knowledge about cars. You need to know *why* carburetors work, not just how.

This book is written for people that want to look under the hood of their IBM Personal Computer. There are certain things you can do to soup up your PC, to make it do more in the specific areas that will be of use to you. This isn't an introductory book, it assumes that you have some basic knowledge of assembly language programming. This book is not a cookbook approach to programming. There are examples, and you may choose to assemble and run them, but the way to get the most out of them is to take the examples apart and put them back together again, slightly differently each time, and see what happens.

The code in this book is written with two things in mind: clarity of design and readability. The programs are not optimized for speed or size. You may read through them and say: "I could have done that with five fewer instructions." Please feel free to do so. This code is not necessarily robust. There is no guarantee that everything works all the time. That isn't the purpose of this software. You should look at everything here suspiciously, saying to yourself: "What happens if....?" Look for reasons why alternate approaches were *not* taken. If, after reading this book, you can figure out how to rewrite some of the programs to be faster, cleaner, smaller, or more useful, then the book has served its purpose.

1.1   Getting Inside the Box

If you look through an introductory book on computer programming, you are sure to find a section on the difference between *applications* programming and *systems* programming. Applications are programs people write to solve a more-or-less well-defined problem. For example, you might want to sort a file of names alphabetically, or calculate the value of π, or crack the Data Encryption Standard. Systems programming is somewhat different in nature and philosophy. Your computer has a nucleus of programming which is always present. Those programs provide a set of services to enable you to run the applications that you choose. They also provide housekeeping functions that permit those applications to be written fairly easily and run on a variety of machines. In other words, the systems programs manage resources and the application programs exploit those resources. Systems programs are permanent; applications programs are transient. Systems programs take care of the resources of the computer; applications programs actually use those resources.

The resource-manager/resource-exploiter view of computer programming is a fairly popular one, and has served well over the years. But it is only a model of what the designers of a system had in mind, not an iron-clad law. Certainly all computers have systems code, and they may run applications code, but on a personal computer, why must there be such a sharp and inconvienient division of the two? Why can't you have an application that is permanent, such as a pop-up appointment calendar? You may want some kinds of applications to be at your fingertips at all times. The conventional model of applications and systems software does not permit you to do that on a machine such as the IBM PC.

A personal computer differs from other kinds of computers by one major point. It is *personal*. It is yours, and you are allowed to do what you can with it. Buying a personal computer is like buying a tract house. When they are built, all the houses in a development are of a set of similar designs. But when you buy a house, it becomes your personal house, and you can furnish it as you please. After a time you may find that you need to remodel a bit, adding a room or removing a wall, so that it meets your needs better than the generic model you originally purchased.

1.2 Solving Problems

The mere fact that you are capable of remodeling your house is not a good reason to do so. You should think carefully before ripping out a wall; likewise, you should apply equal care to adding features to your computer operating system. A great new whizbang feature that you add in one area could have side effects in other places you might not even suspect. It is very much like knocking out a wall that you didn't suspect was load-bearing. You may regret it later.

The kinds of programs you want to add to an operating system are those functions that will:

- *Be available no matter what else you may be doing.* The changes to your system do not come for free. Every feature you add will cost you something in performance, or available memory, or disk space. New features should be worth the price.

- *Cut down the work you do to solve a common problem.* After all, there is no point in adding a function that makes you work harder to solve a problem that you could solve quicker and easier in a more conventional manner.

Adding an operating system routine to calculate π might be an interesting programming exercise, but it would not make you more productive, nor would it be something you would be likely to use frequently. You want to find those operations that you repeat, and reimplement them in a way that helps your work flow more easily.

- *Allow you to do things that were difficult to do in any other way.* Sometimes there is just no way to get the information that you need from a conventional application. If you want to know how your telecommunications program has configured one of your serial ports, you'll have to figure it out while the communications program is running. The act of leaving the program destroys the information you need.

1.3   The Nature of Good Design

Quality is always a difficult thing to pin down and precisely define. Everyone wants to write a "good" program, as opposed to a "bad" one, but the actual definition of "goodness" in programs is hard to come by. Every time you think you've gotten a handle on what makes a program "good," somebody comes up with an example that contradicts your theory. Nevertheless, it should be possible to come up with some guidelines for building good programs, while minimizing the amount of philosophical tail-chasing and without actually turning this chapter into *"Zen and the Art of Computer Programming."*

One attribute of a good program is that it does what it is supposed to do. A program that does not work correctly is not a good program, no matter how beautifully the code is written. In addition to doing what it is supposed to do, a good program should do *absolutely nothing else*. A program that lists the contents of directories correctly but writes random blocks of garbage on the disk while it does so is less than useless; it is actively harmful.

One of the best ways to ensure that a program has the fewest possible side effects is to clearly define a goal for that program. Make it do one and only one thing, and do it perfectly. "Creeping featurism" is a common disease among computer programmers. There is a powerful temptation to add just a little more power to a program or to handle a special case just a little differently. Sometimes "creative" programming is necessary, but it can almost always be avoided by rethinking the problem. It might be possible to make your pliers do the work of a screwdriver, but there is probably a better solution to the problem.

Another aspect of a good tool is flexibility. The mark of a well-designed tool is its ability to be useful in a situation the designer hadn't thought of. The analogy between system software and tools is an important one. When you make an addition to an operating system, you should think of it as getting another tool for your toolkit. If you have the correct set of tools, the problems you want to solve will become easier for you to solve. That is the whole point of getting the tools in the first place. If you don't have enough tools, then you'll have to approach your problems in a way appropriate for those tools you do have. In other words, if you have only a hammer, then you tend to treat all problems as nails. Sometimes this works; sometimes you just break what you are trying to fix.

Having too many tools can be just as bad. One of the nice things about using a computer to solve problems is that once you have an adequate solution to a particular kind of problem, you can package your solution, and never worry about it again. The machine now knows how to do what you want, and all you have to do is remember to ask it to do so. Having a wide variety of tools with overlapping functions may mean that you solve variations on the same problem over and over without recognizing the areas they have in common. This is a waste of your time and your computer's power.

1.4 Writing Debuggable Programs

An application program enjoys the benevolent protection of an operating system during its entire life. When the application breaks or encounters a situation that the applications programmer didn't think of, the system code is usually there to pick up the pieces.

The life of a system program is more dangerous. Since it is the system code that catches mistakes or prevents them, a system bug can be far more devastating than one in an application. In addition, even if the code works correctly, it may be very difficult for the programmer to find out what is happening, since the act of printing a debugging message may depend on the code being debugged. For instance, if you are replacing the system code that gets a character from the keyboard and it breaks, don't expect to type `Control-C` to make things work again. You have broken the entire system and you'll have to reboot. If you are changing the code that does I/O to the disk and it breaks, you may not be *able* to reboot, because you've written over the bit of code on the disk that performs that function.

- *Don't get tricky.* This is also known as "Don't reinvent the wheel." Once you figure out a way to do something correctly, keep doing it that way. Consistency is a good way to save time and energy. It may not be as interesting to write a loop the same way each time, but it will certainly be more likely to work.

- *Don't guess, measure.* Many people make the mistake of optimizing code for speed, or size, before they know whether or not it really works. If you do something once, quite often it doesn't matter how fast it runs. If you are sorting a list of twenty things, a simple sort algorithm will probably work just about as fast as a fancy one. You are much more likely to make the simple one work quickly. The time you save in the cases where it doesn't matter will more than make up for the few cases in which you must go back and optimize.

- *Don't get tricky.* You may understand a piece of code perfectly now, but will you be able to read it in two months, when you have to fix or extend it? Doing things in the most obvious fashion possible will often be a blessing months later or when you are trying to debug it.

- *How do you get to Carnegie Hall? Practice.* Rehearsal is a much bigger part of a musician's life than the performances. Don't write programs where everything needs to work at once. If you *can* debug a piece of code as an application before you put it in your operating system, then do so. If you are writing a pop-up text editor, for example, you might try writing it as a text editor application first and worry about the pop-up part later.

- *Don't get tricky.*

- *Write in modules.* Approach the problem as if you were a diamond cutter. If you hit the problem in just the right way, you'll find that it splits into several clear-cut modules, and maybe just a bit of leftover dust. Hit it wrong and you'll end up with a lot of dust and loose ends that you'd probably rather not deal with. Don't duplicate your efforts if you can possibly avoid it.

- *Don't get tricky.* Sometimes you can "rough-code" an application as a prototype by simplifying portions of your problem. You can simulate the input or the output or the algorithm. Get things to work with known parameters, then write the code that lets you specify different parameters. There is no need to write the program all at once. By writing it in chunks and making each chunk work separately, you'll get to a working program much faster. Besides saving time by prototyping, you are quite likely to find things that you didn't think of in the first place.

- *Expect to do it twice.* It's quite likely that you'll need to write a complicated program at least two times before you get it entirely correct. By making a completed, working prototype and then redesigning it from scratch for the final version, you have a much better chance of really understanding all the issues involved. Your second design should be much cleaner and much easier to write. If you don't go through this second phase, you may find yourself stuck with the shortsighted mistakes of the first.

- *Dare to be lazy.* One of the most useful characteristics that a programmer can develop is "creative laziness," the ability to spot repetitive tasks, and come up with a way of automating them. Each task you can encapsulate within a shell of programming leaves you with more time to move on to other more creative or profitable pursuits. The danger here is one of spending a hundred hours automating a task that cost you only one hour per month. Jobs like that may be fun, but they are not really worth the time. Repetitive things you do often are fair game, however.

Each person develops a style of solving problems when creating computer programs. Like a style of writing or a style of painting, your programming style will evolve. But facets of it will remain the same. Many veteran programmers have had the odd experience of picking up an old program listing and recognizing their own style without remembering that they had written the code. The programs you write are fingerprinted with your thoughts and moods at the time they are written. A good style is probably the most valuable tool a programmer can develop.

A program can be a kind of "living poetry" if you take the time and trouble to write it correctly. A good programmer writes beautiful code, and a great programmer writes beautiful code quickly. Both write code that works.

Chapter 2

Fundamental Arcana

If you have never written any program for your IBM PC, and you are sensible enough to avoid ever doing so, this is not the book for you.

If you have written some regular programs in Pascal, or C, or FORTRAN, but have never heard of assembly language and are curious, give it a try. If you get into trouble, don't get discouraged. Turn to Appendix D, which lists the books that were invaluable in writing this one. Try looking for answers in some of the books mentioned there. Answers may be tough to dig up but the search is usually worthwhile.

If you have written any sort of assembly-language program, even one that just prints "Hello, world", dig in and have fun. You have the basics already, and that ought to be enough.

This book is not *Introduction to Assembly Language Programming on the IBM PC*. That book has been written by several other people, under several other titles. Some of those titles are listed in Appendix D. You'll need an assembler and an assembly-language reference manual to try any of the code in this book. You'll also need good typing skills or a few bucks to buy the disk that goes with this book. And of course, you'll need an IBM PC, or its equivalent.

This book can be read in one of two ways. You can sit down, read through the chapters, and when you are done, go off and play with the programs. Or you can read and play at the same time. This book is as much about designing and creating good programs as it is about writing memory resident programs. You'll probably have a lot more fun if you can sit in front of the keyboard, drink too much coffee, swear at the typos (yours and mine), and wonder why your machine crashed *this* time. That is how the book was written, and I had a wonderful time.

2.1   The Basics

Even though this isn't a primer for assembly language programming, it can't hurt
to spend a little time on the basic concepts. Any computer has a fundamental
set of instructions that it understands. These basic operations are usually quite
simple, being along the lines of `MOVE THE NUMBER 6 INTO THE AX REGISTER` or
`IF THE ZERO FLAG IS SET, CONTINUE EXECUTING AT ADDRESS 1234`. Obviously,
the machine does not understand these sentences as fundamental operations.
Instead, each kind of operation is assigned a unique pattern of bits. The circuitry of the computer was designed to read successive bit patterns from memory,
and take some action based on these patterns. The actions themselves are quite
simple, but if you put enough of them together, you get a program that actually
does something.

By learning to think like the computer, you could actually learn to write
these bit patterns directly into the computer's memory and thus create programs
that way. It's not impossible. Tens of thousands of programmers have done it.
It's not even difficult, when compared to climbing mountains or understanding
quantum electrodynamics. But it does take a long time to learn, and it takes a
long time to write programs that way.

Long ago, some poor, overworked programmer who actually had learned
to write in bits decided to write a program so that others wouldn't have to
master that arcane skill. This program was called an *assembler*, and it took
such English-like commands as `MOV AX,6` and automatically turned them into
the correct set of bits. Early assemblers were often riddled with bugs and painful
to use. But even so, they were a great deal better than writing programs the
old way. And even a lousy assembler can be used to write a better one. Good
assemblers can be used to write even higher-level languages. Or assemblers for
new computers.

Why write in assembly at all, then? Wouldn't higher-level languages be
better? Well, yes and no. For many kinds of programs, assembly language is
a waste of time. But for others, it is essential. Why? The answer lies in the
trade-offs. Trade-offs are a big part of this book, and for good reason. They
are a very big part of the creation of any program. Programs don't just appear,
they are designed. Any program is the end product of hundreds, even thousands,

of design decisions. A few of these are big, most are very small. Every time a designer makes a choice, there is a trade-off, a compromise. Sometimes, the choice is obvious, and the trade is a good one. But sometimes it is a matter of choosing the lesser of two evils, or the greater of two goods. Or more than two. Sometimes *many* more than two.

When a programming language is being designed, the choices made will affect the kind of programming that can be done in that language. For example, a designer who chooses to create a portable language (one that can run on a large number of very different computers) may omit some features, such as direct access to physical memory or linkages to interrupt handlers, that some special programs (such as the ones in this book) might require. The designer may decide that portability is more important than access to those features. This decision means that some kinds of programs, such as memory resident programs, will not be written in that language.

One way of thinking about computer programming languages is in layers. There are many different types of languages, some very low level, some very high. Many times, you'll find that one kind of language (a C compiler, for example), turns its input into a program in another language (assembler, in this case). The layers of languages draw upon each other for support and power. As you ascend through each layer, writing some kinds of programs becomes easier, others more difficult. The most flexible is the arcane language of the bits. Slightly less flexible is a well-written assembler, and so on up the scale. If you want to write a program and are having a hard time figuring out how to trick the language you are using into letting you do what must be done, one approach is to get closer to the raw bits by using a lower-level language.

Assembly language is the best choice for the kind of programming we will be doing. It is flexible enough to allow us to use the machine to our advantage, readable enough so that we need not make a career out of learning bit patterns, and fast enough to permit us to get the job done without wasting too much time. Sophisticated assembly programs can be made small enough to be left resident without eating a major portion of our limited memory space.

2.2   The 8086/8088

The IBM PC is built around a microprocessor, the Intel 8088. This device is a smaller version of the Intel 8086. From a programming point of view, the two are virtually identical. The difference lies in their internal architecture. The

8086 requires a 16-bit-wide channel to the rest of the world. Memory access is done 16 bits at a time. Older 8-bit microprocessors required half the number of paths, half the number of chips, and so on. They also had much less than half the computing power. IBM chose the INTEL 8088 as a compromise, halfway between 8-bit and 16-bit machines. The 8088 could be programmed as an 8086, but it spoke to the world through an 8-bit-wide path. This compromise traded speed of execution for hardware cost; 8088-based systems could be built with fewer parts, but they took longer to run programs. IBM deemed this a wise choice, and the PC was born. As hardware costs dropped, other systems with real 8086s began to appear. Processor speed increases, but the software remains the same.

2.2.1   Registers

The 8086/8088 architecture is fairly simple. The machine has a fair number of general purpose 16-bit registers, in particular AX, BX, CX, DX, BP, SI, and DI. Of these, AX, BX, CX, and DX can be used not only as word registers, but can also be split into high and low byte registers: AH, AL, BH, BL, CH, CL, DH, DL. Registers BP, SI, and DI are general purpose, but cannot be split into bytes. SP is available for general use, but typically is used only as the stack pointer. There are also four very important special registers called *segment* registers: CS, DS, SS, and ES. And of course, there is an extremely special-purpose register called *the* IP *or instruction pointer. This register controls which instructions are being executed by the microprocessor.*

The 8086 was designed to be somewhat compatible with the Intel 8080 class of 8-bit microprocessors. These machines had a maximum address space of 64 kilobytes, which is all two bytes, or 16 bits, can represent. Rather than have an address size of 16 bits (a single word), which was what the 8-bit machines had, or 32 bits (two single words), as some more expensive machines use, Intel chose a different approach. Programs would run within a *segment.* Each segment would be a maximum of 64 kilobytes, but there could be more than one segment in memory. For example, the operating system could run in one segment, user programs in another. Within these segments, it would be possible for programs to treat the machine as though it had only 64 kilobytes of address space. This would make the transport of programs from 8-bit machines easier. Furthermore, segments might overlap, so that two different programs could share the same space in memory. Intel chose the *paragraph* as a fundamental unit of segment space. Changing a segment pointer from 0700H to 0701H would advance that segment by 16 bytes (one paragraph) in memory. In effect, the segment is a 16-bit address shifted 4 bits to the left (multiplied by 16, in other words) in a 20 bit field. Thus, the 8086 can directly address only 20 bits, or one megabyte of memory. Of this megabyte, the top 320 kilobytes is reserved by IBM for things like system ROM, cartridge ROM, and display memory. This makes the actual amount of memory for programs 640 kilobytes.

There are four segments that the machine, and anyone writing programs for it, has to worry about. First is the code segment, contained in CS. This segment is the one in which the code is actually executing. Second is the data segment, in DS. When a program tries to read something from memory as data and a segment is not explicitly specified, the processor will look in the data segment. Third is the stack segment, in SS. PUSH and POP stack operations will be done with this segment. Last is the auxiliary segment, in ES. This is a sort of general purpose segment register, for use at the programmer's discretion.

Many computers are designed so that all registers can be read and written in exactly the same ways. Computer architects call these *orthogonal* designs. The 8086, however, was not designed this way. Access to some registers is restricted. For example, one can move immediate values, such as numbers, to any of the general-purpose registers but not to the segment registers. This means that setting BX to 6 can be done in a single instruction:

```
mov    bx,6
```

Setting DS to 6 requires two instructions, since segment registers can be set only from general purpose registers, not constants or other segment registers:

```
mov    bx,6
mov    ds,bx
```

You'll see code similar to this in the examples in this book.

2.2.2   Addressing Modes

Addressing modes are the keys to many sophisticated operations on a computer. The 8086 provides several: immediate, memory indirect; and register indirect.

Immediate. These are values that are represented directly, as numbers. The 6 used in the previous example is an immediately addressed value.

Memory Indirect. These are values that are contained at some address in the data segment. For example:

```
        mov     bx,foo

                .
                .
foo     dw      6
```

This would move the value 6, or whatever value the variable `foo` might be set to, into the `BX`.

Register Indirect. There are two kinds of registers available for this: Base and Index registers. Base registers are `BX` and `BP`. Index registers are `SI` and `DI`. In this mode, the register contains the address in the data segment in which the desired information is stored. For example:

```
        mov     ax,OFOOOH
        mov     es,ax
        mov     si,OFFFEH
        mov     dl,byte ptr es:[si]
```

This code will read the machine ID at location `F000:FFFE` by using the indirect mode through register `SI`. A register indirect reference can have at most one Index and one Base register. This provides an easy means for indexing in arrays, or data structures.

Addressing modes can be used in quite a few different combinations, many more than shown here. For the most part, these are the modes used in the programs in this book. See the IBM documentation for more information.

2.2.3   Flags

The 8086 has nine single-bit flags that indicate various conditions in the machine state.

`CF` (carry flag). Set to 1 if the arithmetic operation exceeds the correct length.

`PF` (parity flag). Set to 1 for even parity, 0 for odd parity.

`AF` (auxiliary carry flag). Same as the `CF`, except that it applies to the low-order 4 bits of the result. This is typically for 20-bit address computation.

`ZF` (zero flag). Set to 1 if the result of an operation is zero, 0 if the result is not zero.

`SF` (sign flag). Set to 1 if the high-order bit of the result of an operation is a 1, zero otherwise.

`TF` (trap flag). Puts the system into single-step mode. In this mode, the completion of each instruction generates a special trap.

IF (interrupt-enable flag). Set to 1 to enable recognition of external interrupts, zero to disable.

DF (direction flag). Used with looping instructions such as MOVS, MOVSB, MOVSW, CMPS, CMPSB, and CMPSW. If set to 1, these instructions will loop through incremented addresses. If set to 0, these instructions will loop through decremented addresses.

OF. (overflow flag). Set to 1 if a signed operation exceeds the correct word length, 0 otherwise.

For the most part, ZF and CF are the two flags used by the code in this book. (See the IBM documentation for a discussion of the others flags.)

All of the conditional branches used in this book are based on the ZF and CF flags. The ZF-based branches are all tests for a condition of zero. This is all of the typical logical operations done in a program, such as a test for equality or a counter running out. The 8086 has several types of branches that check the zero flag. Whenever possible the branches used here reflect the logical intent of the instruction rather than the actual condition. For example:

```
        cmp     ax,6
        jz      foo
```

means exactly the same thing as:

```
        cmp     ax,6
        je      foo
```

The last example conveys more of the *intent* of the program, however. It lets you know that control should be transferred when the AX register is equal to 6.

Another convention closely related to this one is the habitual use of compares, even when not strictly necessary. Once again, this is for clarity and for generality. The code

```
        dec     ax
        cmp     ax,0
        je      foo
```

could be replaced by the more compact

```
        dec     ax
        jz      foo
```

In some cases the number that we are comparing against might be any number, not just zero. The first case, in which we explicitly compare for a number, conveys that sense of generality. The second example does not. But that is a minor issue compared to readability. The first example is obviously decrementing a counter of some kind and branching when that counter has reached a certain value. The second example is a little more vague, so the code in this book tends to avoid using branches of this kind. There is nothing wrong with them; if you wish to rewrite portions of this code to take advantage of the saving in size, feel free to do so.

The other type of branch used here is based on the carry flag. This is very rare in the code in this book. Some DOS routines return a set or cleared CF as a signal of success or failure. A JC *(Jump if Carry Set)* or a JNC *(Jump if Carry Not Set)* does precisely what you might expect in that case.

2.2.4 Jumping Through Loops

Computers never get bored. That is one of the features that makes them so useful. It is easy to program a machine to perform the same task over and over again. In fact, it is vital that they do so. Looping is a basic control-flow mechanism for all programming languages. The faster a particular computer architecture can perform a loop, the better it is thought to be. Since looping is so useful, many machines, including the 8086, have instructions that specialize in loops.

All loop instructions use the CX register as a counter. A loop will continue until the CX counter has reached a particular value. Thus, the code:

```
        mov ax,0
        mov cx,4
next:
        add ax,6
        loop next
done:
```

is a simple way of multiplying two numbers by repeated addition. In this case, the LOOP decrements CX each time and then checks the value of CX. If CX becomes zero, control will fall through to **done**. If not, then control passes back to **next**.

The same thing could be accomplished with this code:

```
        mov ax,0
```

```
        mov cx,4
next:
        add ax,6
        dec cx
        cmp cx,0
        jne next
done:
```

There is a palette of LOOP instructions to choose from, ones that branch when the counter reaches zero, others that branch when the counter is not zero, and so on. These instructions allow you to repeat an arbitrary sequence of instructions, up to the local branching limit, over and over again. The local branching limit is the maximum number of bytes away from the current instruction that a conditional branch can transfer to. That limit is -127 to +128 bytes, which means that you can branch as much as 127 bytes back into code before the current instruction and up to 128 bytes forward into code after the current instruction.

The 8086 has a powerful looping instruction that permits you to repeat a *single* instruction over and over again. One of the most common cases of looping occurs while handling strings of bytes. For example, suppose that you wanted to move the contents of one 60-byte array to another. With the normal LOOP instruction you could do it using the code:

```
        mov si,offset source
        mov di,offset dest
        mov cx,60
mvloop:
        mov ds:byte ptr [di],ds:[si]
        inc di
        inc si
        loop mvloop
```

This is a fairly tight loop, but if this piece of code were critical, you would want to make it tighter yet. The 8088 provides several string move instructions that duplicate some of the pieces of this code. One way you could optimize the loop would be to use the special instruction MOVSB, which reduces the code to:

```
        mov si,offset source
        mov di,offset dest
        mov cx,60
        cld
mvloop:
        movsb
        loop mvloop
```

The CLD instruction clears the direction flag, DF. The string instructions change the values of the source and destination pointers in SI and DI. The direction flag determines *how* those pointers change. If the flag is cleared, via the CLD instruction, the pointers will be incremented, and successive addresses will move forward (low to high) through memory. Thus, CLD is the same as saying SET DIRECTION TO FORWARD. If the direction flag is set, via the STD, the pointers will be decremented and successive addresses will move backward (high to low) in memory. Thus, STD is the same as saying SET DIRECTION TO REVERSE.

On the 8086/8088, this tiny loop can be reduced even further. The 8086 provides a special repetition instruction that will reduce this loop to a single instruction. There are only certain circumstances in which the REP instruction can be used, and a special convention has been adopted for typing repeated instructions. Using that convention, the move loop can be tighted to:

```
        mov si,offset source
        mov di,offset dest
        mov cx,60
        cld
    rep movsb
```

2.2.5   Organization of Data within Memory

The 8088 is a byte-oriented machine with delusions of grandeur. The entire machine is based on an 8-bit byte-oriented memory structure, but the processor itself manipulates 16-bit words. Finding the right byte in memory can sometimes be a little tricky.

The memory of any machine is a vast array of cells. On many machines, those cells are a single byte wide. On others, they are 16 bits, or 32 bits. Some larger machines have cell widths that are not based on powers of two, such as a 36-bit word. But even though the size of the words may be different, these machines can all be classed into some general categories. If your machine can pick out a single byte from memory, without being forced to resort to loading an entire word and trimming away the extraneous bytes (assuming that the word size is different from the byte size, as it is on the 8088), that machine has a *byte-addressible* architecture. If you must fetch an entire word just to examine a single byte, your machine is said to have a *word-addressible* architecture.

The 8086/8088 is a byte-addressible machine. It is possible to directly address an individual byte in memory. For example, we could fetch the contents of a given byte in this fashion:

```
mov     si,1234H
mov     al,[si]
```

This would copy the contents of the byte at the location in the SI register (in this case 1234H) into the AL register. If we wanted to set that byte to 6, we might suspect that this code would do the trick:

```
mov     si,1234H
mov     [si],6
```

That code will generate an assembler error, because there is no way for the assembler to deduce if you want to set the byte at 1234H to the byte 06H, or the word at 1234H to the word 0006H. The size of the source and destination must be the same. In the previous example, the assembler knew that AL was a byte register. Thus, the pointer in SI must have been a pointer to a byte. In this case, because there is insufficient information to determine the size, the assembler will complain. The correct code would be

```
mov     si,1234H
mov     byte ptr [si],6
```

If we had said WORD PTR instead, we would have set a 16-bit quantity rather than an 8-bit quantity.

Suppose we had chosen to set the word at 1234H to be 0006H. Obviously, one byte in memory would be set to 00H and another would be set to 06H. But which ones? You could dig through manuals to find out, or you might skip ahead to see the answer, but if you do then you will have just simply read the answer. The best way to find out is to *check for yourself*. After all, the manuals might be wrong, eh? And if they are not wrong here, they might be wrong somewhere else.

A simple program to determine the placement of bytes within a word in memory would look like this:

```
cseg    segment para public 'CODE'
        org     100H
        assume  cs:cseg,ds:cseg

start:
        mov     bx,cs
```

```
        mov      ds,bx

        mov      ah,'H'
        mov      al,'L'
        mov      test,ax
        mov      si,offset test
        mov      al,[si]           ; First byte of test
        call     dchar
        mov      al,[si+1]         ; Second byte of test
        call     dchar
        ret

; Display the character contained in AL
dchar              proc     near
        push     ax
        push     bx
        mov      bh,1
        mov      ah,0EH
        int      10H
        pop      bx
        pop      ax
        ret
dchar              endp

test    dw

cseg    ends
        end      start
```

DCHAR is a utility routine that prints a single character on the terminal. (We will be seeing much more of that routine later; for now, simply treat it as a black box that does the right thing.) We build a word in **AX** that has as its high-order (bits 15-8) byte the ASCII character "H", and as its low-order (bits 7-0) byte the ASCII character "L". Then we store this in the data word **TEST**. Printing the individual bytes will determine their order.

The high-order byte is sometimes called the most significant byte, or MSB. The low-order byte is correspondingly called the least significant byte or LSB (You may also see the individual bits referred to with the terms most significant or least significant bit, terms which unfortunately have exactly the same acronyms.) Significance, in these cases, refers to numerical significance. The most significant bit of a word is the bit that adds the most numerically to its value. If you change the low-order bit, the magnitude of a word hardly changes at all. Changing the high-order bit results in the greatest possible magnitude change for a single-bit fluctuation. On the 8086/8088, the most significant bit is bit 15, or 2 to the fifteenth power. The least significant bit is bit 0, or 2 to the zeroth power. Bit 15 is also known as the leftmost bit, bit 0 the rightmost. Shifting a value to the right (without rotation) decreases the value by a factor of two. Shifting to the left will increase a value by a factor of two.

Some machines follow the exact opposite in philosophy. Bit 0 on the 8086 is the least significant bit. This makes the 8086 what is known as a *Little-Endian* machine. On other machines, bit 0 is the most significant bit. They are known as *Big-Endian* machines. These odd terms come from *Gulliver's Travels*, by Jonathan Swift, in which two kingdoms fight a war over which end of an egg should be cracked first, the big end or the little end.

Running this test program may surprise some people. Your intuition may tell you that you should see the string "HL". But what you get is "LH". This means that the 8086 stores the low-order byte *first*. We could recode the declaration of TEST as

```
test    db      ?       ; Low byte of register
        db      ?       ; High byte of register
```

This same pattern repeats itself in the storage of double words. A double word would be a 32-bit quantity. If we were to have in memory a double-word variable, containing perhaps the full address of some subroutine, we would declare it like this:

```
subaddr dd      ; A subroutine address
```

An equivalent representation might be

```
subaddr dw      ; Low word of address
        dw      ; High word of address
```

Finally, in individual bytes, we would see this organized as

```
subaddr db      ? ; Low byte of low word of address
        db      ? ; High byte of low word of address
        db      ? ; Low byte of high word of address
        db      ? ; High byte of high word of address
```

Pushing words onto the stack will cause them to follow this same convention. The code

```
mov     ah,'H'
mov     al,'L'
push    ax
```

will push the word in `AX` onto the stack. The `PUSH` operation means that the stack pointer, in `SP`, is decremented by 2, and the specified register is then stored at that location. Stacks grow toward low memory. You might suspect that the byte ordering would be reversed, but it is not. Examining the stack after execution of the previous example, you would find that the stack pointer `SP` pointed at the low byte (containing "L") and that `SP`+1 pointed at the high byte (containing "H").

2.3   Details of the 8086 Architecture

A good painter knows the feel of paint, the smell and the taste of it. By knowing every detail of the materials with which they work, artists can create within the bounds set by those materials. Sometimes, a great artist can transcend those boundaries and create works that merely good artists thought impossible.

We have seen the basic details of the canvas on which we will paint and the colors we have at our disposal. There is material for an entire book in the subtle variations of these details. Some information can be found in the Microsoft *Macro Assembler* manual. Other details can be found in the books mentioned in *Appendix D*.

Chapter 3

Interrupt Vectors

In many ways, the idea of a memory resident program is tightly coupled with the way the IBM PC handles interrupts. Hard and soft interrupts are the main mechanism of communication and control between an application program and the operating system. Thus, understanding how interrupts work on the IBM PC is a vital part of learning to write memory resident applications.

Interrupts are one of the fundamental ideas that make modern computers work. As the name implies, interrupts are short-term distractions to a computer that is doing other work. The processor suspends the work in progress in such a way that the job can be resumed later. Control is then transferred to a special program called an *interrupt handler*. The handler does something useful such as adding a character to the keyboard input queue or managing a disk I/O operation. When the handler has finished its task, it returns control to the interrupted program. The interrupted program is restarted in such a way that it may not even be aware of the interruption. When you run any application on the IBM PC, it is interrupted dozens of times per second, yet it seems to you as if the application has sole access to the processor.

Without interrupts, the processor in a computer system would have to examine the status of each and every device on the system over and over again. This technique is called *polling*. Writing the system code that would permit continuous polling and still allow user programs to run would be quite a bit more difficult than the code used on the interrupt-driven IBM PC. In addition to reducing the complexity of the code, interrupts manage the flow of information to and from the equipment connected to the IBM PC. In a polled system, the design of those peripheral components would be considerably complicated. Additional circuitry would be required to ensure that information is not lost between the time the processor last polled a device and the next time it is scheduled to do so. Because an interrupt-driven system can rely upon the central processor for a great deal of data management, it can be simpler in design.

It is not impossible to build sophisticated computer systems without interrupts, just more difficult and more costly. Many important systems have been designed around polling systems, including some military systems and some used in the space program. In the case of a desktop personal computer, however, there are overwhelming reasons for choosing an interrupt-driven architecture. Interrupt-based systems can be designed and built cheaper than polled systems. Each component can depend on the central processor to manage the flow of data rather than guarantee that data internally. Interrupt-driven systems are easier to program than polled systems, at both the systems and the applications level. Interrupt-driven systems are also more flexible than polled systems, especially for interactive applications.

If some unforeseen event hangs up a program running on a polled system (with an accidental infinite loop, for example), there may be little choice but to reboot, since the code that will reset the state of the system can never run. On an interrupt-based system, you may be able to force the termination of that program, perhaps by typing CONTROL-C, and recover without restarting from scratch. This is possible is because the CONTROL-C keystroke was processed by means of an interrupt handler, which suspended the execution of the infinite loop long enough to kill the program.

(A note about checking for CONTROL-C on an IBM PC. The IBM PC checks for CONTROL-C or CONTROL-BREAK in a somewhat unusual fashion. For reasons of its own, IBM originally wrote DOS to check for CONTROL-C only during I/O operations. Programs that did not perform I/O operations could not be interrupted. Later versions of DOS fixed this problem to a certain degree but for reasons of compatibility with older versions of DOS, some of the interrupt checking is optional. Consult the manual for your version of DOS to determine how far you can extend CONTROL-C checking.)

3.1   Interrupts Available on the IBM PC

The IBM PC has two basic kinds of interrupts. *Hard* interrupts are those generated by the devices physically connected to the microprocessor in the IBM PC, such as the keyboard, disk drives, clock, and so on. These devices are connected by means of an interrupt controller that arranges these interrupts in order of their importance and allows the IBM PC to manage these hardware signals effectively. *Soft* interrupts, sometimes called *traps*, are generated by programs running on the IBM PC. Although they are handled in exactly the same way as a hard interrupt, they are really requests for some operating system service rather than an indication of some condition in the hardware.

These are the interrupts available on the IBM PC, by interrupt number and vector address.

Number	Address	Function	Number	Address	Function
0H	000-003H	Divide by Zero	16H	058-05BH	Keyboard I/O Call
1H	004-007H	Single Step	17H	05C-05FH	Printer I/O Call
2H	008-00BH	Non-Maskable	18H	060-063H	ROM Basic Entry Code
3H	00C-00FH	Breakpoint	19H	064-067H	Bootstrap Loader
4H	010-013H	Overflow	1AH	068-06BH	Time of Day Call
5H	014-017H	Print Screen	1BH	06C-06FH	Get Control on BREAK
6H	018-01BH	Reserved	1CH	070-073H	Get Control on Timer
7H	01C-01FH	Reserved	1DH	074-077H	Video Initialization Table
8H	020-023H	Timer (18.2 per second)	1EH	078-07BH	Diskette Parameter Table
9H	024-027H	Keystroke	1FH	07C-07FH	Graphics Char Table
AH	028-02BH	Reserved	20H	080-083H	DOS Program Terminate
BH	02C-02FH	RS-232 Port 1	21H	084-087H	DOS Universal Function
CH	030-033H	RS-232 Port 0	22H	088-08BH	DOS Terminate Address
DH	034-037H	Hard Disk	23H	08C-08FH	DOS Control-Break
EH	038-03BH	Diskette	24H	090-093H	DOS Fatal Error Vector
FH	03C-03FH	Reserved	25H	094-097H	DOS Absolute Disk Read
10H	040-043H	Video I/O Call	26H	098-09BH	DOS Absolute Disk Write
11H	044-047H	Equipment Check Call	27H	09C-09FH	DOS Terminate/Stay Resident
12H	048-04BH	Memory Check Call	28-3FH	0A0-0FFH	Reserved for DOS
13H	04C-04FH	Diskette I/O Call	40-7FH	100-1FFH	Not Used
14H	050-053H	Serial Port I/O Call	80-F0H	200-3C3H	Reserved By BASIC
15H	054-057H	Cassette I/O Call	F1-FFH	3C4-3FFH	Not Used

Hard interrupts are rarely touched directly by an IBM PC user or applications programmer, unless special hardware is being used, or tighter control is required. The most commonly modified hard interrupt is the keystroke interrupt. Text editing programs in particular often need a more flexible way of dealing with the keyboard than that provided by IBM. For the most part, hard interrupts are of concern only to component designers and system programmers; several, in particular the keyboard and timer interrupts, are of use to a designer of memory resident applications.

Soft interrupts, on the other hand, are vitally important to anyone writing assembly-language programs, or even to programmers writing high-level code for the IBM PC. These interrupts are the gateway from applications code into the operating system of the IBM PC. It is through these doors that requests for system services and operations are performed; thus, for programs that want to do more than simply contemplate their binary navels, these operations are the key.

First and foremost among the software interrupts that are be of use to an assembly-language programmer is DOS `INT 21H`, the DOS Universal Function. This interrupt is a general-purpose call into DOS that permits the programmer to perform essentially any DOS operation directly.

The next most useful set of software interrupts are those provided by the ROM-BIOS (Basic Input Output System). These functions provide a basic set of operations for using the low-level services provided by the IBM PC, such as keyboard input, display output, and raw disk I/O.

(A note on using ROM-BIOS services. IBM does not license IBM standard BIOS ROMs for use by other manufacturers; in fact, it has actively prosecuted those "clone" manufacturers foolish enough to include a byte-for-byte copy of the IBM ROM in their products. Since the code in clone ROMs legally cannot be exactly the same as the code in an IBM ROM, the small differences may mean that code written to use the ROM-BIOS calls directly may not be portable between IBM and IBM-like systems. This is not always the case for DOS calls, as MS-DOS, which is very similar to PC-DOS, can be licensed by other manufacturers. Thus, programs using only MS-DOS calls on one MS-DOS machine are portable to practically all other MS-DOS machines, regardless of ROM type.)

3.2   The Keyboard Input Mechanism

A good example of the way interrupts work can be seen in the mechanism the IBM PC uses to read characters from the keyboard. Two different interrupts are used, one hard and one soft interrupt. When a key is struck, a signal is sent from the keyboard circuitry to the processor. This signal causes a hard interrupt, which triggers the low-level keyboard interrupt handler. This handler immediately reads the character from the keyboard hardware, and places it into a queue. If the queue is full, the handler causes the IBM PC to beep. After the character is queued or beeped, control returns to the interrupted program. When a program wants to read a character from the keyboard, it issues a soft interrupt. This routine examines the queue and returns the first character available on that queue.

This approach is extremely common in interrupt-driven systems. In a way, it is a shock absorber between the application that needs input and the actual details of the gathering of that input. It is a decoupling mechanism that separates the handling of the keyboard from a request for information from the keyboard. The same general approach can be used for any number of different types of input and output devices.

3.3 Replacing Interrupt Vectors

Interrupt vectors are stored in the first 400H bytes of IBM PC memory. Each vector is four bytes long and contains a pointer to the interrupt-handler code that should be executed when the interrupt occurs. The first two bytes contain the offset portion of the pointer, the last two contain the segment portion.

There are two ways to modify interrupt vectors. You can either set the interrupt-vector locations directly, or call the DOS service designed to set them.

3.3.1 Setting the Vector Directly

Since an interrupt vector is just a location in memory, the obvious way of setting an interrupt vector, for example, the keyboard vector, would look like this:

```
mov ax,0                        ; We can't move to ES directly
mov es,ax                       ; Use AX to clear segment register
                                ; Install offset of handler
mov word ptr es:24,offset keyboard
                                ; Install segment of handler
mov word ptr es:26,seg keyboard
```

In many cases, this code would actually work. Suppose, however, a key was typed *exactly* as this code was executing. Under the worst case, this would happen after the first MOV but before the second. During that time, the keyboard interrupt vector would be meaningless, and the keyboard interrupt could crash the machine. One obvious fix would be to disable interrupts, such as

```
mov ax,0                        ; We can't move to ES directly
mov es,ax                       ; Use AX to clear segment register
cli                             ; Disable interrupts
                                ; Install offset of handler
mov word ptr es:24,offset keyboard
                                ; Install segment of handler
mov word ptr es:26,seg keyboard
sti                             ; Enable interrupts
```

This approach would work in almost all cases. However, the `CLI` instruction does not suspend the NMI *(non-maskable interrupt)*. So this approach is adequate for every interrupt vector save that one. A slightly more complicated approach, useful for every vector *including* the NMI vector, would be this:

```
                                    ; Make a correct vector address
                                    ;   containing interrupt vector
        mov word ptr kbd-ptr[0],offset keyboard
        mov word ptr kbd-ptr[2],seg keyboard
        mov di,0                    ; Use DI to set ES to zero
        mov es,di                   ; Set ES to destination segment
        mov di,24                   ; Set DI to destination offset
        mov si,offset kbdptr        ; Set SI to source offset
        mov cx,2                    ; Set word count to 2
        cld                         ; Set direction to forward
        cli                         ; Disable interrupts
    rep movsw                       ; Copy the new vector
        sti                         ; Enable interrupts
        .
        .
        .
kbdptr  dd
```

In this code, `kbdptr` is a double word containing a pointer to the `keyboard` interrupt handler. The advantage of this somewhat more complicated approach is that at no time is the interrupt vector ever invalid. The `rep` operation repeats the `movsw` the number of times specified in `CX`, behaving as a single instruction. The NMI cannot occur within an instruction, and since the entire move is contained within a single instruction, it will be immune to any possible interrupt.

3.3.2   Using DOS to Set the Vector

Since safely setting an interrupt vector can be a somewhat tricky operation, DOS provides a special service for setting the value of an interrupt vector securely. If you limit yourself to using this service, you won't have to worry about the race conditions described earlier. DOS also provides a service for reading the value of an interrupt vector. Since this operation does not modify the state of the system, there is no danger at all in this, and thus a direct read is just as safe. A direct read, however, requires that you calculate the correct address for the interrupt vector. Since DOS already has resident code to do this for you, there is no sense in duplicating the effort.

To read the value of an interrupt vector (INT 16H *(keyboard I/O)* in this example) under DOS requires the use of INT 21H function 35H *(read interrupt vector)*. This function performs the calculation to get a vector address from a vector number and then returns the contents of that slot in the vector table.

```
old_keyboard_io dd                       ; A double word to hold the value
        .
        .
        .
        mov     al,16H                   ; The interrupt number to be read
        mov     ah,35H                   ; READ INTERRUPT VECTOR function
        int     21H                      ;   under DOS Universal Function
                                         ; Offset of interrupt handler
        mov     old_keyboard_io,bx
                                         ; Segment of interrupt handler
        mov     old_keyboard_io[2],es
```

The **old_keyboard_io** variable is defined as a double word, since we need both a segment and an offset to describe the correct location of the interrupt handler at any location in memory. Note the order of segment and offset within the four-byte range of **old_keyboard_io**. The offset must be placed in the first two bytes, and the segment in the last two. There is great intuitive pressure to reverse this ordering, but the architecture of the machine has a fixed idea as to how addressing information should be ordered, and the machine is the final judge of correctness in this case.

The following code sets the value of an interrupt vector (INT 16H *(keyboard I/O)*, in this example), under DOS:

```
new_keyboard_io         proc    far
        .
        iret
new_keyboard_io         endp
        .
        .
        mov     bx,cs                    ; Make DS point to the segment
        mov     ds,bx                    ; That our code is in (i.e. CS)
                                         ; DX holds offset to new code
        mov     dx,offset new_keyboard_io
        mov     al,16H                   ; The interrupt number to set
        mov     ah,25H                   ; The SET INTERRUPT VECTOR function
        int     21H                      ; under the DOS Universal Function
```

The new interrupt handler, **new_keyboard_io**, replaces the previous interrupt handler. **DS:DX** is a double word pointer to the new handler, with **DS** containing the segment of the new routine and DX containing the offset within that segment. Since this routine is located within the current code segment, we can simply copy CS (by way of BX, due to the limited interregister move instructions on the 8086/8088), into DS. Another possibility would have been to set DS to the segment of new_keyboard_io by use of the assembler SEG pseudooperation.

3.4   Examining the Interrupt Vectors

Since we are about to spend quite a bit of time poking about under the hood of the IBM PC, jostling the spark plug wires, and generally getting greasy, perhaps we should begin by acquiring a tool or two. One useful operation that we can perform immediately is to write a small application program to read and display the value of all the interesting interrupt vectors in the IBM PC.

Much of this book depends on your ability to create runnable programs from source written in IBM Macro Assembler. Turning a piece of source code, the human readable text representation of a program into an executable program takes three, well, actually two-and-a-half steps.

If we have an assembly source program called GLOP.ASM, from which we want to make an executable program called GLOP.COM, we must first run it through an assembler. All the assembly code in this book was written for the *IBM Macro Assembler* MASM, version 1.0. To assemble GLOP.ASM, at the DOS command prompt enter:

```
MASM GLOP;
```

The semicolon causes MASM to use several defaults. The output file, GLOP.OBJ, contains relocatable, unlinked machine code. MASM will not generate a listing file or a cross reference file.

The second step is to turn GLOP.ASM into an executable program. To do this, you must use the linker. All the programs in this book are linked with the *Microsoft Linker* LINK, version 2.2, which is included with DOS. To link a single object file, including no special libraries, at the DOS prompt, enter:

```
LINK GLOP;
```

The semicolon causes LINK to use several defaults. The output file, GLOP.EXE, is a general-format executable program. Link does not generate listing files, and no libraries are included.

The last step, although not necessary for all programs, is required for the assembly code shown in this book. The final step is to turn the general format .EXE file into the faster-loading and smaller .COM file. This is done with the EXE2BIN program. All assembly programs in this book are converted with the EXE2BIN program that comes with DOS. To convert GLOP.EXE into GLOP.COM, at the DOS prompt, enter:

```
EXE2BIN GLOP.EXE GLOP.COM
```

This creates a new file, GLOP.COM, which is much smaller than the original .EXE and which loads and starts faster. The original file, GLOP.EXE, remains untouched.

Developing a resident application takes some amount of trial and error. This means that you may find yourself typing these last three DOS commands over and over again. Since repetition is best left to a computer rather than fingers, the same result can be achieved with a small .BAT file:

```
MASM GLOP;
LINK GLOP;
EXE2BIN GLOP.EXE GLOP.COM
```

Conceivably, you could create a MAKE.BAT for each and every program that you care to develop. However, since the assembly language source in this book can be compiled using this same basic template, and changing only the names, the parameterization facility of .BAT files might be a bit more appropriate:

```
MASM %1;
LINK %1;
EXE2BIN %1.EXE %1.COM
```

DOS replaces %1 with the first argument of the command. Thus

```
MAKE GLOP
```

is an entirely adequate replacement for the previous special purpose MAKE file.
If you later want to create a MACRO.COM, then MAKE MACRO will work with no
changes.

With later versions of DOS, various error conditions can be detected and
execution of this .BAT file can be aborted, for example if the assembly fails.
This file should work under all versions of DOS. Ambitious programmers are
heartily encouraged to improve upon this foundation.

3.5   IVEC.ASM – Listing Interrupt Vectors

The IVEC.ASM program runs as a normal application and lists the current values
of the interrupt vectors in a form that fits on a single screen. On a generic IBM
PC with no resident applications installed, you'll notice that many of the vectors
appear to originate from the same set of segments. These are the ROM routines.
As you change handlers and rerun the program you'll see the changes appear in
the vector table.

```
cseg    segment para public 'CODE'
        org     100H
        assume  cs:cseg,ds:cseg
start:
        mov     bx,cs                   ; Make Data Seg be the
        mov     ds,bx                   ; same as the Code Seg
        call    vectors
        ret


        ; Scan through display table, printing two vectors per line
        ; If any record has an interrupt # = zero, this indicates
        ; end of the table.
vectors          proc    near
        mov     di,offset disptab       ; Pointer to start of table
        mov     dh,0                    ; Zero out top half of DX
vloop:
        mov     dl,[di]                 ; Get the interrupt number
        cmp     dl,0                    ; If it is zero, we are done
        je      vdone                   ;   so exit loop
        add     di,1                    ; Advance pointer 1 byte
        mov     si,[di]                 ; Get pointer to description
        call    dvector                 ; Call the display routine
        add     di,2                    ; Advance to the next record
```

```
            mov     dl,[di]                 ; Get the interrupt number
            cmp     dl,0                    ; If it is zero, we are done
            je      vdone                   ;   so exit loop
            add     di,1                    ; Advance pointer 1 byte
            mov     si,[di]                 ; Get pointer to description
            call    dvector                 ; Call the display routine
            add     di,2                    ; Advance to the next record

            call    dcrlf                   ; Print a carriage return
            jmp     vloop
vdone:
            call    dcrlf                   ; Print final CRLF
            ret
vectors endp

            ; Displays an interrupt vector.  Display is in the form of
            ; <banner>  <interrupt #> <seg>:<offset>
            ; where <interrupt #>, <seg> and <offset>
            ;  are all hexadecimal numbers.
;
            ; Call with
            ;       DX       - interrupt number
            ;       DS:SI    - pointer to banner string
dvector proc    near
            call    dstring                 ; Display the string in DS:SI
            call    dbyte                   ; Display the byte in DL
            call    dspace                  ; Display a space

            mov     al,dl                   ; Move the interrupt number to AL
            mov     ah,35H                  ; Function is GET INTERRUPT VECTOR
            int     21H
            mov     dx,bx                   ; Move BX to DX so we can display
            call    ddword                  ; double-word in ES:DX
            call    dspace                  ; Display a space
            ret
dvector endp

            ;       DS:SI points to ASCIIZ string to be printed
dstring proc    near
            push    si
            push    ax
dis:
            mov     al,[si]                 ; Fetch the next character
            cmp     al,0                    ; If it is zero, we are done
            je      disdone
```

```
        call    dchar               ; If not, print it
        inc     si                  ; Advance pointer to next char
        jmp     dis
disdone:
        pop     ax
        pop     si
        ret
dstring endp


        ;           ES:DX contains doubleword to be displayed
ddword  proc    near
        push    dx                  ; Save offset temporarily
        mov     dx,es               ; Move Segment to DX
        call    dsword              ; Display segment
        call    dcolon              ; Print a ";"
        pop     dx                  ; Restore offset to DX
        call    dsword              ; Display offset
        ret
ddword  endp


        ;           DX contains singleword to be displayed
dsword  proc    near
        push    dx                  ; Save low byte temporarily
        mov     dl,dh               ; Move high byte to low byte
        call    dbyte               ; Display high byte
        pop     dx                  ; Restore low byte to DL
        call    dbyte               ; Display low byte
        ret
dsword  endp


        ;           DL contains byte to be displayed
dbyte   proc    near
        push    ax                  ; Save any registers used
        push    dx
        push    si

        push    dx                  ; Save low nybble temporarily
        push    cx                  ; Save CX
        mov     cl,4                ; Set shift count to 4
        shr     dx,cl               ; Shift high nybble into low nybble
        and     dx,000FH            ; Mask out all but low nybble
        mov     si,dx               ; Use low nybble as index into
        mov     al,hextab[si]          ; hexadecimal character table
        call    dchar               ; Display character
        pop     cx                  ; Restore CX
```

```
        pop     dx                      ; Restore low nybble

        and     dx,000FH                ; Mask out all but low nybble
        mov     si,dx                   ; Use low nybble as an index into
        mov     al,hextab[si]              ; hexadecimal character table
        call    dchar                   ; Display character
        pop     si                      ; Restore registers
        pop     dx
        pop     ax
        ret
dbyte   endp

        ; Display a ":"
dcolon  proc    near
        mov     al,':'
        call    dchar
        ret
dcolon  endp

        ; Display a " "
dspace  proc    near
        mov     al,' '
        call    dchar
        ret
dspace  endp

        ; Display a Carriage Return/Line Feed
dcrlf   proc    near
        mov     al,0DH
        call    dchar
        mov     al,0AH
        call    dchar
        ret
dcrlf   endp

        ; Display the character contained in AL
dchar   proc    near
        push    ax
        push    bx
        mov     bh,1
        mov     ah,0EH
        int     10H
        pop     bx
        pop     ax
        ret
```

```
dchar    endp

hextab   db      '0123456789ABCDEF',0

disptab db      05H             ; Print screen
        dw      v05
        db      19H             ; Bootstrap loader
        dw      v19

        db      08H             ; Timer tick
        dw      v08
        db      1AH             ; Real-time clock
        dw      v1A

        db      09H             ; Keyboard input
        dw      v09
        db      1BH             ; CTRL-Break handler
        dw      v1B

        db      0BH             ; Comm. port 1
        dw      v0B
        db      1CH             ; Timer control
        dw      v1C

        db      0CH             ; Comm. port 0
        dw      v0C
        db      1DH             ; Pointer to video parameter table
        dw      v1D

        db      0DH             ; Hard disk controller
        dw      v0D
        db      1EH             ; Pointer to disk parameter table
        dw      v1E

        db      0EH             ; Floppy disk controller
        dw      v0E
        db      1FH             ; Pointer to graphics character table
        dw      v1F

        db      0FH             ; Printer controller
        dw      v0F
        db      20H             ; Program terminate
        dw      v20

        db      10H             ; Video driver
```

```
        dw      v10
        db      21H             ; DOS universal function
        dw      v21

        db      11H             ; Equipment check
        dw      v11
        db      22H             ; Pointer to termination handler
        dw      v22

        db      12H             ; Memory size check
        dw      v12
        db      23H             ; Pointer to CTRL-C handler
        dw      v23

        db      13H             ; Disk driver
        dw      v13
        db      24H             ; Pointer to critical error handler
        dw      v24

        db      14H             ; Communications driver
        dw      v14
        db      25H             ; Absolute disk read
        dw      v25

        db      15H             ; Cassette driver
        dw      v15
        db      26H             ; Absolute disk write
        dw      v26

        db      16H             ; Keyboard driver
        dw      v16
        db      27H             ; Terminate and stay resident
        dw      v27

        db      17H             ; Printer driver
        dw      v17
        db      2FH             ; Print spooler
        dw      v2F

        db      18H             ; ROM BASIC
        dw      v18
        db      0
        dw      0

v05     db      'Print screen:           ',0
```

```
v08      db       'Timer tick controller:     ',0
v09      db       'Keyboard input:            ',0
v0B      db       'Communication port 1:      ',0
v0C      db       'Communication port 0:      ',0
v0D      db       'Hard disk controller:      ',0
v0E      db       'Floppy disk controller:    ',0
v0F      db       'Printer controller:        ',0
v10      db       'Video driver:              ',0
v11      db       'Equipment check:           ',0
v12      db       'Memory size check:         ',0
v13      db       'Disk driver:               ',0
v14      db       'Communication driver:      ',0
v15      db       'Cassette driver:           ',0
v16      db       'Keyboard driver:           ',0
v17      db       'Printer driver:            ',0
v18      db       'ROM BASIC:                 ',0
v19      db       'Bootstrap loader:          ',0
v1A      db       'Real-time clock:           ',0
v1B      db       'Ctrl-Break handler:        ',0
v1C      db       'Timer control:             ',0
v1D      db       'Video parameter table:     ',0
v1E      db       'Disk parameter table:      ',0
v1F      db       'Graphic character table:   ',0
v20      db       'Program terminate:         ',0
v21      db       'DOS universal function:    ',0
v22      db       'Terminate vector:          ',0
v23      db       'Ctrl-C vector:             ',0
v24      db       'Critical error vector:     ',0
v25      db       'Absolute disk read:        ',0
v26      db       'Absolute disk write:       ',0
v27      db       'Terminate/stay resident:   ',0
v2F      db       'Print spooler:             ',0

cseg     ends
         end      start
```

Chapter 4

A Basic Resident Program

A journey of a thousand miles begins with a single step. That phrase has been used to refer to a lot of things, and assembly-language memory resident programming is one of them. To understand how to write a complicated resident application, you should begin, as they say, at the beginning.

In this chapter, we will write an extremely simple resident application, one of no practical use whatsoever, but one that encapsulates the basic features of more important and useful programs. The simplest possible resident application would just install itself and do nothing. This is basically what we intend to write here, but with an additional constraint. We want to be able to tell the difference between a trivial program that works, meaning that it is installed correctly, and a trivial program that fails quietly. To do this, we must complicate our simple program in such a way that we can determine whether or not it is installed and working.

Quite a number of trivial goals are available to us, if our only constraints are simplicity and detectability. The goals we choose depend on the kind of resident application that we choose to write. One of the simplest and most useful resident applications involves intercepting keyboard input and replacing the characters that were typed with characters of our own choosing. This type of application is easy to write and understand, yet the basic design can be extended to include the vastly more useful functions found in keyboard macro expanders, or input line editors.

Having decided on the basic structure, a keyboard input interceptor, we must decide on the method of detectability. Since we plan to intercept characters from the keyboard and to pass those characters, at our discretion, to DOS, one method of detecting the presence of our modifications would be to alter what the user types in a predictable fashion. If the alterations show up, our application was successfully installed. If they aren't present, something was wrong, either a flaw in the design or the construction.

A simple way to alter the input would be to detect a character and do something predictable when that character, and only that character, is typed. For example, we could design our application to detect the typing of a "Y" and replace it with a "#" when it is passed to DOS. An injudicious choice, however, would break the machine while the application was installed. In the case of the "Y" replaced by a "#", we would be unable to use the TYPE command while the application is resident. We would be breaking DOS deliberately to detect the presence of our resident application.

A better choice would be to alter something in a way that we could detect, but that would not break the operating system. Case shifting is a good example. If we shift the case of the "Y", returning a "y" instead, we can detect the presence of our application. DOS will not care if we use the "TyPE" command. Only a few programs, those in which case is important (such as word processors) will be affected. If we then add a few more lines of code, we can detect a "y" and return a "Y". Thus, we will not prevent any character from being typed, we simply complicate matters a little by reversing the sense of the SHIFT key for the "Y". Nothing is made unusable, but we can detect our success or failure.

4.1   A Simple Resident Application

A program is more than just a series of instructions that a computer can execute. It is a sort of frozen thought, a glimpse into the mind of the designer. A designer of machinery captures types of actions and encapsulates them in steel and plastic in such a way that the actions can be performed after the designer is no longer present. A programmer can capture certain types of ideas into a program in such a way that those captured thoughts can be systematically rethought after the programmer is no longer present. The meaning of all this philosophizing is a fact of writing programs: it's more important to worry about the way that *you*, the programmer, think about your program than it is to worry about how the computer thinks about it.

Books that discuss programming commonly present the source code for a program in a line-by-line fashion. If you talk with experienced programmers, however, you'll probably find that programs are never written line by line. Some programmers see their code as a tree of successively refined ideas, others as view it as a woven tapestry of threads of thought or a network of interconnected ideas. There are many different ways that you can model a problem in your mind, not all of them easily articulated. Building a mental model of a program is the first ninety percent of writing a program. Turning a well-formed idea into code is the next ninety percent.

The programs in this book were designed and written as a series of nested boxes within boxes. The outermost box is the requirements of making a working .COM program. Within that are two boxes, the code that makes up the application and the installation code that makes the application an extension of the operating system. Within each of those are functions within functions that make up the individual concepts of each segment of the program. When possible, the listings discussed in this and subsequent chapters will be shown in the perspective of the nested functions of the code.

4.2   A Basic .COM Program

The memory resident programs discussed in this book are all written to assemble into .COM programs. These programs are one of the two types of executable files that DOS understands. The .COM file is designed to load and begin execution quickly. Like most design choices, the trade-off necessary to achieve this speed of loading was in flexibility. The .COM format is limited in how the program can use the full power of the IBM PC. The .COM file is small, less than 64 kilobytes, and can load into only one segment. The more general, but slower loading form of executable file is the .EXE. The .EXE format can load into multiple segments and be larger than 64 kilobytes. It is possible to create resident applications that load in .EXE format, but typically this is more trouble than it is worth. Resident applications are usually much less than 64 kilobytes and usually need to be loaded at exactly the portion in memory that .COM files are loaded into. Thus, .COM-format executable files are the best choice for the envelope that surrounds a resident application.

The code that will assemble into a legal, working, empty .COM file looks like this:

```
                        ; section 1
cseg    segment
        assume  cs:cseg,ds:cseg
        org     100H
```

```
                                    ; section 2
start:
        ret
                                    ; section 3
cseg    ends
        end     start
```

This code can be broken down into three obvious parts. Section 1 defines the segment that the code will be relative to. It defines the assumptions that the assembler will make about the segment that the code resides in, and it defines the starting point of the executable code.

Section 2 is the actual code itself, in this case, simply a return statement to transfer control back to DOS. Execution begins at the **start** label.

Section 3 ends the segment and the program. The end statement contains a label name that refers to the address at which execution should begin. In this case, the **start** label is where we want the program to start.

If you assemble, link, and convert this minimum program, you might expect it to be 257 bytes long,–256 bytes of program segment prefix and 1 byte for the RET opcode. However, if you follow the sequence described above, you'll find that the .COM file is only 1 byte long. The reason for this is quite simple: all .COM files are loaded with identical program segment prefixes, and thus DOS does not need to save a copy with each .COM file. DOS automatically generates a correct program segment prefix in memory when it loads a .COM file. If necessary, a program can alter its program segment prefix during its run, but all .COM programs start with the same basic program segment prefix. All .COM program segment prefixes have the same format:

The Program Segment Prefix

Offset	Meaning
0000H	Termination Handler Address
0002H	Segment, end of allocation block
0004H	Reserved
0005H	Long call to MS-DOS function dispatcher
000AH	Previous termination handler vector
000EH	Previous CONTROL-C vector
0012H	Previous critical error handler vector
0016H	Reserved
002CH	Segment address of environment block
002EH	Reserved
005CH	Default File Control Block #1
006CH	Default File Control Block #2
0080H	Command tail and default Disk Transfer Area

4.3 A Minimum Resident Program

The minimum `.COM` file shown here is not yet a memory resident program. It is simply a DOS program like most others. This program loads at the beginning of available memory; when the program terminates, the memory this program it consumed will be freed for use by subsequent programs.

A basic program that terminates, but remains resident, looks like this:

```
                           ; section 1
cseg    segment
        assume  cs:cseg,ds:cseg
        org     100H
                           ; section 2
start:
        nop
done:
                           ; section 3
        mov     dx,offset done
        int     27H
                           ; section 4
cseg    ends
        end     start
```

The first and last sections of this code are unchanged from our minimum `.COM` program. The middle two sections are the interesting ones. Section 2 is the code that actually remains resident. In this case we simply leave a NOP as an empty resident application. In fact, any code that we put in between the **start** and **done** labels remains resident.

Section 3 is the part of the code that terminates this program, leaving it resident. In this case, we use INT 27H as the terminate and stay resident function. This function requires us to set a pointer to the first available location of memory, in effect setting where the next `.COM` file will load. If we had wished to do so, we could have used INT 21H function 31H *(keep process)*, which requires that we specify the amount of memory to reserve, rather than a pointer. That function has the advantage of being able to send an exit code to DOS. No exit code is generated by INT 27H.

INT 27H requires a pointer to the first available address for DOS to use to load subsequent programs. DOS contains a pointer to a base address used for loading `.COM` and most `.EXE` files. INT 27H resets this pointer to the new value, which makes all the memory between the old and new pointer values inaccessible to DOS for loading transient programs. It also makes this memory inaccessible to transient programs that either allocate their own memory directly as buffers or implicitly in their size. Thus, if you keep loading memory resident programs, you'll whittle away at the amount of memory available for normal programs.

The pointer to the next available byte of memory is a **FAR** pointer, meaning that it consists of an offset pointer, contained in **DX**, which points to a location within a 64-kilobyte range, and a segment pointer, contained in **DS**, which points to a paragraph-aligned segment within the 640-kilobyte address space of the IBM PC. **DS** need not be set explicitly, since **DS** is set to the same value as **CS** when the .**COM** file is loaded.

A common mistake in writing assembly language programs for the IBM PC is to confuse the preloading of **DS** with the **assume ds:cseg** statement in the assembler source. It is important to realize that the **assume** statements in assembler source have *absolutely no relation* to the value of the **DS** register or any other register. These statements produce no code whatsoever. Their function is to tell the assembler to make certain assumptions necessary to correctly assemble the code. For example:

```
cseg     segment
         . . .
         assume  ds:cseg
         mov     ah,radix
         . . .
radix    db      16
         . . .
cseg     ends
```

The type of move instruction generated when the assembler sees the **mov ah,radix** is directly related to the **assume ds:cseg** statement. With the **assume** pseudooperation, you tell the assembler to pretend that the data segment is in the current code segment, a key issue for memory resident programs. If the actual value of **DS** is not the same as the value of **CS** when this code is executed, this code will fail, despite the **assume** statements.

4.4   A Refined Resident Program

The code for the minimum resident program does nothing but take up space in memory. In fact, if you actually were to place useful code between **start** and **end**, you'd quickly find that it would be executed only once, at the time you ran the .COM initialization file. After that, the code would be permanently locked in memory, but inaccessible except by direct far jump to the **start** address. The actual value of the **start** address for this code is not fixed, but varies according to the state of the machine when the program was loaded. At this point we have created a small program that causes some code to be loaded into the appropriate area and retained, but we have not actually created a *resident application.*

The next step is to create a .COM program that executes the installation code at the time it is run, and install the resident code correctly without running it. To achieve this, we must modify the previous program in this fashion:

```
                              ; section 1
cseg    segment
        assume  cs:cseg,ds:cseg
        org     100H
                              ; section 2
start:
        jmp     initialize
                              ; section 3
app_start:
        nop
initialize:
                              ; section 4
        mov     dx,offset initialize
        int     27H
                              ; section 5
cseg    ends
        end     start
```

The first thing that this program does upon being run as a .COM file is to branch around the actual code of the resident application directly to the initialization code that correctly installs the resident application. Note that **done** has been changed to **initialize** and that the actual code of the resident application falls between **app_start** and **initialize**.

You may wonder why **initialize** is not made the starting address. The starting address of all .COM programs is 100H. In this program, **start** is located at 100H, but **initialize** is not. If you specify **initialize** as the starting address, which is done by putting it after the **end** statement (see the last line of the previous example, where the starting address was set to **start**), EXE2BIN tells you that the file cannot be converted. If you cannot make a .COM file, you must handle the segmentation issues directly.

4.5   Elimination of Memory Overhead

By now you may have noticed that nothing has been done about the program
segment prefix. Since we are basically advancing a pointer to the first available
byte of memory when we use INT 27H, anything below that pointer will be
retained including the program segment prefix of the .COM file used to start the
resident application. The last time the program segment prefix will be of any
use is while the .COM file is exiting, since INT 27H restores information from the
program segment prefix on exit. So we cannot get rid of the program segment
prefix until *after* the .COM file has exited.

   This interesting fact requires us to make another design choice. If the program segment prefix can be removed only after the .COM installation program
has exited, the program segment prefix must be removed by *resident* code. We
can do this by copying the entire resident application down in memory by 256
bytes. But how will this copying code be started? One way might be to set a flag
on loading that indicates whether or not the resident application has been run.
The first time the resident application is run, the copying code is invoked, and
the resident application relocated. However, what if the resident application is
not run for a long time after installation? What if a .COM file is running? What if
more resident applications have been loaded? These are important issues, which
may require some code to solve. If this code requires more than 256 bytes, it is
more cost-effective to waste the space taken up by the program segment prefix.
Some designers have implemented cost-effective solutions to this problem, but
they are usually quite subtle. For the most part, unless available memory is so
limited that 256 bytes becomes critical, you will probably make your programs
more readable and cleaner by simply ignoring the program segment prefix.

   Another bit of overhead is the `jmp initialize` instruction. These few bytes
are retained along with the program segment prefix and the resident application.
Once again it is a small price to pay, but if you are sufficiently interested in
removing this overhead, it can be done.

4.6   Invoking the Resident Application

Now that we know how to load code in memory and retain it after the initialization program has terminated, we must look at how our resident application
is to be called into service.

   Each memory resident program is invoked in a way that is closely related

to what it is designed to do. A keyboard input interceptor is quite likely to be
linked via the keyboard input soft interrupt or possibly the keystroke interrupt.
Other programs may involve linking to a sophisticated combination of interrupts,
timers, and system calls. These linkages may be established at any time, but
at least one must be established at the time the installation .COM shell is run.
If this first link is not established, the code will never be invoked to establish
more. Typically, all the necessary linkages are established at initialization time,
with the program simply responding to the linked events.

What is meant by the term *linkage*? An IBM PC is driven by events such
as keystrokes, timer ticks, or soft interrupt system calls. These events can be
intercepted, and actions can be performed based on these events. By linkage,
we mean the mechanism that causes *our* code to be run rather than the code
that came with the system.

In the case of the trivial keyboard input interceptor that we are designing,
the linkage will be to the keyboard input ROM system call. When DOS or an
application wants a character from the keyboard, it calls INT 16H. If we can
arrange to have our code called instead, then we can place a layer of code that
we can control between the application and the generic operating system. It
is this interposition of layers that is the fundamental mechanism of all resident
applications.

To install the linkage, we use INT 21H function 25H *(set interrupt vector)* to
replace the interrupt vector for the ROM system call with a pointer to our own
code.

```
cseg    segment
        assume  cs:cseg,ds:cseg
        org     100H
start:
        jmp     initialize
                                        ; Section 1
new_keyboard_io         proc    far
        sti
        nop
        iret
new_keyboard_io         endp
                                        ; End Section 1
initialize:
                                        ; Section 2
        mov     dx,offset new_keyboard_io
        mov     al,16H
        mov     ah,25H
```

```
        int     21H
                                        ; End Section 2
        mov     dx,offset initialize
        int     27H

cseg    ends
        end     start
```

In this version of the code, several important changes have been made. These changes are shown in Sections 1 and 2 of the listing.

In Section 1, we rewrote the portion of the code that makes up our resident application as a Macro Assembler procedure. This was done to aid readability. By making a procedure out of the special code that is to remain resident, it becomes distinct from the rest of the code in the program. A simple label at the beginning would have been just as effective, but not visually distinct.

Of greater practical importance, two instructions were added to our null resident application. The first of these is the STI *(set interrupt flag/enable interrupts)* instruction.

When an interrupt occurs, the hardware of the 8086/8088 turns off the flag that permits any further interrupts from being serviced. In effect, the system is giving its undivided attention to servicing the interrupt in progress. This devotion to duty is commendable and important, but it comes with a price. While interrupts are disabled, any hardware signals, such as keystrokes, timer ticks, disk signals, and modem interrupts will be ignored. If interrupts remain disabled, the system will lose valuable information, and things will begin to fail. Thus, while there may be a valid reason for operating for a time with interrupts disabled, this time is precious, and should not be squandered.

The second important instruction is the IRET *(return from interrupt)*. As RET is used to return from CALLed subroutines, IRET is used to return from interrupt handlers. IRET differs from RET only in that the CPU state flags are restored from the stack after the return address has been popped off the stack. These flags are pushed onto the stack by the interrupt mechanism built into the hardware. By restoring the flags to their previous state, IRET restores the interrupt enable flag to its previous state, thus reenabling interrupts. Strictly speaking, for the null resident application in this example, using an STI and an IRET is redundant. However, both instructions are crucial for real interrupt handlers, so for the sake of clarity, they both are shown here.

4.7 Chaining Interrupt Handlers

It is often more useful to replace part of an interrupt handler rather than replace the entire handler, as has been done in the previous example. If the code shown in the previous example was used, keyboard input would not be possible. Characters would continue to be read and queued by the hard interrupt handler until the keyboard input queue was filled. With the null resident application shown, no method of dequeuing characters is possible.

Suppose we want to install an interrupt handler that simply calls the original keyboard interrupt handler. Once we are capable of doing this, modifying the parameters or taking action based on the results of the existing code is easily within our power. We can sucessfully insert a layer of code under our control.

```
cseg    segment
        assume  cs:cseg,ds:cseg
        org     100H
start:
        jmp     initialize
                                        ; Section 1
old_keyboard_io dd
                                        ; End Section 1
new_keyboard_io         proc    far
        sti
                                        ; Section 2
        pushf
        assume  ds:nothing
        call    old_keyboard_io
                                        ; End Section 2
        iret
new_keyboard_io         endp

initialize:
        assume  cs:cseg,ds:cseg
                                        ; Section 3
        mov     bx,cs
        mov     ds,bx

        mov     al,16H
        mov     ah,35H
        int     21H
        mov     old_keyboard_io,bx
        mov     old_keyboard_io[2],es
                                        ; End Section 3
```

```
        mov     dx,offset new_keyboard_io
        mov     al,16H
        mov     ah,25H
        int     21H

        mov     dx,offset initialize
        int     27H

cseg    ends
        end     start
```

In Section 1, we created a place to store the value of the old vector. Since we were constrained to operate within a single segment, the data statements had to be in the same segment as the code. Of course, we should avoid inadvertently transferring control to these bits of data mixed in with our code.

Since it was not likely that the original interrupt handler would be in the same segment as our interrupt handler, we had to allocate a double word to contain the segment and the offset of the target handler.

There is no reason that this double word could not have been allocated at any convenient place in resident application memory. You may find it more convenient, however, to locate the double word immediately after the jump to the initialization code. By putting the address of the previous vector in a known location (the four bytes preceding the start address of the new handler) you make it easier to find with a debugger and, if necessary, by a program.

Section 2 is the body of the resident application, which consists of a simulated interrupt call to the old interrupt handler. Since any interrupt handler that you replace was designed to be called by an INT rather than a CALL, you must simulate the actions of the INT by first pushing the flags onto the stack with a PUSHF instruction.

The next line is an assembler directive, not an opcode. It tells the assembler to assume nothing about the data segment flag when generating subsequent machine code. This causes the assembler to generate the proper double-word address in the next instruction.

The CALL instruction transfers control to the old keyboard interrupt handler as if it were a subroutine. When this function is completed, it executes an IRET instruction and control returns to this code, just as a normal subroutine call would happen. By doing this, we can use the old function to do work for us, without giving up control. If we chose to, we simply could have JMPed to the old handler, without pushing the flags. Control would have left our code permanently, with the old handler actually returning from the interrupt for us.

Section 3 is the initialization code. Here, we determine the setting of the interrupt vector we are about to replace and squirrel that value away in a place that will remain resident, where the resident application can use it.

The first two lines of Section 3 actually copy the `DS` register from the `CS` register. The 8086/8088 has no instruction to copy one segment register to another, so this must be done through an intermediate register, in this case, `BX`. When the `.COM` file terminates, these register changes will be flushed; thus, we cannot count on them at the time our resident application is invoked.

We then use `INT 21H` function `35H` *(get interrupt vector)* to determine the value of the interrupt vector. This value is returned in two registers, with `ES` containing the segment of the old vector and `BX` containing the offset. These values are copied into the double word set aside for them. Please note that the offset precedes the segment within the double word.

Running this program should have no apparent effect on the behavior of DOS or any normal application. Keyboard input should behave normally.

`INT 21H` function `31H` is somewhat more modern than `INT 27H`, but it performs basically the same function. This function requires that you calculate the number of paragraphs (16-byte chunks of memory) that you wish to reserve. In addition, it also permits you to return an exit code. In the long run, you might be better off using it instead of `INT 27H`. In this book we stick with `INT 27H` simply because it is easier to use, is more obvious in function, and runs under a wider range of DOS versions.

4.8 Detecting Our Resident Application

Now that we have successfully insinuated our code between applications and what DOS does to read a character from the keyboard, we can begin to modify the results. In this example, we will simply be reversing the case on a single letter. Certainly it is trivial, but it also proves that modification can be performed successfully.

One design issue that must be resolved is that of duplication of function. Clearly, we are not interested in duplicating what DOS or the ROMs do to check the status of the keyboard. In fact, we are not even interested in intercepting that function. We are interested only in intercepting the read, `INT 16H` function `0H` *(read character)*. Since we can let the original handler manage functions other than the read, we must add a little code to let the ROMs (or whatever other handler might be in place) handle the other functions.

```
cseg    segment
        assume  cs:cseg,ds:cseg
        org     100H
start:
        jmp     initialize

old_keyboard_io dd

new_keyboard_io         proc    far
        assume  cs:cseg,ds:cseg
        sti
                                ; Section 1
        cmp     ah,0
        je      ki0
        assume  ds:nothing
        jmp     old_keyboard_io
                                ; End Section 1
                                ; Section 2
ki0:
        pushf
        assume  ds:nothing
        call    old_keyboard_io

        cmp     al,'y'
        jne     ki1
        mov     al,'Y'
        jmp     kidone
ki1:
        cmp     al,'Y'
        jne     kidone
        mov     al,'y'
kidone:
                                ; End Section 2
        iret
new_keyboard_io         endp

initialize:
        assume  cs:cseg,ds:cseg
        mov     bx,cs
        mov     ds,bx

        mov     al,16H
```

```
        mov     ah,35H
        int     21H
        mov     old_keyboard_io,bx
        mov     old_keyboard_io[2],es
        mov     dx,offset new_keyboard_io
        mov     al,16H
        mov     ah,25H
        int     21H

        mov     dx,offset initialize
        int     27H

cseg    ends
        end     start
```

Section 1 of this code detects whether the operation is function 0H *(read character)*. If it is not, control is transferred entirely to the old handler, which then deals with the other functions function 1H *(read keyboard status)*, and function 2H *(read keyboard flags)*. By doing a jump, rather than simulating an interrupt with a subroutine call, we let the original handler return from the interrupt for us.

Even though we have already reenabled interrupts, the original handler will perform this operation again. STI is not a toggle; it always sets the interrupt flag. Repeatedly setting the IF will have no unusual side-effects.

Section 2 of the code handles the case in which a read request has been detected. Here we must simulate an interrupt to the old routine by pushing the flags and then calling the old vector as a subroutine. In this case, we want control to return to our code before it returns to the program that generated the read request, function 0H *(Read Character)* (which returns its results in AL). The next few lines of code determine if it is the character we are interested in (in this case the "Y" or the "y") and modify that character by returning it with the opposite case.

This basic application could be called an existence proof. By running this code, we prove that it is possible to place a controlled layer of code between the operating system and the application. That layer can then selectively enforce or replace DOS functions, modifying the results to suit us. From this basic premise, we can move on to much more interesting applications and make deeper explorations into the workings of DOS.

Chapter 5

A Keystroke Expander

We can now build quite a variety of applications using the foundation of our basic resident application. The first few steps, which we have already taken, are the hardest. From here, we can find out what these techniques of resident programming are good for.

Given that we can construct a basic program that will replace one keystroke with another, perhaps the next step is a program that will replace one keystroke with a sequence of keystrokes. After all, how many times do you find yourself typing the same commands over and over again? If you could do the same work with fewer keystrokes, you could do something else with the time and effort you save, if only put your feet up on the table and sip coffee while the machine does the work. Dare to be creatively lazy.

Let's take another look at our minimal keyboard interrupt resident application:

```
cseg    segment
        assume  cs:cseg,ds:cseg
        org     100H
start:
        jmp     initialize


old_keyboard_io dd

new_keyboard_io             proc    far
        assume  cs:cseg,ds:cseg
        sti
        iret
new_keyboard_io             endp
```

```
initialize:
        assume  cs:cseg,ds:cseg
        mov     bx,cs
        mov     ds,bx

        mov     al,16H
        mov     ah,35H
        int     21H
        mov     old_keyboard_io,bx
        mov     old_keyboard_io[2],es
        mov     dx,offset new_keyboard_io
        mov     al,16H
        mov     ah,25H
        int     21H

        mov     dx,offset initialize
        int     27H

cseg    ends
        end     start
```

By changing just the **new_keyboard_io** routine, we can modify this code into a variety of keyboard applications. Since only **new_keyboard_io** will change, we need to list only the code involved with that routine, since the envelope of installation code remains the same. This will be the basis for our keystroke expander. Before we write that program, however, we must examine the problem and resolve several design issues.

First, of course, we must decide what kind of keystrokes to expand. Expanding a printing character, such as a letter or number, would make typing simple text quite an adventure. Expanding a control character ought to work, but DOS already interprets some control characters (for example CONTROL-H) as special operators. A set of characters that are used great deal with word processing programs, but rarely outside them, are the extended characters. Extended characters are used for such things as the function keys, and the ALT-keys. These characters are a good choice for expandable keystrokes. DOS identifies these characters by preceding them with a zero byte; thus, they are easily identifiable. By using extended characters, we will have essentially no impact on normal DOS programs and commands. By choosing carefully which extended characters to expand we will have a minimal impact on programs that make use of the extended character set.

The Extended Character Set

1		34	ALT-G	67	F9	100	CONTROL-F7
2		35	ALT-H	68	F10	101	CONTROL-F8
3	Pseudo-NULL	36	ALT-J	69		102	CONTROL-F9
4		37	ALT-K	70		103	CONTROL-F10
5		38	ALT-L	71	Home	104	ALT-F1
6		39		72	UpArrow	105	ALT-F2
7		40		73	PgUp	106	ALT-F3
8		41		74		107	ALT-F4
9		42		75	LeftArrow	108	ALT-F5
10		43		76		109	ALT-F6
11		44	ALT-Z	77	RightArrow	110	ALT-F7
12		45	ALT-X	78		111	ALT-F8
13		46	ALT-C	79	End	112	ALT-F9
14		47	ALT-V	80	DownArrow	113	ALT-F10
15	SHIFT-TAB	48	ALT-B	81	PgDn	114	CONTROL-PrtSc
16	ALT-Q	49	ALT-N	82	Insert	115	CONTROL-LeftArrow
17	ALT-W	50	ALT-M	83	Delete	116	CONTROL-RightArrow
18	ALT-E	51		84	SHIFT-F1	117	CONTROL-End
19	ALT-R	52		85	SHIFT-F2	118	CONTROL-PgDn
20	ALT-T	53		86	SHIFT-F3	119	CONTROL-Home
21	ALT-Y	54		87	SHIFT-F4	120	ALT-1
22	ALT-U	55		88	SHIFT-F5	121	ALT-2
23	ALT-I	56		89	SHIFT-F6	122	ALT-3
24	ALT-O	57		90	SHIFT-F7	123	ALT-4
25	ALT-P	58		91	SHIFT-F8	124	ALT-5
26		59	F1	92	SHIFT-F9	125	ALT-6
27		60	F2	93	SHIFT-F10	126	ALT-7
28		61	F3	94	CONTROL-F1	127	ALT-8
29		62	F4	95	CONTROL-F2	128	ALT-9
30	ALT-A	63	F5	96	CONTROL-F3	129	ALT-0
31	ALT-S	64	F6	97	CONTROL-F4	130	ALT-Hyphen
32	ALT-D	65	F7	98	CONTROL-F5	131	ALT-=
33	ALT-F	66	F8	99	CONTROL-F6	132	CONTROL-PgUp

Second, we must examine the kind of strings we will expand a keystroke into. For example, how do we terminate such a string, indicating the boundaries of the expansion? One possible choice might be a carriage return (standard ASCII code ODH). This would be a logical choice, since commands are normally terminated with a carriage return. However, if we choose this as a termination character, we cannot easily represent multiple line expansions. Another choice might be the $ character. Unfortunately, some DOS system calls use the $ as a string terminator. If we used the $ (or any other printing character) we could not incorporate that character into our expansion strings.

The C programming language has the convention that strings are terminated by a zero byte. This type of string is sometimes called an ASCIIZ (ASCII Zero-terminated) string by assembly-language programmers. By zero-terminating (sometimes called null-terminating) the strings, we can represent any printing

character, as well as all the nonprinting ASCII characters. Since there is no way
to enter a zero byte from the keyboard, there will never be a conflict between
the stored representation and the actual keystrokes for ASCII.

For the purpose of this first example, we will redefine the meaning of the `F1`
key (extended character 59), to have it generate a `DIR<CR>` command and list a
directory. Both choices are arbitrary. We could just as easily define `F1` to mean

```
MASM MACRO;
LINK MACRO;
EXE2BIN MACRO.EXE MACRO.COM
```

where each line is ended with a carriage return (`0DH`). We could have chosen
another character to expand.

Third, how is the information to be passed back to DOS? DOS normally
expects one keystroke at a time from the keyboard input queue. Somehow, we
must contrive to fool DOS into accepting a stream of characters in the place of
our single character.

DOS determines when a character is available for input by checking the
status of the keyboard. A subfunction of the keyboard input ROM call returns
a set (1) `ZF` if no characters are waiting and a cleared (0) `ZF` if a character
is ready. Obviously, it would be unacceptable to require a separate keystroke,
a space perhaps, for each matching character in the expanded string. If we
assume control of this subfunction, we can feed any number of characters to
DOS by repeatedly deceiving DOS into believing that a character is ready at
the keyboard and then simply returning a character from our stored stream
when the corresponding read is requested.

5.1 A Basic Expander

We can replace the empty `new_keyboard_io` routine with a new piece of code
that will intercept the functions that we require:

```
new_keyboard_io          proc    far
      sti
      cmp     ah,0                  ; A READ request?
      je      ksread
      cmp     ah,1                  ; A STATUS request?
      je      ksstat
      assume  ds:nothing            ; Let original routine
```

```
        jmp     old_keyboard_io      ; do remaining subfunction.
ksread:
        call    keyread              ; Get next char to return
        iret
ksstat:
        call    keystat              ; Get status.
        ret     2                    ; Important!!!
new_keyboard_io         endp
```

Using this routine, we place function 0H *(read character)* and function 1H *(get keyboard flags)* under our control. The code is straightforward, but there is one key portion that makes this entire application work. A keyboard status check returns its results by setting or clearing ZF. We have already discussed how the IRET instruction pops the flags, pushed by the interrupt, and thus restores them. Properly setting the value of ZF and then following with an IRET would be purposeless, since ZF would immediately be reset to the value it held before the interrupt. Thus, we must return from the interrupt *without* altering the value of ZF. This is done by using the optional parameter of the RET instruction.

The RET instruction has an optional argument that indicates the number of bytes to pop off the stack. Usually this is done when a subroutine in a high-level language has a number of parameters or variables that it wishes to flush off the stack when it returns. In this case, we want to flush the original flags from the stack so our altered set of flags can be returned instead. Any flags that have been changed in our interrupt handler will return to the interrupted program in their altered state, including the critical ZF flag.

```
        assume  ds:nothing

        ; If expansion is in progress, return a fake status
        ; of ZF=0, indicating that a character is ready to be
        ; read.  If expansion is not in progress, then
        ; return the actual status from the keyboard.
keystat         proc    near
        cmp     cs:current,0
        jne     fakestat
        pushf                        ; Let original routine
        call    old_keyboard_io      ; get keyboard status.
        ret
fakestat:
        mov     bx,1                 ; Fake a "char ready"
        cmp     bx,0                 ; by clearing ZF.
        ret
```

```
keystat          endp

          ;  Read a character from the keyboard input queue,
          ;  if not expanding or the expansion string,
          ;  if expansion is in progress.
keyread          proc    near
        cmp      cs:current,0
        jne      expandchar
readchar:
        mov      cs:current,0          ; Slightly peculiar
        pushf                          ; Let original routine
        call     old_keyboard_io       ; get keyboard status.
        cmp      al,0
        je       extended
readdone:
        ret
extended:
        cmp      ah,59                 ; Is this character to expand?
        jne      readdone              ; If not, then return it normally.
                                       ; If so, then start expanding
        mov      cs:current,offset string
expandchar:
        push     si
        mov      si,cs:current
        mov      al,cs:[si]
        inc      cs:current
        pop      si
        cmp      al,0                  ; Is this end of string?
        je       readchar              ; If so, then read a real char?
        ret
keyread          endp

          ;  Pointer to where we are in the expansion string
current dw       0

          ;  String we will return when an F1 is typed.
          ;  0dH is ASCII Carriage Return
string  db       'DIR',0dH,0
```

We have a pointer, current, that points to the next character to be returned
to DOS. If that pointer is zero, we are not expanding anything. If it is not zero,
then the pointed-at character is to be returned, unless that character is a zero
byte. If the pointed-at character is a zero byte, we must turn expansion off and
get a character from the keyboard. Both keystat, the status checking routine,

and `keyread`, the character-input routine have two halves, one side for when expansion is happening, (`current is not 0`), and one side for when it is not, (`current is 0`).

If expansion is not happening, the status routine simply calls the old keyboard routine to determine the state of the keyboard input queue. If expansion is happening, `ZF` is cleared, meaning that a character is available. `ZF` can be set or cleared by performing an operation whose result is zero or not zero, respectively. By setting `BX` to 1 and then comparing it to see if it is equal to zero, we are performing an operation whose result is guaranteed to be not zero (not equal/false). Thus, the zero flag is cleared. There are, of course, more clever, less bulky ways of ensuring that `ZF` is cleared. This way was chosen for clarity.

The character-input routine is by far the most complicated part of the whole program. This routine determines what the next character to be sent to DOS will be. If expansion is off, the older keyboard input routine is called to fetch the next character. When that character has been acquired, it must be checked to see if it is an expanded character. Normally, the character-input routine returns its results in the low byte of `AX`. `AL` will contain the ASCII character that was typed. If an extended character, such as a function key or an ALT key, is typed, `AL` will be zero. In these cases, the extended character code (see the table earlier in this chapter) will be contained in the high byte of `AX`.

If the character read is an extended character and that extended character is the `F1` key, we want to begin expansion. We do this by setting the `current` pointer to the start of the expansion string. A frequent mistake is to do a `mov cs:current,string` rather than a `mov cs:current,offset string`. The difference here is that the first would fail, since we would be trying to move a byte into a word, and the assembler would force us to make the types match for the source and the destination of the move. The second is correct because what we want is not the **value** of the string, but a pointer to the beginning of the string.

If we are expanding, we will fetch the byte at the `current` pointer and stuff it into `AL`. As long as `AL` is not zero, we need not worry about the value of `AH`; nothing will examine it. If `AL` does become zero, we have reached the end of our expansion string. This means that we should not return a zero, but instead call `old_keyboard_io` once again to fetch another character from the keyboard.

In this bit of code there is one slightly peculiar line. You may have noticed that, upon entry to this routine, and after checking to be sure that `current` was zero, the very next thing we did in the case in which `current` was known to be zero was to set it to zero again. By itself, this is a harmless, if somewhat odd, thing to do. It is useful, however, in the case we have just been discussing. When we have reached the end of the expansion string, `current` will be non-zero but will be pointing at a byte immediately following the one containing the zero that indicated the end of the string, since we incremented `current` immediately after fetching what it pointed to. We know that the expansion is completed, and thus we need to turn it off. To do this in a straightforward fashion, we would jump to an intermediate bit of code that sets `current` to zero and then unconditionally jump to `readchar`. By wasting one harmless instruction, we save a step, reduce the code size a little, and make things just a little less convoluted.

In this code, it is important that each reference to memory include a segment specification. When control enters our interceptor, we have no idea what is in the `DS` register, but we can make two guesses about the value of `DS`. It is almost certainly not a value that will do us any good, and its value is probably quite important to the program that was interrupted. Therefore, we must take pains to ensure that each reference we make to memory uses the correct segment, which will always be the same value as `CS`. We must also be sure not to alter any register without making provisions to restore its value before releasing control.

5.2   Expanding on Multiple Keys

The preceeding program expanded *one* special key into *one* string. Sometimes, as they say, once is not enough. Suppose we want to paint in broader stripes, expand a set of keys in some reasonable fashion. How might this be done?

One obvious way would be to modify our simple single-character program to take its character and expansion string as arguments. That way we might define a bunch of keys in the `AUTOEXEC.BAT` file like this:

```
        . . .
MACRO F1 DIR
MACRO F2 DIR/W
MACRO F3 DIR *.ASM
MACRO F4 DIR *.COM
MACRO F5 DIR *.EXE
        . . .
```

By doing this, we could stack each successive key expander on the next. The values of individual macros would be defined in the `AUTOEXEC.BAT` file and could be changed at each reboot. Some of the design choices for our key expander have a positive impact on this approach. Since we concerned ourself only with the expanded (zero-prefixed) character set and designated, in the C fashion, that our expansion strings be terminated by a zero, our macro strings cannot contain any expanded characters. This is quite a lucky break for us, because having expanded characters in macro strings in this design could be disastrous. Each time we run `MACRO` in `AUTOEXEC.BAT`, it will link a new copy of the program to the previous keyboard handler. The first time we do so, we will add a layer between the call and the original ROM handler. The second time, we will add a layer *above* the first additional layer. The next time, we add a third layer, and so on. Each character we type must filter through each and every layer. Each expanded character must filter through any layers above the one at which it was declared. As long as no two calls replace the same special character, there is no need to impose any order on the invocations of `MACRO`. If any character is declared twice, the last one to be called will be used. Imagine, however, if each and every layer could alter the meaning of the expansion string as the character filters upstream. You might get things to work, but chances are you would be pulling your hair out over unexpected peculiarities.

For a very small number of characters, this layer-upon-layer method is acceptable. Since our expander is approximately a hundred bytes of resident code, each layer will remove a hundred bytes or so from available memory. To add new values for all 128 function keys would cost about 13 kilobytes of memory. Surely, some less piecemeal approach would let us do this in less memory, with less overhead per character.

As you may have guessed, that last statement was a bit of rhetoric. If we can recognize one character in a small program, we can easily recognize more than one. By using the expanded key to index into a table of strings, we can bind any of the possible expanded characters to a string.

A character is a single byte. A pointer to a string is two bytes. For 128 expanded characters, this adds up to a total table size of 384 bytes. Estimating the additional code necessary to be about 50 bytes gives us a total code size of roughly half a kilobyte. Add to that the size of the total set of expansion strings (say, 20 bytes each), and you can see that we need about 2.5 kilobytes to expand all 128 keys, or about 10 kilobytes less than the piecemeal approach. Since we have less overhead per character, this approach is clearly a winner.

It may be that we don't want to replace all the extended characters. For example, we may want to leave the cursor keys and the page keys alone. We may

not have useful things to bind to all the other keys either. For this reason, we
probably don't want to blindly use the key code as an index into a sparsely filled
table. Instead, we want to replace only the keys that we choose and have the rest
pass through unchanged. If we replace roughly half the keys, our total cost in
memory becomes something in the neighborhood of 1 kilobyte, with additional
memory costs that track exactly with the size of the expansion string, plus a
byte to indicate the character and a byte to terminate the string. By rethinking
the problem, we have dropped more than an order of magnitude in size, for the
typical case.

The only code that must change to go from a single-key expander to a
multiple-key expander is the `keyread` routine and the data area:

```
                ;  Read a character from the keyboard input queue,
                ;  if not expanding or the expansion string,
                ;  if expansion is in progress.
keyread         proc    near
        push    si
        cmp     cs:current,0
        jne     expandchar
readchar:
        mov     cs:current,0            ; Slightly peculiar
        pushf                           ; Let original routine
        call    old_keyboard_io         ; get keyboard status.
        cmp     al,0
        je      extended
        jmp     readdone
extended:
        mov     si,offset keytab
nextext:
        cmp     byte ptr cs:[si],0  ; Is this end of table?
        je      readdone
        cmp     ah,cs:[si]
        je      startexpand
        add     si,3
        jmp     nextext
startexpand:
        push    bx
        add     si,1
        mov     bx,cs:[si]
        mov     cs:current,bx           ; If so, start expanding
expandchar:
        mov     si,cs:current
        mov     al,cs:[si]
```

```
            inc     cs:current
            cmp     al,0                    ; End of string?
            je      readchar                ; If so, read a char?
readdone:
            pop     si
            ret
keyread             endp

current dw          0

keytab      db      59
            dw      dir_cmd
            db      60
            dw      dir_wide
            db      61
            dw      dir_asm
            db      62
            dw      dir_com
            db      63
            dw      dir_exe
            db      50
            dw      make_macro
            db      0           ; This must be last in key table

dir_cmd             db      'DIR',0dH,0
dir_wide            db      'DIR/W',0dH,0
dir_asm             db      'DIR *.ASM',0dH,0
dir_com             db      'DIR *.COM',0dH,0
dir_exe             db      'DIR *.EXE',0dH,0
make_macro          db      'MASM MACRO;',0dH,
                            'LINK MACRO;',0dH,
                            'EXE2BIN MACRO.EXE MACRO.COM',0dH,0
```

Of course, as with any design choice, there are trade-offs. By choosing to
search an unordered table rather than indexing into a sorted table, we make the
time it takes the system to act on an expanded character dependent on that
character's position in the table. If this search time becomes excessive, we could
manually sort the table and then use one of the classic searching algorithms to
look for the correct entry. The search loop used in the above code, however, is
just six instructions long. The maximum table size is 128 entries. For a worst-
case match, the machine must execute approximately 768 (6 * 128) instructions.
On a generic IBM PC, 768 instructions would take on the order of a millisecond
to execute. We could make this a little faster at the cost of making the code a

little larger, but it hardly seems worth it.

Compare this to the case in which we simply accumulated key expanders for each "search", meaning the operation necessary to compare the current character with the target character. We would require about eight to ten instructions, one of which would be a subroutine call. Subroutine calls can be quite expensive on some machines. On an 8086/8088, subroutines calls are time consuming, but not vastly more so than other branching instructions (this is not the case for subroutine calls in a high level language, however). Anyway, the worst case time here is something around 1200 instructions. Not too bad, since the perceptible time is roughly the same, but still less efficient.

So by rethinking the problem, we have saved a little time and a lot of important memory. We also have made the human interface a little less convenient, since we have moved the definition of the strings to the assembly source. There is nothing preventing us from rewriting this program to load the strings from a file at initialization time, however. This should not change the resident size at all, since all the initialization code to load the file can be discarded, like the first stage of a rocket, after it has done its job. The loader code need not take up space in resident memory at all.

5.3 MACRO.ASM – Single-key Expander

The following program expands a single keystroke into a command string.

```
cseg      segment
          assume  cs:cseg,ds:cseg
          org     100H
start:
          jmp     initialize


old_keyboard_io dd

          assume  ds:nothing
new_keyboard_io         proc    far
          sti
          cmp     ah,0            ; Is this call a READ request?
          je      ksread
          cmp     ah,1            ; Is it a STATUS request?
          je      ksstat          ; Let original routine
          jmp     old_keyboard_io ; handle remaining subfunction.
ksread:
```

```
        call    keyread         ; Get next character to return
        iret
ksstat:
        call    keystat         ; Return appropriate status.
        ret     2               ; Important!!!
new_keyboard_io         endp


keyread         proc    near
        cmp     cs:current,0
        jne     expandchar
readchar:
        mov     cs:current,0    ; Slightly peculiar
        pushf                   ; Let original routine
        call    old_keyboard_io ; determine keyboard status.
        cmp     al,0
        je      extended
readdone:
        ret
extended:
        cmp     ah,59           ; Is this character to expand?
        jne     readdone        ; If not, return it normally.
                                ; If so, start expanding
        mov     cs:current,offset string
expandchar:
        push    si
        mov     si,cs:current
        mov     al,cs:[si]
        inc     cs:current
        pop     si
        cmp     al,0            ; Is this end of string?
        je      readchar        ; If so, then read a real char?
        ret
keyread         endp

keystat         proc    near
        cmp     cs:current,0
        jne     fakestat
        pushf                   ; Let original routine
        call    old_keyboard_io ; determine keyboard status.
        ret
fakestat:
        mov     bx,1            ; Fake a "Character ready" by
        cmp     bx,0            ; clearing ZF.
        ret
```

```
keystat         endp

current dw      0
string  db      'masm macro;',0dH,
                'link macro;',0dH,
                'exe2bin macro.exe macro.com',0dH,0

initialize:
        assume  cs:cseg,ds:cseg
        mov     bx,cs
        mov     ds,bx

        mov     al,16H
        mov     ah,35H
        int     21H
        mov     old_keyboard_io,bx
        mov     old_keyboard_io[2],es
        mov     dx,offset new_keyboard_io
        mov     al,16H
        mov     ah,25H
        int     21H

        mov     dx,offset initialize
        int     27H

cseg    ends
        end     start
}
```

5.4   MACTAB.ASM – General Keystroke Expander

This program expands any number of extended keys into individual command strings by means of a lookup table.

```
cseg    segment
        assume  cs:cseg,ds:cseg
        org     100H
start:
        jmp     initialize


old_keyboard_io dd

        assume  ds:nothing
```

```
new_keyboard_io         proc    far
        sti
        cmp     ah,0            ; Is this call a READ request?
        je      ksread
        cmp     ah,1            ; Is it a STATUS request?
        je      ksstat          ; Let original routine
        jmp     old_keyboard_io ; do remaining subfunction.
ksread:
        call    keyread         ; Get next character to return
        iret
ksstat:
        call    keystat         ; Return appropriate status.
        ret     2               ; Important!!!
new_keyboard_io         endp

keystat         proc    near
        cmp     cs:current,0
        jne     fakestat
        pushf                   ; Let original routine
        call    old_keyboard_io ;   determine keyboard status.
        ret
fakestat:
        mov     bx,1            ; Fake a "Character ready" by
        cmp     bx,0            ; clearing ZF.
        ret
keystat         endp


        ; Read a character from the keyboard input queue,
        ; if not expanding or expansion string,
        ; if expansion is in progress.
keyread         proc    near
        push    si
        cmp     cs:current,0
        jne     expandchar
readchar:
        mov     cs:current,0    ; Slightly peculiar
        pushf                   ; Let original routine
        call    old_keyboard_io ;   get keyboard status.
        cmp     al,0
        je      extended
        jmp     readdone
extended:
        mov     si,offset keytab
nextext:
```

```
        cmp     byte ptr cs:[si],0  ; End of table?
        je      readdone
        cmp     ah,cs:[si]
        je      startexpand
        add     si,3
        jmp     nextext
startexpand:
        add     si,1
        push    bx
        mov     bx,cs:[si]
        mov     cs:current,bx
        pop     bx
expandchar:
        mov     si,cs:current
        mov     al,cs:[si]
        inc     cs:current
        cmp     al,0              ; End of string?
        je      readchar         ;   then read a real char
readdone:
        pop     si
        ret
keyread         endp

current dw      0

keytab  db      59
        dw      dir_cmd
        db      60
        dw      dir_wide
        db      61
        dw      dir_asm
        db      62
        dw      dir_com
        db      63
        dw      dir_exe
        db      50
        dw      make_macro
        db      0

dir_cmd         db        'DIR',0dH,0
dir_wide        db        'DIR/W',0dH,0
dir_asm         db        'DIR *.ASM',0dH,0
dir_com         db        'DIR *.COM',0dH,0
dir_exe         db        'DIR *.EXE',0dH,0
make_macro      db        'MASM MACRO;',0dH,
```

```
                        'LINK MACRO;',0dH,
                        'EXE2BIN MACRO.EXE MACRO.COM',0dH,0

initialize:
        assume  cs:cseg,ds:cseg
        mov     bx,cs
        mov     ds,bx

        mov     al,16H
        mov     ah,35H
        int     21H
        mov     old_keyboard_io,bx
        mov     old_keyboard_io[2],es
        mov     dx,offset new_keyboard_io
        mov     al,16H
        mov     ah,25H
        int     21H

        mov     dx,offset initialize
        int     27H

cseg    ends
        end     start
```

Chapter 6

Using the Timer

Up to this point, we have concentrated on linking to the keyboard interrupt of the IBM PC. The keyboard is a good linkage for functions that should happen "at the touch of a button"–in other words, applications that we run sporadically. But sometimes we want to perform a small job continuously while still using the IBM PC for its normal work.

Larger, more powerful computer systems have the ability to run several tasks at what appears to be the same time. This is known as *multi-tasking*. The design of the IBM PC does not permit us to run several large jobs at once. By being slightly clever, however, we can manage to do one large job and a few very small jobs at the same time. In the jargon of larger computer systems, such small tasks would be known as a "lightweight processes." A good example of a lightweight process is a clock display that appears somewhere on the screen, always telling us the correct time of day. A pleasant, well-placed clock display is a useful addition to a personal computer, especially a portable computer. The one listed in this chapter kept the author from missing several airplanes.

One of the devices an IBM PC has built into it is a timer. This timer sends an interrupt to the IBM PC exactly 18.2 times per second. DOS uses this interrupt to manage its time-of-day clock. By linking to this timer interrupt, we can have our "lightweight process" run 18.2 times per second as well.

The timer is a tricky interrupt to plug into. Since it occurs regularly while other programs are running, there is no telling what function was interrupted. If the function that was running is used within the body of the timer interrupt handler and that function is not reentrant, there is a good chance that the system will crash.

6.1 Reentrant code

Let's talk for a moment about what it means for a process or function to be *reentrant*. This is a term used a great deal by designers of multi-tasking operating systems. A reentrant routine is one that can be successfully interrupted by itself. That definition may sound a little circular and confusing, so further explanation is in order. Imagine that you are a designer of a multi-tasking operating system. You will have several processes running at the same time, meaning each gets a few processor cycles in turn, over and over again. Each of these processes may wish to write characters to the console terminal, for example, status messages.

Your current job is to write the routine that prints characters on the console terminal. Since there are many processes that need to do this exact operation, you'd like to write your code so that each process can use the same print routine. Since all of these processes will be running in the same memory space, you'd rather they not have to make individual copies of each common routine, such as the print routine. That would be a waste of space.

If you arrange things so that only one copy will be used, then how you write that particular routine becomes very important. Let's say that this is a piece of the assembly language for such a routine:

```
printchar       proc    far
        . . .
        mov     temp,al         ; Section 1
                                ;   move char to temp storage
        . . .
        mov     al,temp         ; Section 2
                                ;   retrieve the char
        . . .
printchar       endp

temp    db      0
```

Suppose an interrupt occurred, causing control to shift (called a *context switch*) to another running task that also happened to be printing. Worse yet, suppose the context switch occurred after Section 1 and before Section 2 in the interrupted code and allowed Section 1 of the interrupting code to run. The next time the interrupted code was allowed to run, the value that should have been in **temp** will be gone. It was overwritten by the interrupting routine.

Suppose we rewrote that routine to store values on the stack. Since each task has its own program counter and stack pointer, switching contexts would allow the same code to run without interfering with itself.

```
printchar       proc    far
        . . .
        push    ax              ; Section 1
                                ;   move char to temp storage

        . . .
        pop     ax              ; Section 2
                                ;   retrieve the char

        . . .
printchar       endp
```

This is all fine for true multi-tasking systems. The IBM PC, however, has no mechanism for doing a real context switch. A great many of the DOS and ROM routines cannot be interrupted by themselves. By linking to the DOS timer interrupt, we push the system in a direction it was not intended to go. Extreme care is necessary when writing timer-based code.

The best way to avoid problems with non-reentrant routines is never to call any from within a timer interrupt handler. This limits the kinds of problems you can run into. Another thing to avoid is any lengthy I/O. This means input or output to the disk, from the keyboard, and the communications ports. You should be able to do output to the screen safely enough.

A timer interrupt has a "window" of about 55 milliseconds in which to operate, since it would be disastrous for the next timer interrupt to come in before the last one has finished processing. But don't get the idea that your code can use up all that time. Part of that time is taken up by what DOS must do to handle its timer services. This must happen at all costs, or DOS will grind to a halt. Any remaining milliseconds are used to run the current application. Processor cycles that you consume by adding to the timer overhead reduce the amount of processing time that the main application will have available. Thus, it is important to be frugal with the amount of code you put in a timer interrupt handler.

6.2 Building a Desk Clock

Even though there are many things that should *not* be done from within a timer interrupt handler, there are still many useful things that can be done with one.

Probably the most familiar timer-based application is that of a desk clock. This is a small resident application that continuously displays the time of day

somewhere on the screen. The sources for these programs are usually quite
popular on bulletin boards, so they are easily available. We will write one here,
one of a slightly different design, so as not to duplicate what others have done.
Perhaps we can also shed some light on the conventional design by looking at a
desk clock in a slightly different perspective.

A normal program can determine the system time in several ways. It can
read the current tick count, which is the internal counter DOS uses to keep
track of the time of day. This count is then used to compute the time. Another
approach uses the DOS function that performs this computation for you and
simply returns the time of day.

Within a timer interrupt handler, calling either of these functions is only
slightly more difficult.

For our desk clock, we'll take a somewhat different approach. We won't do
any calculations or make any DOS calls, save the minimum necessary display
calls. Instead, we will compute the time in an "open-loop" fashion. This method
makes for a very small, very fast program, one that gives considerably less
overhead for the timer than the other methods. The disadvantage here is that
we are computing the time forward from when the program was first installed.
If you change DOS time you must reboot and reinstall the clock before the desk
clock time will agree.

By "open loop" we mean a method by which we set the initial time and then
compute the current time incrementally, without ever rechecking with DOS. A
"closed loop" program would be one in which we continually asked DOS for
the time and then displayed the result. Either method is acceptable in the
short run. In the long run, the only difference is that of cumulative error. The
clock shown here has been measured to track within a few seconds of the real
clock over a period of some two days. The total error would be one of about a
minute per month. Since few IBM PC systems go for an entire month without
a reboot, this clock should be perfectly acceptable. By applying a somewhat
fancier initialization algorithm and tightening up the code (which was written
for clarity, not speed), the accuracy of this clock would approach that of the
DOS clock.

To start, we need to rewrite our basic resident application to replace the
timer vector. By modifying the interrupt number and the variable names, we
can get a good start on this code. The application shown here simply interposes
a layer between the normal timer interrupt handler, which we control.

```
cseg     segment para public 'CODE'
```

```
        org     100H
        assume  cs:cseg,ds:cseg
start:
        jmp     initialize

old_timer       dd

timer_int       proc    far
        sti
        pushf
        assume  ds:nothing
        call    old_timer
        iret
timer_int       endp

initialize:
        mov     bx,cs
        mov     ds,bx

        mov     al,08H
        mov     ah,35H
        int     21H
        mov     old_timer,bx
        mov     old_timer[2],es

        mov     dx,offset initialize
        int     27H

cseg    ends
        end     start
```

Next, to construct a clock, we must modify our `timer_int` routine so that it calls a routine of our own devising to handle the needs of our desk clock. In the past, we have called the standard routine just after our custom code had completed. In the case of the timer, we want to call the timer routine *first*. The reason for this is simple: it is much more important that the system clock be updated on the tick than our desk clock. Since both the system routine and our routine take time to execute, and the system routine expects to be called directly on the timer tick, we must permit it to run first. Our code, being less critical, can run after the system routine without significant gain in error. In fact, since the system routine runs more or less in a fixed length of time, there should be very little cumulative error by running our code after the system code. If the system code were to run last, the cumulative error would be greater, since this routine does not run in constant time. Even worse, the error would be in the master system clock, used for marking files and so on, and thus have a greater impact on the system as a whole.

As a first pass, we modify timer_int to display an empty time string in the upper right corner of the screen. This location was chosen as the least obtrusive area of the display; the position is entirely up to the discretion of the programmer. The clock can actually be positioned anywhere on the screen.

One design choice we must make is how the time is to be displayed. Most civilians prefer the twelve-hour format, midnight to noon, and one to eleven, rather than the twenty-four-hour format used by the armed services and the IBM PC. Showing hours and minutes is quite adequate. A seconds display can sometimes be useful, but it may make the screen too active, and distract from normal work. For this example, we will display the hour and the minute, in twelve-hour format. Another frill will be the absence of a leading zero on hours between one and nine. The hour and the minute will be separated by a colon.

Since we want to display a maximum of five characters, we could either write this into the program or use code already written to display an arbitrary string, using the ROM display routines. Since we may want to modify this code to do other things, the previous code we wrote to display a string and position the cursor is probably the better choice.

```
timer_int       proc    far
        sti
        pushf
        assume  ds:nothing
        call    old_timer
        call    timer
        iret
timer_int       endp

timer           proc    near
        assume  cs:cseg,ds:cseg
        push    ds              ; Save modified registers
        push    bx

        mov     bx,cs           ; Set data segment to be same
        mov     ds,bx           ;   as code segment via BX
        call    dtime           ; Else redisplay

        pop     bx              ; Restore registers
        pop     ds
```

```
        ret
timer           endp

dtime           proc    near
        push    si                  ; Save modified registers
        push    bx

        call    get_pos  ; Save previous cursor position
        push    bx   ;  on stack
        mov     bx,position  ; Go to upper right corner
        call    set_pos
        mov     si,offset time   ; Display current time string
        call    dstring
        pop     bx   ; Restore from stack
        call    set_pos   ;  old cursor position

        pop     bx
        pop     si
        ret
dtime           endp

dstring         proc    near
        push    si
        push    ax
        cmp     si,0                ; Check for a null pointer
        je      dsdone
dloop:
        mov     al,[si]             ; Get a character from string
        cmp     al,0                ; A NULL? (termination char)
        je      dsdone              ; If so, quit
        call    dchar               ; If not, display character
        inc     si                  ; move pointer to next char
        jmp     dloop               ; and go around again
dsdone:
        pop     ax
        pop     si
        ret
dstring         endp

dchar           proc    near
        push    ax
        push    bx
        mov     bh,1
        mov     ah,0EH
        int     10H
```

```
            pop     bx
            pop     ax
            ret
dchar               endp

get_pos             proc    near
            push    ax
            push    bx
            push    cx
            push    dx

            mov     ah,03H          ; Function is GET POSITION
            mov     bh,0
            int     10H
            mov     bx,dx

            pop     dx
            pop     cx
            pop     bx
            pop     ax
            ret
get_pos             endp

set_pos             proc    near
            push    ax
            push    bx
            push    dx

            mov     dx,bx
            mov     ah,02H              ; Function is SET POSITION
            mov     bh,0
            int     10H

            pop     dx
            pop     bx
            pop     ax
            ret
set_pos             endp

position    dw      004BH
time        db      '12:00',0
```

This code should display a "12:00" in the upper right corner of the screen, regardless of the screen activity of the system. If the characters are scrolled off the screen, they will be refreshed 55 milliseconds later. Because the display process happens on every timer tick, the clock will appear to be fairly stable but you may notice a slight flicker around the base of the characters as the cursor continually goes to that position to refresh the display. For this application, 18.2 times per second is somewhat faster than necessary for a refresh, and the flickering is vaguely annoying. One way to reduce the number of times per second is to introduce another counter loop within `timer` that reduces the number of times `dtime` is called. For example:

```
timer           proc    near
        assume  cs:cseg,ds:cseg
        push    ds              ; Save modified registers
        push    bx

        mov     bx,cs           ; Set data segment to be same
        mov     ds,bx           ;   as code segment via BX
        inc     refresh         ; 18.2 times per second causes
        cmp     refresh,3       ;  flicker.  Try 4.5/second
        jl      rdone           ; If not a whole refresh, skip
        call    dtime           ; Else redisplay
        mov     refresh,0       ; and reset refresh counter.
rdone:

        pop     bx              ; Restore registers
        pop     ds
        ret
timer           endp
```

You will see this delay technique used several times in this code. Another use for this is to stagger the computational load on the interrupt handler. By carefully selecting the loop number, we could perform a computation on one cycle, a display on the next, and so on. By doing this, we can reduce the maximum length of any given interrupt-handler call, and still do the same work.

6.3 What Time Is It, Anyway?

At this point, there are two remaining portions of the clock to be constructed. We have the portion that will display a valid time string in the correct location on the screen. What we need now is a module that will advance that time correctly, from minute to minute, and a module that will determine the correct time. The next step is to build the mechanism of the clock; we'll worry about setting the time later.

Building a program is like capturing a thought. New ways of thinking about a problem often provide new mechanisms for solving problems. Many people would design a clock with a byte for the hour and a byte for the minute, and write a conversion routine that takes a byte and makes it into an ASCII string. But this is not the only way of thinking about a clock, and it may not be the best way. As an exercise in alternatives, let's look at a different kind of clock. We might look at the five characters as two numbers separated by a colon, with the first going from 1 to 12, and the second going from 0 to 59. Or we might look at them and see five separate characters. The first may be a space or a 1; the second, 0 through 9; the third, always a colon; the fourth 1 through 6; and the last 0 through 9. We could imagine a small machine, clicking through successive combinations of characters, always producing a valid time. After all, this is how clock makers have seen mechanical digital clocks for years.

If you are given the time "11:48" and are asked to produce the next valid time one minute later, you can do it without hesitation. For that example, it may seem very much like adding a 1 to the number 48. If, however, you are given the time "12:59", and are asked the same question, you would not use simple addition at all. You have learned the rules for valid timekeeping and apply them daily. Why not write your program to follow the rules you yourself use, rather than transposing those rules into an unfamiliar domain?

As we all know, in a twelve-hour clock, one moves from each minute to its successor using these rules, applied successively from top to bottom:

- If advancing the minutes column and the minutes column is a nine, the minutes column becomes zero and the tens-of-minutes column advances by one.

- If advancing the tens-of-minutes column and the tens-of-minutes column is a five, the tens-of-minutes column becomes a zero, and the hours column advances by one.

- If advancing the hours column and the hours column is a two, and the tens-of-hours column is a one, the hours column becomes a one and the the tens-of-hours column becomes empty.

Let's convert these rules into an assembly-language routine, sort of a miniature expert system, that will correctly advance the time for us. In computer science, the type of routine where the rules for moving from one state to the next are defined and repeatedly applied is known as a *finite-state machine*, or FSM.

The characters are located in the time string, with the tens-of-hours at `time[0]`, the hours at `time[1]`, the colon at `time[2]`, the tens-of-minutes at `time[3]`, and the minutes at `time[4]`.

```
settime        proc    near
        cmp     byte ptr time[4],'9' ; Compute the one minutes
        je      tenthmin          ; If minutes = "9", advance the ten
        inc     byte ptr time[4]
        jmp     setdone
tenthmin:                         ; Minutes must advance past 9.
        mov     byte ptr time[4],'0' ; Compute the ten minutes
        cmp     byte ptr time[3],'5' ; If "59", then advance one hour
        je      nexthour
        inc     byte ptr time[3]
        jmp     setdone
nexthour:                         ; Total minutes must advance past 59
        mov     byte ptr time[3],'0' ; Compute the hours
        cmp     byte ptr time[1],'2' ; Might be " 2" or "12"
        je      twelvethhour      ; Wrap around at 12?
        cmp     byte ptr time[1],'9' ; If " 9", to to "10"
        je      tenthhour
        inc     byte ptr time[1]
        jmp     setdone
twelvethhour:                     ; Advance from 12 or 03?
        cmp     byte ptr time[0],' ' ; Is it " 2"
        je      thirdhour         ; If so, then go to " 3"
        mov     byte ptr time[0],' ' ; If not, it must be "12"
        mov     byte ptr time[1],'1' ; so go to " 1"
        jmp     setdone
thirdhour:                        ; Go from 03 to 04
        inc     byte ptr time[1]; Go to " 3"
        jmp     setdone
tenthhour:                        ; Go from 09 to 10
        mov     byte ptr time[0],'1' ; Go to "10"
        mov     byte ptr time[1],'0'
setdone:
        ret
settime        endp
```

Now that we have the `settime` routine, we can try it out by changing `timer` slightly, adding a call to `settime` after the call to `dtime`. We want to add the call *after* rather than *before* so that our displayed sequence will start with 12:00, rather than 12:01.

```
timer           proc    near
        assume  cs:cseg,ds:cseg
        push    ds              ; Save modified registers
        push    bx

        mov     bx,cs           ; Set data segment to be same
        mov     ds,bx           ;   as code segment via BX
        inc     refresh         ; 18.2 times per second causes
        cmp     refresh,3       ;   flicker.  Try 4.5/second
        jl      rdone           ; If not a whole refresh, skip
        call    dtime           ; Else redisplay
        call    settime         ; Advance to next logical time
        mov     refresh,0       ; and reset refresh counter.
rdone:

        pop     bx              ; Restore registers
        pop     ds
        ret
timer           endp
```

By building an application with just the code shown here, we can cycle through all the possible clock values in a short time. Because we are running `settime` at the display rate, it will crank through all the possible time values at very high speed. We can see if there are any incorrect times displayed, such as 12:60 or 13:00. By spending a few minutes watching the display, we can find out if our finite-state machine is correct.

6.4   Winding the Watch

A wristwatch has four basic subsystems. Most familiar to us is the dial and the hands. This portion of a watch actually displays the time in a form that we can read. Underneath that is the gearing that turns the hands according to some basic rules, such as the amount of arc that a second will sweep out and what happens when the second, minute, or hour hand reaches the twelve. Behind all that is sort of a metronome, a device that sends a pulse once per second or minute to the turning mechanism. This is the heart of the watch, the driving function that makes all the other pieces useful. The last piece is the overall control mechanism that lets us set the correct time from which all else will proceed smoothly.

We have built the display, and the gears that turn the hands. What we need now is the device that ticks, once per second, and the method for setting the correct time.

Ticking is easy. We know that our routine will be called 18.2 times per second. We know that there are usually 60 seconds per minute. By multiplying these two, we get 1092 ticks per minute, a nice integer number. If we rewrite `timer` one more time, we can arrange things so that `settime` is called once per minute, while `dtime` is called 4.5 times per second, as before. In a concession to digital watches, we can also add a nice little frill that blinks the semicolon approximately once per second, just for fun.

```
timer           proc    near
        assume  cs:cseg,ds:cseg
        push    ds
        push    bx

        mov     bx,cs           ; Set the data segment to be the same
        mov     ds,bx           ;    as the code segment via BX
        inc     tick            ; Advance one tick
        cmp     tick,1092       ; There are 1092 ticks per minute
        jl      tdone           ; If not a whole minute, just redisplay
        call    settime         ; Else recompute the time
        mov     tick,0          ; and reset the tick counter
tdone:
        inc     refresh         ; Refreshing 18.2 times per second causes
        cmp     refresh,3       ;  flicker.  Try only 4.5 times per second
        jl      rdone           ; If not a whole refresh period, do nothing
        call    dtime           ; Else redisplay
        mov     refresh,0       ; and reset the refresh counter.
rdone:
        inc     blinker
        cmp     blinker,9       ; Approximately,but not exactly,half a second
        jl      bdone
        call    blink
        mov     blinker,0
bdone:
        pop     bx
        pop     ds
        ret
timer           endp
```

```
blink           proc    near
        cmp     byte ptr time[2],':' ; Is the colon on
        je      bloff           ; If so turn it off
        mov     byte ptr time[2],':'; If not, turn it on
        jmp     bldone
bloff:
        mov     byte ptr time[2],' '; Replace colon with space
bldone:
        ret
blink           endp
```

Of course, we have to add the new variables to the data area:

```
tick            dw      0
refresh         dw      0
blinker         dw      0
```

Now we have all of our clock built except the time-setting function. We have made this an open-loop design, one that simply needs a tick to advance the time correctly. If we place the correct time of day in the **time** string, we can just let the clock run free from that point. Since we need only to set the time to start, we can do this in the installation portion of our .COM program, the part that will not remain resident. By doing this, only the bare minimum of clock functions have to remain locked in memory.

To set the time, we will use the DOS function INT 21H function 2CH (*get system time*). This function computes the system's idea of the correct time of day and returns it to us, with the hour in CH and the minute in CL. The hour ranges from 0 to 23, with 0 being midnight and 23 being 11 PM. The minute ranges from 0 to 59.

The second is also returned to us, in DH, which can go from 0 to 59. DL contains the hundredths of seconds, but we will ignore that value for this application. Because the IBM PC provides us with a clock tick 18.2 times per second, we cannot easily measure an exact second. We can either go for 18 clock ticks, which is 0.98 seconds, or 19 clock ticks, which is 1.04 seconds. For the purposes of a desk clock that displays only hours and minutes, we need not worry too much about actual seconds. The nearest integer multiple of 18.2 is 91 (5×18.2). If we can get the clock set correctly to within 91 ticks, it will have a maximum error of 5 seconds, which is pretty good for a pocket watch.

We must modify the installation code just a bit for this application, by adding the code that sets the time correctly. We want be sure that the very last thing we do is modify the timer interrupt. If we modified the interrupt first, and the time-setting code took more than 55 milliseconds to run in the best case, or a timer tick interrupt occurred before the time was correctly set in the worst case, we would have two "processes" competing for the same five bytes of memory. To ensure that everything occurs in the proper order, we simply do not reset the timer interrupt until we are ready to exit.

Our modifications to the initialization code need not be optimized in any way. The only impact optimization would have is to slightly reduce the start-up time or slightly reduce the amount of space this application takes up on disk. The initialization code is thrown away when the .COM file exits, so we can write it to suit our fancy.

In this case, the initialization code is written in the same style as the resident application. Another method might have been to apply a byte-printing algorithm to the hour and minute bytes, simply printing them into the string rather than to the screen or the printer.

By treating the hour byte as a key that determines how we set our clock characters, just as we did in the clock algorithm for the resident application, we can, except for midnight, use the same code for the afternoon that we use for the morning. To explain further, if we have an algorithm for setting the clock correctly in the hours from 1 to 12, we can use the same code for the afternoon hours, from 13 to 23 on the IBM PC, by simply subtracting 12 and looping back through the code. We needn't have another set of cases for the afternoon. The only special case is midnight, the zeroth hour according to IBM.

Applying this same reducing principle, we can use the same algorithm for the hours column, by determining if the hour is greater than or equal to ten. If we start by putting a space in the tens-of-hours column, then we compute the hour column. If the hour is less than ten, we simply convert the number to an ASCII digit and put it in the hours column. If the hour is greater than ten, put a one in the tens-of-hour column, subtract ten, and apply the algorithm for less than ten.

Converting a byte in the range of 0 to 9 to an ASCII character in the range "0" through "9" is easy. We know that the characters "0" through "9" fall sequentially in the ASCII character set. If we simply add an ASCII zero to the byte we want to convert, we will have the correct character. Incidentally, it is exactly this reason that allows us to advance a digit by simply adding one to its ASCII character code in the clock.

After we have the hours set, we can set the minutes by applying the division method you learned in grade school: repeated subtraction. We could have done a division in about the same number of instructions, but the repeated subtraction method is easily understood, simple to use, and somewhat novel. It never hurts to look for alternative ways to code a particular function.

```
initialize:
        mov     bx,cs
        mov     ds,bx

        mov     al,08H
        mov     ah,35H
        int     21H
        mov     old_timer,bx
        mov     old_timer[2],es

        mov     ah,2CH                  ; Get the time of day from DOS
        int     21H

        cmp     ch,0                    ; Is it the witching hour?
        jg      hour                    ; If not, handle it normally
        add     ch,12                   ; Else convert to noon and handle that
hour:
        cmp     ch,12                   ; Is it after noon?
        jle     day                     ; If not, just compute normally
        sub     ch,12                   ; If so, subtract 12 and use same code
        mov     byte ptr time[0],' '; Set initial value of tens column
day:                    ; Set time for the twelve hour clock
        cmp     ch,10                   ; Is it after 10?
        jl      early                   ; If not, just deal with the one hours
        sub     ch,10                   ; Else subtract 10
        mov     byte ptr time[0],'1'; set tens column, and handle the ones
early:                  ; Set the time for the one hour column
        add     ch,'0'                  ; Convert number to digit.
        mov     byte ptr time[1],ch ; And set the ones hour column
minute:                 ; Set the tens of minutes
        cmp     cl,10                   ; Determine how many tens of minutes
        jl      minset                  ; we need to set the clock to by
        sub     cl,10                   ; means of repeated subtraction.
        inc     byte ptr time[3]        ; Initialized to '0'
        jmp     minute
minset:                 ; Set the minutes, by simply converting the remainder
        add     cl,'0'
        mov     byte ptr time[4],cl

        mov     tick,0                  ; Clear the tick
```

```
second:
        cmp     dh,5                    ; 5 seconds is the smallest integer
        jle     clockstart              ; granularity we can measure.
        add     tick,91                 ; 5 seconds is exactly 91 clock ticks.
        sub     dh,5                    ; Get to the nearest 5 seconds by
        jmp     second                  ; repeated subtractions.

clockstart:             ; Start the clock by installing the interrupt vector
        mov     dx,offset timer_int
        mov     al,08H
        mov     ah,25H
        int     21H

        mov     dx,offset initialize
        int     27H

cseg    ends
        end     start
```

All the parts of the clock are in place. All that remains is to wind it and let it run.

6.5   CLOCK.ASM – A Resident Desk Clock

This program displays the time of day, in twelve-hour format in the upper right hand corner of the screen. Just for fun, it will also blink the colon about once per second.

```
cseg    segment para public 'CODE'
        org     100H
        assume  cs:cseg,ds:cseg
start:
        jmp     initialize

old_timer       dd

timer_int       proc    far
        sti
        pushf
        assume  ds:nothing
        call    old_timer
        call    timer
        iret
```

```
timer_int       endp

timer           proc    near
        assume  cs:cseg,ds:cseg
        push    ds
        push    bx

        mov     bx,cs   ; Set data segment to be same
        mov     ds,bx   ;   as code segment via BX
        inc     tick    ; Advance one tick
        cmp     tick,1092   ;There are 1092 ticks per minute
        jl      tdone   ; If not a whole minute, just redisplay
        call    settime ; Else recompute time
        mov     tick,0  ; and reset tick counter
tdone:
        inc     refresh ; Refreshing 18.2/second causes
        cmp     refresh,3   ;   flicker.  Try only 4.5/second
        jl      rdone   ; If not a whole refresh, do nothing
        call    dtime   ; Else redisplay
        mov     refresh,0   ; and reset refresh counter.
rdone:
        inc     blinker
        cmp     blinker,9
        jl      bdone
        call    blink
        mov     blinker,0
bdone:
        pop     bx
        pop     ds
        ret
timer           endp

blink           proc    near
        cmp     byte ptr time[2],':'
        je      bloff
        mov     byte ptr time[2],':'
        jmp     bldone
bloff:
        mov     byte ptr time[2],' '
bldone:
        ret
blink           endp

settime         proc    near
        cmp     byte ptr time[4],'9'; Compute one minutes
```

```
        je      tenthmin        ; If "x9", advance to next ten
        inc     byte ptr time[4]
        jmp     setdone
tenthmin:
        mov     byte ptr time[4],'0'; Compute ten minutes
        cmp     byte ptr time[3],'5'; If "59", then advance one hour
        je      nexthour
        inc     byte ptr time[3]
        jmp     setdone
nexthour:
        mov     byte ptr time[3],'0'; Compute hours
        cmp     byte ptr time[1],'2'; Might be " 2" or "12"
        je      twelvethhour     ; See if we'll wrap around at 12
        cmp     byte ptr time[1],'9'; If " 9", to to "10"
        je      tenthhour
        inc     byte ptr time[1]
        jmp     setdone
twelvethhour:
        cmp     byte ptr time[0],' '; Is it " 2"
        je      thirdhour        ; If so, then go to " 3"
        mov     byte ptr time[0],' '; If not, then it must be "12"
        mov     byte ptr time[1],'1'; so go to " 1"
        jmp     setdone
thirdhour:
        inc     byte ptr time[1]; Go to " 3"
        jmp     setdone
tenthhour:
        mov     byte ptr time[0],'1'; Go to "10"
        mov     byte ptr time[1],'0'
setdone:
        ret
settime         endp

dtime           proc    near
        push    si
        push    dx

        call    get_pos         ; Save previous cursor position
        push    dx              ;   on stack
        mov     dx,position     ; Go to upper right corner
        call    set_pos
        mov     si,offset time  ; Display current time string
        call    dstring
        pop     dx              ; Restore from stack
        call    set_pos         ;   old cursor position
```

```
        pop     dx
        pop     si
        ret
dtime           endp

dstring         proc    near
        push    si
        push    ax
        cmp     si,0
        je      dsdone
dloop:
        mov     al,[si]
        cmp     al,0
        je      dsdone
        call    dchar
        inc     si
        jmp     dloop
dsdone:
        pop     ax
        pop     si
        ret
dstring         endp

dchar           proc    near
        push    ax
        push    bx
        mov     bh,1
        mov     ah,0EH
        int     10H
        pop     bx
        pop     ax
        ret
dchar           endp

get_pos         proc    near
        push    ax
        push    bx
        push    cx
        mov     ah,03H
        mov     bh,0
        int     10H
        pop     cx
        pop     bx
        pop     ax
```

```
            ret
get_pos         endp

set_pos         proc    near
        push    ax
        push    bx
        mov     ah,02H
        mov     bh,0
        int     10H
        pop     bx
        pop     ax
        ret
set_pos         endp

position        dw      004BH
tick            dw      0
refresh         dw      0
blinker         dw      0
time            db      '12:00',0

initialize:
        mov     bx,cs
        mov     ds,bx

        mov     al,08H
        mov     ah,35H
        int     21H
        mov     old_timer,bx
        mov     old_timer[2],es

        mov     ah,2CH          ; Get time of day from DOS
        int     21H

        cmp     ch,0            ; Set correct hour
        je      midnight        ;   which will be in range 0-23
        cmp     ch,12
        jg      afternoon
day:
        cmp     ch,10
        jge     late
early:
        add     ch,'0'
        mov     byte ptr time[0],' '
        mov     byte ptr time[1],ch
        jmp     minute
```

```
late:
        sub     ch,10
        add     ch,'0'
        mov     byte ptr time[0],'1'
        mov     byte ptr time[1],ch
        jmp     minute
afternoon:
        sub     ch,12
        jmp     day
midnight:                               ; Hour is 0 (midnight)
        mov     byte ptr time[0],'1'
        mov     byte ptr time[1],'2'
minute:
        cmp     cl,10                   ; Determine how many tens of minutes
        jl      minset                  ; we need to set clock to by
        sub     cl,10                   ; means of repeated subtraction.
        inc     byte ptr time[3]; Initialized to '0'
        jmp     minute
minset:
        add     cl,'0'
        mov     byte ptr time[4],cl

        mov     tick,0
second:
        cmp     dh,5                    ; 5 seconds is smallest integer
        jle     clockstart              ; granularity we can measure.
        add     tick,91                 ; 5 seconds is exactly 91 clock ticks.
        sub     dh,5                    ; Get to nearest 5 seconds by
        jmp     second                  ; repeated subtractions.

clockstart:
        mov     dx,offset timer_int
        mov     al,08H
        mov     ah,25H
        int     21H

        mov     dx,offset initialize
        int     27H

cseg    ends
        end     start
```

Chapter 7

Building a Front Panel

There are other uses for the timer interrupt besides a simple desk clock. By making clever use of the timer, and understanding how the IBM PC really does what it does, you can create some interesting and useful applications.

One problem with writing assembly-language programs is that it is sometimes difficult to know what your machine is really doing. When a program does not change the display, is not reading the disk, is not talking to the serial ports, it may be either dead or simply thinking. With normal programs, there is no way to tell what is happening. When debugging a complicated program, it would be useful to peek into the brain of the machine, without disturbing its thinking.

In the early days of computing, a machine of roughly the same computational capacity as an IBM PC would fill a reasonably large room. Early computers must have caused a boom in the air conditioning industry, because the rooms they filled were chilled by huge devices that would otherwise be suitable for entire office buildings. A giant mainframe computer was a significant capital outlay for even a large company, and time and money could not be wasted on a leisurely repair of buggy programs. These giant electronic brains had panels full of blinking lights, a wonderful public relations device that became synonymous with the idea of giant computers, and that occasionally helped in debugging programs, too. Typically, the replacement cost of just the light bulbs for the front panel exceeded the cost of a modern, fully loaded IBM PC.

The information available to a mainframe programmer from a front panel was quite detailed and often unavailable through any other means. First and foremost in importance among the displays was the instruction pointer, or IP. (Well, perhaps the *most* important was the HALT light, indicating that the

95

machine had stopped.) The IP indicated where the computer was finding the instructions it was currently executing. Other information might be the contents of various registers, the state of various flags within the system, and so on.

Reading the front panel of a mainframe was a high art, even among programmers. The displays were in binary, meaning that the lights were either on or off. There were no digital displays. Either you learned to read binary or you got another job. Nevertheless, people not only learned to read these displays, they excelled at it. Many system operators could read the state of the system from across a crowded room, knowing when a tape should be mounted or a disk changed simply by the pattern of lights on the display. Programmers could know what part of the operating system was running simply by reading the lights. The amount of information a skilled programmer could get from a single glance at the front panel was astonishing.

An IBM PC does not have a front panel; for the most part, this is a blessing. Computers no longer fill a room or keep a staff of engineers, programmers, and operators busy. But there is still something to be said for being able to sneak a peek into a machine and see what it is doing.

Because of the timer interrupt on the IBM PC, we can do a little peeking into the guts of our machine. In this chapter, we will create a program that displays and updates the program counter on the screen. With a little practice and a little research, you can get a surprising amount of information from a simple flickering display. Don't worry, though, we won't display the IP in binary. But we could, if we wanted to.

7.1   Peeking at the Instruction Pointer

At first, it may seem unreasonable to talk of displaying the IP from an interrupt handler. After all, won't the program counter always show that the computer is executing the timer interrupt? Well, since we aren't interested in the address of the timer routine, we may need to fudge our concepts a little. What we are interested in displaying is the IP that was being used just as the interrupt occurred. How can we get this information? Well, two things we know about interrupt handlers might be expressed like this: First, if an interrupt handler is running, an interrupt has occurred. Second, when the interrupt handler has completed its work, it will return control to the interrupted program via an IRET instruction.

If the interrupt handler has any hope of returning successfully, the stack

will contain two things on entry. At the top of the stack will be the program
counter that indicates where execution was interrupted. Below that will be the
old processor flags. We cannot modify these values, but we can examine them.
The stack pointer does not change when an interrupt routine is run. It is the
responsibility of the interrupt routine to manage the stack in such a fashion that
no garbage is left on the stack. Therefore, we can read and use the values of the
old PC and flags as we choose, so long as we don't change them.

In the previous chapter, we constructed a basic timer interrupt skeleton. We
can use that same code as a starting point for this application.

```
cseg      segment para public 'CODE'
          org     100H
          assume  cs:cseg,ds:cseg
start:
          jmp     initialize

old_timer         dd

timer_int         proc    far
          sti
          pushf
          assume  ds:nothing
          call    old_timer
          call    timer
          iret
timer_int         endp

timer             proc    near
          assume  cs:cseg,ds:cseg
          ret
timer             endp

initialize:
          mov     bx,cs
          mov     ds,bx

          mov     al,08H
          mov     ah,35H
          int     21H
          mov     old_timer,bx
          mov     old_timer[2],es

          mov     dx,offset timer_int
          mov     al,08H
```

```
        mov      ah,25H
        int      21H

        mov      dx,offset initialize
        int      27H

cseg    ends
        end      start
```

Now that we have the basic form, we must address some basic design issues. First, where will the display be located? There is no "right" answer; it is again at the discretion of the programmer. In order not to interfere with the clock display that we have just written, we will place the IP in the upper right corner of the screen, just to the left of the clock. Since this is a debugging tool and not one you would care to run all the time, you may be better off putting the IP display in the far right corner and not run the clock at all. This would reduce the load on the timer interrupt and provide more cycles for your application programs to run. Nevertheless, since the possibility exists that both will run simultaneously, in this example we will position the display to compensate for the clock.

Second, in what format will the IP be displayed? In both the resident and the regular interrupt-vector display programs, we showed the addresses in hexadecimal, with segment first, then a separator colon, and finally the offset. While the possibilities of binary are tantalizing, hexadecimal is probably the most useful.

To some degree, this resident application will resemble the clock resident application. We can use the same cursor read and positioning routines and the same character-display function. We will also need the double word hexadecimal conversion routine that we wrote for the interrupt-vector display. In the first chapter, we discussed the importance of not getting tricky. This application is a good example of why that is important. If we had cleverly optimized these basic toolbox routines, we would not be able to steal them so easily for use in other applications. As with everything, there are trade-offs. In this case, the trade was portablility and speed of later development against speed and size of the current project. But one of the great things about program development is that nothing need ever be permanent. If you can whip up a prototype with the components from your toolbox, you can try out your basic idea. Later on, you can pull the stock parts out and replace them with high-performance custom components.

Now that we have some idea of the outline of this project, let's take a look at the basic code we have acquired for it:

```
timer_int       proc    far
        sti
        pushf
        assume  ds:nothing
        call    old_timer
        call    timer
        iret
timer_int       endp

timer           proc    near
        assume  cs:cseg,ds:cseg
        ret
timer           endp

; Get the current cursor position and return it in BX
getpos          proc    near
        push    ax
        push    cx
        push    dx

        mov     ah,03H
        mov     bh,0        ; Page zero
        int     10H
        mov     bx,dx       ; Return the position in BX

        pop     dx
        pop     cx
        pop     ax
        ret
getpos          endp

; Set the current cursor position to the value in BX
setpos          proc    near
        push    ax
        push    bx
        push    dx

        mov     ah,02H
        mov     dx,bx
        mov     bh,0
        int     10H

        pop     ax
```

```
        pop     bx
        pop     dx
        ret
setpos          endp


;       ES:DX contains doubleword to be displayed
ddword          proc    near
        push    dx              ; Save offset temporarily
        mov     dx,es           ; Move Segment to DX
        call    dsword          ; Display segment
        call    dcolon          ; Print a colon
        pop     dx              ; Restore offset to DX
        call    dsword          ; Display offset
        ret
ddword          endp


;       DX containes singleword to be displayed
dsword          proc    near
        push    dx              ; Save low byte
        mov     dl,dh           ; Move high byte to low byte
        call    dbyte           ; Display high byte
        pop     dx              ; Restore low byte to DL
        call    dbyte           ; Display low byte
        ret
dsword          endp


;       DL contains byte to be displayed
dbyte           proc    near
        push    ax              ; Save any registers used
        push    dx
        push    si

        push    dx              ; Save low nybble temporarily
        push    cx              ; Save CX
        mov     cl,4            ; Set shift count to 4
        shr     dx,cl           ; Move high nybble to low
        and     dx,000FH        ; Mask out all but low nybble
        mov     si,dx           ; Use low nybble as index into
        mov     al,hextab[si]   ; hex char table
        call    dchar           ; Display character
        pop     cx              ; Restore CX
        pop     dx              ; Restore low nybble

        and     dx,000FH        ; Mask out all but low nybble
        mov     si,dx           ; Use low nybble as index into
```

```
        mov     al,hextab[si]   ; hexa char table
        call    dchar           ; Display character
        pop     si              ; Restore registers
        pop     dx
        pop     ax
        ret
dbyte           endp

; Display a colon
dcolon          proc    near
        mov     al,':'
        call    dchar
        ret
dcolon          endp

; Display the character contained in AL
dchar           proc    near
        push    ax
        push    bx
        mov     bh,1
        mov     ah,0EH
        int     10H
        pop     bx
        pop     ax
        ret
dchar           endp

location        dw      0041H
hextab          db      '0123456789ABCDEF',0
```

From here, the first step we can take is to get the code to display a zero double word in the correct location on the screen. We must change the `timer` routine by adding the code to save the registers on the stack, save the old cursor location, move to the new one, display the value, and restore the cursor position and registers.

```
timer           proc    near
        assume  cs:cseg,ds:cseg
        push    ax
        push    bx
        push    cx
        push    dx
        push    si
        push    di
```

```
        push    es
        push    ds

        mov     bx,cs           ; Set DS to be same as CS
        mov     ds,bx           ; by means of BX
        call    getpos          ; Save current cursor loc
        push    bx              ;  on stack
        mov     bx,location     ; Move to upper right corner,
        call    setpos          ;  just left of clock
        mov     dx,0            ; Set SEG:OFS to zeros
        mov     es,dx
        call    ddword          ; Display 0000:0000
        pop     bx              ; Move cursor back to old
        call    setpos          ;  saved location

        pop     ds              ; Restore registers
        pop     es
        pop     di
        pop     si
        pop     dx
        pop     cx
        pop     bx
        pop     ax
        ret
timer           endp
```

The application should now display a zero segment and offset just to the left of the clock display. If you install this code and then hit enough carriage returns to scroll the screen, the zeros should appear to remain fixed on the screen. The IP display should seem more "solid" than our clock display because the refresh rate is faster.

7.2   Using a Stack-Frame Pointer

Armed with a timer-based program that writes zeros in the correct form to the screen many times per second, we can now complete this application and make it do something useful. We know that somewhere on the stack is the information that we need, namely the return address for the interrupt routine. Unfortunately, at the place we need it, in the middle of the timer routine, is some number of bytes deep on the stack. One way to retrieve them would be to count the number of push instructions we have used and then compute the offset from the current location pointed to by SP. This technique will work, but it will also make modification of the program somewhat difficult. Adding code that uses the stack will mean that this number must be recomputed.

A better approach would be to use what is called a *stack-frame pointer*. This is a common technique used in compilers for high-level languages. If a language uses the stack to pass parameters to subroutines, it is important to know how to find those parameters easily. This is done by using a register as a sort of bookmarker. What you do is copy the value of the stack pointer as early as possible in a subroutine, when you know that nothing has been added to the stack. Then you can use that register as a surrogate stack pointer, since it remembers where the top of the stack was and thus where the stack information you need can be found.

On the IBM PC, the convention is to use the BP register as a stack-frame pointer. Since there is no pressing reason to alter this convention, we will adopt it. We don't want to lose the contents of BP every time we reuse the stack-frame pointer, however, so we must save it first on the stack.

There are three characteristics of 8086/8088 stack management that become important at this point. First, only registers can be pushed onto the stack. Since all registers are 16 bits (one word) long, only words, not bytes, can be pushed. Second, the stack pointer always points to the last word pushed on the stack. Third, the PUSH operation *decreases* the stack pointer, POP increases it. This means that the stack starts at a high address and, as it grows, moves toward the lower addresses. To reach something pushed onto the stack, you must *add* to the stack pointer.

Thus, if we modify the timer_int routine as shown here we will have saved a stack-frame pointer from the start of the timer interrupt handler:

```
timer_int       proc    far
        sti
        push    bp
        mov     bp,sp
        pushf
        assume  ds:nothing
        call    old_timer
        call    timer
        pop     bp
        iret
timer_int       endp
```

Since the SP points to what was just pushed, we know that [BP] will point to its own old value, which brings us to an interesting and important digression. Since [BP] points to the previous value of BP, if we were writing a high-level language, and made sure that each subroutine established a stack-frame pointer using the method shown here and that every program started with BP = 0, we would have a chain that could be followed back through all the calls made to get to a point in a given subroutine. How? Well, since [BP] points to its last value and that last value points to the value before it and that value to an even earlier one, until one value finally points to the zero that was the original value, there is a chain that can be followed. Between each successive value are the contents of the stack, including any parameters passed. If enough information is available about the code that was running, these parameters can be examined. Why is this so important? It is this technique that is used very extensively in many high-level language debuggers. If stack-frame chaining is used, and the value of the stack-frame pointer at the time of a program crash is known, this technique may help pinpoint, via a debugger, what went wrong.

We know that [BP] contains its old value. Since the stack grows toward low memory, [BP+2] will contain the offset of the calling address, and [BP+4] will contain the segment. [BP+6] contains a word that holds the system flags at the time of interrupt. Conceivably, this information could be added to the front panel display, but to keep things simple we will not do so here.

Now that we know how to find the return address, we can complete our program by modifying **timer** to display the return segment and offset instead of zeros:

```
timer           proc    near
        assume  cs:cseg,ds:cseg
        push    ax
        push    bx
        push    cx
        push    dx
        push    si
        push    di
        push    es
        push    ds

        mov     bx,cs           ; Set DS to be same as CS
        mov     ds,bx           ;   by means of BX
        call    getpos          ; Save current cursor loc
        push    bx              ;   on stack
        mov     bx,location     ; Move to upper right
        call    setpos          ;   corner, left of clock
```

```
                ; The stack frame looks like this:
                ; [BP]      word    Old value of BP
                ; [BP+2]    word    Offset of calling address
                ; [BP+4]    word    Segment of calling address
                ; [BP+6]    word    Flags at interrupt
        mov     dx,word ptr ss:[bp+2] ; Offset of addr
        mov     es,word ptr ss:[bp+4] ; seg of addr
        call    ddword              ; Display 0000:0000
        pop     bx                  ; Move cursor back to its
        call    setpos              ;  saved location

        pop     ds
        pop     es
        pop     di
        pop     si
        pop     dx
        pop     cx
        pop     bx
        pop     ax
        ret
timer           endp
```

The front-panel resident application *must* be the last application to link with the timer interrupt. If it is not, the address displayed will always be that of the layer that was installed afterward, from which this would be called as a subroutine.

7.3   FPANEL.ASM – An Instruction Pointer Display

This program displays the program counter at frequent intervals in the upper right corner of the screen.

```
cseg    segment para public 'CODE'
        org     100H
        assume  cs:cseg,ds:cseg
start:
        jmp     initialize

old_timer       dd
```

```
timer_int        proc      far
        sti
        pushf
        assume  ds:nothing
        call    old_timer
        push    bp
        mov     bp,sp
        call    timer
        pop     bp
        iret
timer_int        endp

timer            proc      near
        assume  cs:cseg,ds:cseg
        push    ax
        push    bx
        push    cx
        push    dx
        push    si
        push    di
        push    es
        push    ds

        mov     bx,cs
        mov     ds,bx
        call    getpos
        push    bx
        mov     bx,location
        call    setpos
          ; The stack looks like this:
          ;                       New stack since BP saved
          ;       [BP]     word   Old value of BP
          ;       [BP+2]   word   Offset of calling address
          ;       [BP+4]   word   Segment of calling address
          ;       [BP+6]   word   Flags at interrupt
        mov     dx,word ptr ss:[bp+2] ; Offset of addr
        mov     es,word ptr ss:[bp+4] ; Seg of addr
        call    ddword
        pop     bx
        call    setpos

        pop     ds
        pop     es
        pop     di
        pop     si
```

```
        pop     dx
        pop     cx
        pop     bx
        pop     ax
        ret
timer           endp

; Get the current cursor position and return it in BX
getpos          proc    near
        push    ax
        push    cx
        push    dx

        mov     ah,03H
        mov     bh,0            ; Page zero
        int     10H
        mov     bx,dx           ; Return the position in BX

        pop     dx
        pop     cx
        pop     ax
        ret
getpos          endp

; Set the current cursor position to the value in BX
setpos          proc    near
        push    ax
        push    bx
        push    dx

        mov     ah,02H
        mov     dx,bx
        mov     bh,0
        int     10H

        pop     ax
        pop     bx
        pop     dx
        ret
setpos          endp

;       ES:DX contains doubleword to be displayed
ddword          proc    near
        push    dx              ; Save offset temporarily
        mov     dx,es           ; Move Segment to DX
```

```
        call    dsword          ; Display segment
        call    dcolon          ; Print a colon
        pop     dx              ; Restore offset to DX
        call    dsword          ; Display offset
        ret
ddword          endp

;       DX containes singleword to be displayed
dsword          proc    near
        push    dx              ; Save low byte temporarily
        mov     dl,dh           ; Move high byte to low byte
        call    dbyte           ; Display high byte
        pop     dx              ; Restore low byte to DL
        call    dbyte           ; Display low byte
        ret
dsword          endp

;       DL contains byte to be displayed
dbyte           proc    near
        push    ax              ; Save any registers used
        push    dx
        push    si

        push    dx              ; Save low nybble temporarily
        push    cx              ; Save CX
        mov     cl,4            ; Set shift count to 4
        shr     dx,cl           ; Move high nybble into low
        and     dx,000FH        ; Mask out all but low nybble
        mov     si,dx           ; Use low nybble as index into
        mov     al,hextab[si]   ; hex char table
        call    dchar           ; Display character
        pop     cx              ; Restore CX
        pop     dx              ; Restore low nybble

        and     dx,000FH        ; Mask out all but low nybble
        mov     si,dx           ; Use low nybble as index into
        mov     al,hextab[si]   ; hex char table
        call    dchar           ; Display character
        pop     si              ; Restore registers
        pop     dx
        pop     ax
        ret
dbyte           endp

; Display a colon
```

```
dcolon          proc    near
        mov     al,':'
        call    dchar
        ret
dcolon          endp

; Display the character contained in AL
dchar           proc    near
        push    ax
        push    bx
        mov     bh,1
        mov     ah,0EH
        int     10H
        pop     bx
        pop     ax
        ret
dchar           endp

location        dw      0041H
hextab          db      '0123456789ABCDEF',0

initialize:
        mov     bx,cs
        mov     ds,bx

        mov     al,08H
        mov     ah,35H
        int     21H
        mov     old_timer,bx
        mov     old_timer[2],es

        mov     dx,offset timer_int
        mov     al,08H
        mov     ah,25H
        int     21H

        mov     dx,offset initialize
        int     27H

cseg    ends
        end     start
```

Chapter 8

An Interrupt-Vector Display

To write resident applications on an IBM PC, you must understand the interrupt structure. This mechanism is the key to all the I/O and system operations under DOS. We have already constructed some tools to help us examine the interrupt-vector table. This tool is quite useful, but it runs only as an application at the DOS level. Suppose a program changes an interrupt vector on entry and restores it on exit. A vector-display application would not tell us a thing about these transient vectors, since to examine them we must leave the program that permits them to exist. Is there a way for us to examine the interrupt-vector table without leaving the current application? The answer is, of course, yes. We can modify our earlier program to make it memory resident.

A memory resident vector display program solves some problems, but it raises other questions that we must think about before we can begin to write code. First and foremost among these questions is that of linkage: if we use this program to examine and debug memory resident applications and it is in fact a memory resident application itself, won't it interfere with other resident applications since it must be linked somehow into the interrupt-vector table? One might find an analogy here to physics, where the act of measuring some characteristic of a particle alters the behavior of that characteristic. How can we install a vector display program so that its effect on the system will be minimal while still permitting us to see the information we requre?

Obviously, binding it to a key on the keyboard is not the solution. The keyboard interrupt is probably the most frequently replaced interrupt vector under DOS. If we were to insert a linkage there, the next memory resident application that came along might erase that link and replace it, rendering our code useless. However, there is no other generally accessible signaling mechanism on the IBM PC. Well, almost no other....

There are three key sets on the IBM PC that can bypass the normal keyboard interrupt mechanism. The most well known is CONTROL-ALT-DEL, which generates an interrupt to the reboot vector The second is CONTROL-BREAK, which generates an interrupt to the CONTROL-BREAK handler. The last is PrtSc. This generates an INT 5H, which is supposed to call a routine to print a copy of the screen on the printer. If we decide that, for a time, the display of interrupts is more important than the printing of screens, we can use PrtSc as the link for our vector display without interfering with other, more common vectors and without significantly impairing the operation of the system.

Let's rewrite our basic resident program so that it will replace the PrtSc interrupt rather than the communications interrupt.

```
cseg      segment
          assume  cs:cseg,ds:cseg
          org     100H
start:
          jmp     initialize

old_prtsc_io    dd

new_prtsc_io                proc    far
          assume  cs:cseg,ds:cseg
          sti
          iret
new_prtsc_io                endp

initialize:
          assume  cs:cseg,ds:cseg
          mov     bx,cs
          mov     ds,bx

          mov     al,05H
          mov     ah,35H
          int     21H
          mov     old_prtsc_io,bx
          mov     old_prtsc_io[2],es
          mov     dx,offset new_prtsc_io
          mov     al,05H
          mov     ah,25H
          int     21H
```

```
        mov     dx,offset initialize
        int     27H

cseg    ends
        end     start
```

All we did was replace 16H with 05H and keyboard with prtsc. Nevertheless, these small changes will cause this program to link to the PrtSc vector. By adding to new_prtsc_io, we can bend the PrtSc function to our will.

The next question is one of display. How do we cause our vector listing to appear on the screen? Will normal output calls work directly? Clearly, we are asking for trouble if we try to use the file control block or handle-based I/O functions, unless we take some pains to save the old file control block or handle and use one of our own. It is possible to do so, but is it necessary? The ROM screen output calls are the best bet here. They are low-level calls, unencumbered by the idea of file control blocks or handles. We can modify our basic PrtSc resident application to display a simple ASCIIZ string. Since we have already written code to do that in our non-resident vector display, we will simply add that code here.

```
new_prtsc_io            proc    far
        assume  cs:cseg,ds:cseg
        sti
        push    ds
        push    bx
        push    si
        mov     bx,cs
        mov     ds,bx
        mov     si,offset string
        call    dstring
        pop     si
        pop     bx
        pop     ds
        iret
new_prtsc_io            endp

;       DS:SI points to ASCIIZ string to be printed
dstring proc    near
        push    si
        push    ax
dis:
        mov     al,[si]                 ; Fetch the next character
```

```
          cmp      al,0            ; If it is zero, we are done
          je       disdone
          call     dchar           ; If not, print it
          inc      si              ; Advance to next char
          jmp      dis
disdone:
          pop      ax
          pop      si
          ret
dstring endp

; Display the character contained in AL
dchar     proc     near
          push     ax
          push     bx
          mov      bh,1
          mov      ah,0EH
          int      10H
          pop      bx
          pop      ax
          ret
dchar     endp

string  db       'Hello world',0dH,0aH,0
```

Before you run the .COM file this program assembles into, run the IVEC
vector-display application. Note the value for the Print Screen vector. After
running the .COM file use IVEC again to see that the vector has changed. You
should notice that the new value is :0107H. The segment may change,
but for this program, (and many others in this book), the offset will always be
107H. The program segment prefix is 100H bytes long, the jmp initialize adds
another 3 bytes, and the double word that holds the old vector is 4 bytes. For
other programs, the offset may not be 107H, but it can be deduced from the
code. An offset that is vastly different from what you expect may indicate a
bug.

To invoke this code, hit the PrtSc key (actually, SHIFT-PrtSc on most machines). This should cause the "Hello world" message to appear. You'll notice
that the DOS prompt does not reappear until you hit a carriage return. This
odd behavior stems from the fact that DOS is unaware of the "Hello world"
message, and thus has no reason to generate a new prompt. The carriage return
is actually seen by DOS, and it behaves as it would normally. You could have
typed a command, followed by carriage return, and it would have been

interpreted properly. You have generated a display on the screen, behind DOS's back.

This fact has one major implication. By doing output in this manner, it is possible to mess up the screen, with the currently running program being unaware of the changes. This has great bearing on the mannerisms of "well-behaved" resident applications. In some cases, such as the debugging tool we are writing now, one does not mind if a display of information trashes the contents of the screen. In the case of "pop-up" programs such as notepads or calculators, we demand better manners.

8.1 Listing the Vectors

Since we have successfully stolen the output routine from our vector display application, and since this code does not use the interrupt we are replacing, there is no reason we cannot try to steal the rest of the code.

```
new_prtsc_io            proc    far
        sti
        push    bx
        push    ds
        mov     bx,cs
        mov     ds,bx
        call    vectors
        pop     ds
        pop     bx
        iret
new_prtsc_io            endp

; Scans through the display table, printing two vectors per line.
; If any record has an interrupt number of zero, this indicates the
; end of the table.
vectors         proc    near
        mov     di,offset disptab; Pointer to start of table
        mov     dh,0            ; Zero out top half of DX
vloop:
        mov     dl,[di]         ; Get interrupt number
        cmp     dl,0            ; If it is zero, we are done
        je      vdone           ;   so exit loop
        add     di,1            ; Advance pointer 1 byte
        mov     si,[di]         ; Get pointer to description string
        call    dvector         ; Call display routine
```

```
        add     di,2                    ; Advance to next record

        mov     dl,[di]                 ; Get interrupt number
        cmp     dl,0                    ; If it is zero, we are done
        je      vdone                   ;   so exit loop
        add     di,1                    ; Advance pointer 1 byte
        mov     si,[di]                 ; Get pointer to description string
        call    dvector                 ; Call display routine
        add     di,2                    ; Advance to next record

        call    dcrlf                   ; Print a carriage return
        jmp     vloop
vdone:
        call    dcrlf                   ; Print a final carriage return
        ret
vectors endp

; Displays an interrupt vector.  Display is in the form of
; <banner string> <interrupt number> <vector seg>:<vector offset>
; where <interrupt number>, <vector seg> and <vector offset> are all
; hexadecimal numbers.
;
; Call with
;       DX      - interrupt number
;       DS:SI   - pointer to banner string
dvector proc    near
        call    dstring ; Display string in DS:SI
        call    dbyte   ; Display byte in DL
        call    dspace  ; Display a space

        mov     al,dl   ; Move interrupt number to AL
        mov     ah,35H  ; Function is GET INTERRUPT VECTOR
        int     21H
        mov     dx,bx   ; Move BX to DX so we can display the
        call    ddword  ; double-word in ES:DX
        call    dspace  ; Display a space
        ret
dvector endp


;       DS:SI points to ASCIIZ string to be printed
dstring proc    near
        push    si
        push    ax
dis:
        mov     al,[si] ; Fetch next character
```

```
        cmp     al,0      ; If it is zero, we are done
        je      disdone
        call    dchar     ; If not, print it
        inc     si        ; Advance pointer to next character
        jmp     dis
disdone:
        pop     ax
        pop     si
        ret
dstring endp

;       ES:DX contains doubleword to be displayed
ddword  proc    near
        push    dx        ; Save offset temporarily
        mov     dx,es     ; Move Segment to DX
        call    dsword    ; Display segment
        call    dcolon    ; Print a ":"
        pop     dx        ; Restore offset to DX
        call    dsword    ; Display offset
        ret
ddword  endp

;       DX containes singleword to be displayed
dsword  proc    near
        push    dx        ; Save low byte temporarily
        mov     dl,dh     ; Move high byte to low byte
        call    dbyte     ; Display high byte
        pop     dx        ; Restore low byte to DL
        call    dbyte     ; Display low byte
        ret
dsword  endp

;       DL contains byte to be displayed
dbyte   proc    near
        push    ax        ; Save any registers used
        push    dx
        push    si

        push    dx        ; Save low nybble temporarily
        push    cx        ; Save CX
        mov     cl,4      ; Set shift count to 4
        shr     dx,cl     ; Shift high nybble into low nybble
        and     dx,000FH  ; Mask out all but low nybble
        mov     si,dx     ; Use this low nybble as an index into the
        mov     al,hextab[si]   ; hexadecimal character table
```

```
        call    dchar     ; Display character
        pop     cx        ; Restore CX
        pop     dx        ; Restore low nybble

        and     dx,000FH  ; Mask out all but low nybble
        mov     si,dx     ; Use low nybble as an index into the
        mov     al,hextab[si]   ; hexadecimal character table
        call    dchar     ; Display character
        pop     si        ; Restore registers
        pop     dx
        pop     ax
        ret
dbyte   endp

; Display a ":"
dcolon  proc    near
        mov     al,':'
        call    dchar
        ret
dcolon  endp

; Display a " "
dspace  proc    near
        mov     al,' '
        call    dchar
        ret
dspace  endp

; Display a Carriage Return/Line Feed
dcrlf   proc    near
        mov     al,0DH
        call    dchar
        mov     al,0AH
        call    dchar
        ret
dcrlf   endp

; Display character contained in AL
dchar   proc    near
        push    ax
        push    bx
        mov     bh,1
        mov     ah,0EH
        int     10H
        pop     bx
```

```
        pop     ax
        ret
dchar   endp

hextab  db      '0123456789ABCDEF',0

disptab db      05H     ; Print screen
        dw      v05
        db      19H     ; Bootstrap loader
        dw      v19

        db      08H     ; Timer tick
        dw      v08
        db      1AH     ; Real-time clock
        dw      v1A

        db      09H     ; Keyboard input
        dw      v09
        db      1BH     ; CTRL-Break handler
        dw      v1B

        db      0BH     ; Comm. port 1
        dw      v0B
        db      1CH     ; Timer control
        dw      v1C

        db      0CH     ; Comm. port 0
        dw      v0C
        db      1DH     ; Pointer to video parameter table
        dw      v1D

        db      0DH     ; Hard disk controller
        dw      v0D
        db      1EH     ; Pointer to disk parameter table
        dw      v1E

        db      0EH     ; Floppy disk controller
        dw      v0E
        db      1FH     ; Pointer to graphics character table
        dw      v1F

        db      0FH     ; Printer controller
        dw      v0F
        db      20H     ; Program terminate
        dw      v20
```

```
        db      10H     ; Video driver
        dw      v10
        db      21H     ; DOS universal function
        dw      v21

        db      11H     ; Equipment check
        dw      v11
        db      22H     ; Pointer to termination handler
        dw      v22

        db      12H     ; Memory size check
        dw      v12
        db      23H     ; Pointer to CTRL-C handler
        dw      v23

        db      13H     ; Disk driver
        dw      v13
        db      24H     ; Pointer to critical error handler
        dw      v24

        db      14H     ; Communications driver
        dw      v14
        db      25H     ; Absolute disk read
        dw      v25

        db      15H     ; Cassette driver
        dw      v15
        db      26H     ; Absolute disk write
        dw      v26

        db      16H     ; Keyboard driver
        dw      v16
        db      27H     ; Terminate and stay resident
        dw      v27

        db      17H     ; Printer driver
        dw      v17
        db      2FH     ; Print spooler
        dw      v2F

        db      18H     ; ROM BASIC
        dw      v18
        db      0
        dw      0
```

```
v05     db          'Print screen:               ',0
v08     db          'Timer tick controller:      ',0
v09     db          'Keyboard input:             ',0
v0B     db          'Communication port 1:       ',0
v0C     db          'Communication port 0:       ',0
v0D     db          'Hard disk controller:       ',0
v0E     db          'Floppy disk controller:     ',0
v0F     db          'Printer controller:         ',0
v10     db          'Video driver:               ',0
v11     db          'Equipment check:            ',0
v12     db          'Memory size check:          ',0
v13     db          'Disk driver:                ',0
v14     db          'Communication driver:       ',0
v15     db          'Cassette driver:            ',0
v16     db          'Keyboard driver:            ',0
v17     db          'Printer driver:             ',0
v18     db          'ROM BASIC:                  ',0
v19     db          'Bootstrap loader:           ',0
v1A     db          'Real-time clock:            ',0
v1B     db          'Ctrl-Break handler:         ',0
v1C     db          'Timer control:              ',0
v1D     db          'Video parameter table:      ',0
v1E     db          'Disk parameter table:       ',0
v1F     db          'Graphic character table:    ',0
v20     db          'Program terminate:          ',0
v21     db          'DOS universal function:     ',0
v22     db          'Terminate vector:           ',0
v23     db          'Ctrl-C vector:              ',0
v24     db          'Critical error vector:      ',0
v25     db          'Absolute disk read:         ',0
v26     db          'Absolute disk write:        ',0
v27     db          'Terminate/stay resident:    ',0
v2F     db          'Print spooler:              ',0
```

This code works, but it is somewhat unpleasant to use, since the column position of the first line is dependent on where the cursor was located when **PrtSc** was struck. To fix this, we must decide where the cursor should go to perform this display. Typically, while in the DOS command processor, or any non-screen-oriented program, the cursor will spend most of its time on the bottom line of the screen, several characters to the right of the first column (due to the prompt). For screen-oriented programs, the cursor can be anywhere. Because of this wide variation, there is no "best" choice for the position, but we can adopt a convention. Since we know that all the information in this display will fit on less than one full screen and that a good guess for the cursor position under some circumstances is on the bottom line, why not always start the display from the upper left corner. By doing this, the code will run faster, since no scrolling is necessary. In addition, the columns will always line up, and there is a good chance that we will not overwrite the current command prompt.

To do this, we must learn how to perform two operations. First, we must be able to read the current cursor position, so that we can remember where the cursor was when we started. Second, we must be able to set the cursor position, so that we can move to the upper left corner to begin our display and return to the old position when we have finished. The ROM calls provide us with two routines to do just that, so we need do nothing too complicated.

We can add cursor control to this program at the topmost level, modifying only `new_prtsc_io`, as shown here:

```
new_prtsc_io              proc    far
      sti
      push    bx
      push    ds
      mov     bx,cs           ; Make Data Seg be the same as
      mov     ds,bx           ; the Code Seg

      call    getpos
      push    bx
      mov     bx,0000H        ; Upper left corner position
      call    setpos
      call    vectors
      pop     bx
      call    setpos

      pop     ds
      pop     bx
      iret
new_prtsc_io              endp

; Get the current cursor position and return it in BX
getpos                    proc    near
      push    ax
      push    cx              ; Since this function modifies CX
      push    dx

      mov     ah,03H
      mov     bh,0    ; Page zero
      int     10H
```

```
        mov     bx,dx     ; Return the position in BX

        pop     dx
        pop     cx
        pop     ax
        ret
getpos                    endp

; Set the current cursor position to the value in BX
setpos                    proc    near
        push    ax
        push    dx

        mov     ah,02H
        mov     dx,bx
        mov     bh,0
        int     10H

        pop     ax
        pop     dx
        ret
setpos                    endp
```

With the program now doing a little bit of display management, it becomes much cleaner and easier to read. In addition, by always starting in the upper left corner of the screen, you are guaranteed that the position of each vector on the screen will be the same each time the program is called. By doing this, your eye can learn where a vector display should be and can then find the vector of interest without having to search the screen for the right label. In the human-interface game, permitting users to form habits is highly regarded.

8.2 BASIC.ASM – A Test Display

This program makes an interrupt vector display with a dummy value, just to see if we can successfully link to the PrtSc vector.

```
cseg    segment
        assume  cs:cseg,ds:cseg
        org     100H
start:
        jmp     initialize
```

```
old_prtsc_io     dd

new_prtsc_io               proc    far
        assume  cs:cseg,ds:cseg
        sti
        push    ds
        push    bx
        push    si
        mov     bx,cs
        mov     ds,bx
        mov     si,offset string
        call    dstring
        pop     si
        pop     bx
        pop     ds
        iret
new_prtsc_io               endp

;       DS:SI points to ASCIIZ string to be printed
dstring proc    near
        push    si
        push    ax
dis:
        mov     al,[si]  ; Fetch the next character
        cmp     al,0     ; If it is zero, we are done
        je      disdone
        call    dchar    ; If not, print it
        inc     si       ; Advance pointer to the next character
        jmp     dis
disdone:
        pop     ax
        pop     si
        ret
dstring endp

; Display the character contained in AL
dchar   proc    near
        push    ax
        push    bx
        mov     bh,1
        mov     ah,0EH
        int     10H
        pop     bx
        pop     ax
        ret
```

```
dchar    endp

string   db      'Hello world',0dH,0aH,0

initialize:
         assume  cs:cseg,ds:cseg
         mov     bx,cs
         mov     ds,bx

         mov     al,05H
         mov     ah,35H
         int     21H
         mov     old_prtsc_io,bx
         mov     old_prtsc_io[2],es
         mov     dx,offset new_prtsc_io
         mov     al,05H
         mov     ah,25H
         int     21H

         mov     dx,offset initialize
         int     27H

cseg     ends
         end     start
```

8.3 VECTORS.ASM – An Interrupt Vector Display

The following code will display the current values of the interrupt vector table
when a **PrtSc** command is entered at the keyboard.

```
cseg     segment para public 'CODE'
         org     100H
         assume  cs:cseg,ds:cseg
start:
         jmp     initialize

old_prtsc_io    dd

new_prtsc_io            proc    far
         sti
         push    bx
         push    ds
         mov     bx,cs               ; Make Data Seg be the same as
```

```
        mov     ds,bx                   ; the Code Seg

        call    getpos
        push    bx
        mov     bx,0000H                ; Upper left corner position
        call    setpos
        call    vectors
        pop     bx
        call    setpos

        pop     ds
        pop     bx
        mov     ax,0
        iret
new_prtsc_io            endp

; Get the current cursor position and return it in BX
getpos                  proc    near
        push    ax
        push    cx              ; Since this function modifies CX
        push    dx

        mov     ah,03H
        mov     bh,0    ; Page zero
        int     10H
        mov     bx,dx   ; Return the position in BX

        pop     dx
        pop     cx
        pop     ax
        ret
getpos                  endp

; Set the current cursor position to the value in BX
setpos                  proc    near
        push    ax
        push    dx

        mov     ah,02H
        mov     dx,bx
        mov     bh,0
        int     10H

        pop     ax
        pop     dx
```

```
        ret
setpos                  endp


; Scans through the display table, printing two vectors per line.
; If any record has an interrupt number of zero, this indicates the
; end of the table.
vectors          proc    near
        mov     di,offset disptab; Pointer to the start of the table
        mov     dh,0            ; Zero out the top half of DX
vloop:
        mov     dl,[di]         ; Get the interrupt number
        cmp     dl,0            ; If it is zero, we are done
        je      vdone           ;   so exit loop
        add     di,1            ; Advance pointer 1 byte
        mov     si,[di]         ; Get pointer to description string
        call    dvector         ; Call the display routine
        add     di,2            ; Advance to the next record

        mov     dl,[di]         ; Get the interrupt number
        cmp     dl,0            ; If it is zero, we are done
        je      vdone           ;   so exit loop
        add     di,1            ; Advance pointer 1 byte
        mov     si,[di]         ; Get pointer to description string
        call    dvector         ; Call the display routine
        add     di,2            ; Advance to the next record

        call    dcrlf           ; Print a carriage return
        jmp     vloop
vdone:
        call    dcrlf           ; Print a final carriage return
        ret
vectors endp


; Displays an interrupt vector.  Display is in the form of
; <banner string>  <interrupt number> <vector seg>:<vector offset>
; where <interrupt number>, <vector seg> and <vector offset> are all
; hexadecimal numbers.
;
; Call with
;       DX      - interrupt number
;       DS:SI   - pointer to banner string
dvector proc    near
        call    dstring  ; Display the string in DS:SI
        call    dbyte    ; Display the byte in DL
        call    dspace   ; Display a space
```

```
        mov     al,dl      ; Move the interrupt number to AL
        mov     ah,35H     ; Function is GET INTERRUPT VECTOR
        int     21H
        mov     dx,bx      ; Move BX to DX so we can display the
        call    ddword     ; double-word in ES:DX
        call    dspace     ; Display a space
        ret
dvector endp

;       DS:SI points to ASCIIZ string to be printed
dstring proc    near
        push    si
        push    ax
dis:
        mov     al,[si]    ; Fetch the next character
        cmp     al,0       ; If it is zero, we are done
        je      disdone
        call    dchar      ; If not, print it
        inc     si         ; Advance pointer to the next character
        jmp     dis
disdone:
        pop     ax
        pop     si
        ret
dstring endp

;       ES:DX contains doubleword to be displayed
ddword  proc    near
        push    dx         ; Save the offset temporarily
        mov     dx,es      ; Move the Segment to DX
        call    dsword     ; Display the segment
        call    dcolon     ; Print a ":"
        pop     dx         ; Restore the offset to DX
        call    dsword     ; Display the offset
        ret
ddword  endp

;       DX containes singleword to be displayed
dsword  proc    near
        push    dx         ; Save the low byte temporarily
        mov     dl,dh      ; Move the high byte to the low byte
        call    dbyte      ; Display the high byte
        pop     dx         ; Restore the low byte to DL
        call    dbyte      ; Display the low byte
```

```
        ret
dsword  endp


;       DL contains byte to be displayed
dbyte   proc    near
        push    ax        ; Save any registers used
        push    dx
        push    si

        push    dx        ; Save the low nybble temporarily
        push    cx        ; Save CX
        mov     cl,4      ; Set shift count to 4
        shr     dx,cl     ; Shift the high nybble into the low nybble
        and     dx,000FH  ; Mask out all but the low nybble
        mov     si,dx     ; Use this low nybble as an index into the
        mov     al,hextab[si]   ; hexadecimal character table
        call    dchar     ; Display the character
        pop     cx        ; Restore CX
        pop     dx        ; Restore the low nybble

        and     dx,000FH  ; Mask out all but the low nybble
        mov     si,dx     ; Use the low nybble as an index into the
        mov     al,hextab[si]   ; hexadecimal character table
        call    dchar     ; Display the character
        pop     si        ; Restore the registers
        pop     dx
        pop     ax
        ret
dbyte   endp

; Display a ":"
dcolon  proc    near
        mov     al,':'
        call    dchar
        ret
dcolon  endp

; Display a " "
dspace  proc    near
        mov     al,' '
        call    dchar
        ret
dspace  endp

; Display a Carriage Return/Line Feed
```

```
dcrlf   proc    near
        mov     al,0DH
        call    dchar
        mov     al,0AH
        call    dchar
        ret
dcrlf   endp

; Display the character contained in AL
dchar   proc    near
        push    ax
        push    bx
        mov     bh,1
        mov     ah,0EH
        int     10H
        pop     bx
        pop     ax
        ret
dchar   endp

hextab  db      '0123456789ABCDEF',0

disptab db      05H     ; Print screen
        dw      v05
        db      19H     ; Bootstrap loader
        dw      v19

        db      08H     ; Timer tick
        dw      v08
        db      1AH     ; Real-time clock
        dw      v1A

        db      09H     ; Keyboard input
        dw      v09
        db      1BH     ; CTRL-Break handler
        dw      v1B

        db      0BH     ; Comm. port 1
        dw      v0B
        db      1CH     ; Timer control
        dw      v1C

        db      0CH     ; Comm. port 0
        dw      v0C
        db      1DH     ; Pointer to video parameter table
```

```
        dw      v1D

        db      0DH     ; Hard disk controller
        dw      v0D
        db      1EH     ; Pointer to disk parameter table
        dw      v1E

        db      0EH     ; Floppy disk controller
        dw      v0E
        db      1FH     ; Pointer to graphics character table
        dw      v1F

        db      0FH     ; Printer controller
        dw      v0F
        db      20H     ; Program terminate
        dw      v20

        db      10H     ; Video driver
        dw      v10
        db      21H     ; DOS universal function
        dw      v21

        db      11H     ; Equipment check
        dw      v11
        db      22H     ; Pointer to termination handler
        dw      v22

        db      12H     ; Memory size check
        dw      v12
        db      23H     ; Pointer to CTRL-C handler
        dw      v23

        db      13H     ; Disk driver
        dw      v13
        db      24H     ; Pointer to critical error handler
        dw      v24

        db      14H     ; Communications driver
        dw      v14
        db      25H     ; Absolute disk read
        dw      v25

        db      15H     ; Cassette driver
        dw      v15
        db      26H     ; Absolute disk write
```

```
        dw      v26

        db      16H     ; Keyboard driver
        dw      v16
        db      27H     ; Terminate and stay resident
        dw      v27

        db      17H     ; Printer driver
        dw      v17
        db      2FH     ; Print spooler
        dw      v2F

        db      18H     ; ROM BASIC
        dw      v18
        db      0
        dw      0

v05     db      'Print screen:          ',0
v08     db      'Timer tick controller: ',0
v09     db      'Keyboard input:        ',0
v0B     db      'Communication port 1:  ',0
v0C     db      'Communication port 0:  ',0
v0D     db      'Hard disk controller:  ',0
v0E     db      'Floppy disk controller:',0
v0F     db      'Printer controller:    ',0
v10     db      'Video driver:          ',0
v11     db      'Equipment check:       ',0
v12     db      'Memory size check:     ',0
v13     db      'Disk driver:           ',0
v14     db      'Communication driver:  ',0
v15     db      'Cassette driver:       ',0
v16     db      'Keyboard driver:       ',0
v17     db      'Printer driver:        ',0
v18     db      'ROM BASIC:             ',0
v19     db      'Bootstrap loader:      ',0
v1A     db      'Real-time clock:       ',0
v1B     db      'Ctrl-Break handler:    ',0
v1C     db      'Timer control:         ',0
v1D     db      'Video parameter table: ',0
v1E     db      'Disk parameter table:  ',0
v1F     db      'Graphic character table:',0
v20     db      'Program terminate:     ',0
v21     db      'DOS universal function:',0
v22     db      'Terminate vector:      ',0
v23     db      'Ctrl-C vector:         ',0
```

```
v24        db        'Critical error vector:    ',0
v25        db        'Absolute disk read:       ',0
v26        db        'Absolute disk write:      ',0
v27        db        'Terminate/stay resident: ',0
v2F        db        'Print spooler:            ',0

initialize:
           assume    cs:cseg,ds:cseg
           mov       bx,cs
           mov       ds,bx

           mov       al,05H
           mov       ah,35H
           int       21H
           mov       old_prtsc_io,bx
           mov       old_prtsc_io[2],es
           mov       dx,offset new_prtsc_io
           mov       al,05H
           mov       ah,25H
           int       21H

           mov       dx,offset initialize
           int       27H

cseg       ends
           end       start
```

Chapter 9

Controlling the Machine

One problem with computers is that they are so damn finicky. Most programs are designed to solve a certain set of problems in a certain way. If the set of problems is big enough and the choice of methods clever enough, we call these programs well designed. There are times, however, when it would be nice to do things from within a program that the designers never considered. Quite often, the action you choose is not possible from within the program you are executing. This may or may not be shortsightedness on the part of the designers. No two people solve problems in the same way. Everyone has a style, an approach to getting their work done. People like programs that are similar to their own style or that have a style they agree with. People don't like programs that do things in a way they would never consider reasonable.

We have already built a program that lets you tell DOS what to do by simulating your typing at the keyboard. Sometimes, however, we want to perform an action directly, without standing back and issuing a command to do so. Sometimes we want to look deep into the machine, see what bits are set, and change them ourselves if we don't like the way things look. If there is a program to make the changes we want, we can just run it – if we don't happen to be running something else, that is.

One place in which this happens all the time is the communications ports. There are a lot of programs for telecommunications that let you use the IBM PC as a terminal or transfer files from one computer to another. You connect a modem to one of your serial ports and use that modem to talk across the telephone to another computer. Those computers have communication programs, as well. Each of those programs has a designer, and each designer has an opinion about how telecommunications should be done. Few of those designers share the same opinion. So you discover that, having connected to a computer, you are using the wrong baud rate, or parity, or word length, or something.

If you've chosen your communication program well, you may be able to switch gears and change the mode of your communications port on the fly. Suppose you have a less powerful program, such as many of the public-domain telecom programs. Or suppose you use several programs in the course of a day's work, and can't find the particular manual that explains exactly how to go about doing what you'd like to do. How do you solve the problem?

One way might be to use a resident application. Most programs that fiddle with the communications port parameters don't keep an eye on them to make sure they remain the same. If the mode changes when the communications program isn't looking, everything should still work.

Here we begin to see some of the real dangers and the seductiveness of the "dark side" of resident-application programming. When you can sneak in and change anything in the machine, there is a real temptation to overdo it. This program is an example of one that is on the borderline. There is no chance that this program will work with every telecom program on the market. But it may do some of the right things for some people, and thus it is worth understanding.

9.1   Rewriting the Key Expander

Let's define our goal a little better. What we want is a program that allows us to examine and reset the state of the two serial ports COM1: and COM2:. We want to see what the current settings, such as baud rate, number of stop bits, parity, and bits per character have been set to, and we want to reset those parameters at will.

What sort of control mechanism can we use for this? Well, one way might be to write a resident version of the MODE command that would prompt us for parameters in the system format, and then set them correctly. This is a clumsy approach, however. To write a resident command that prompts for a parameter string and then parses it is certainly possible, but it may be more work than is necessary to solve the problem. Another consideration is that the DOS MODE command, while it is one solution to this problem, is extremely cryptic and difficult to use. The order of parameters is specific, and the correct form of those parameters is obscure and hard to remember. Perhaps a better model for the MODE command is in order.

Another approach is along the same lines as the keystroke expander we have already written. We know that we can easily detect expanded characters and perform actions based on them. In the past, those actions have been similar, namely to begin returning the value of a predefined string. There is no reason we could not use the same sort of mechanism to execute our own specially written code.

What will we need to do this? In a way, this is an easier problem to solve than the general-purpose keystroke expander. Since we are not returning anything via the returned character, as we did with the expanded keys, we need not take control of the keyboard status function. So all the code related to that function can be removed. In general, though, we can use a mechanism extremely similar to that of the keystroke expander. In that program, we had a table of characters, each of which was bound to a pointer to a string. A pointer to a string indicates the location of some information in memory. A pointer to a subroutine does exactly the same thing. We can build exactly the same type of table but simply perform a different operation on the information contained within. In the case of the string, we began returning it as data. In the case of a subroutine, we can execute it.

```
cseg    segment
        assume  cs:cseg,ds:cseg
        org     100H
start:
        jmp     initialize


old_keyboard_io dd

        assume  ds:nothing
new_keyboard_io         proc    far
        sti
        cmp     ah,0                    ; Is this call a READ request?
        je      ksread
        jmp     old_keyboard_io         ; Handle the remaining subfunction.
ksread:
        call    keyread                 ; Get the next character to return
        iret
new_keyboard_io         endp


; Read a character from the keyboard input queue, if not expanding
; or the expansion string, if expansion is in progress.
keyread         proc    near
```

```
        push    si
readchar:
        pushf                           ; Let the original routine
        call    old_keyboard_io         ; determine keyboard status.
        cmp     al,0
        je      extended
        jmp     readdone
extended:
        mov     si,offset keytab
nextext:
        cmp     byte ptr cs:[si],0      ; Is this the end of the table?
        je      readdone
        cmp     ah,cs:[si]
        je      startexpand
        add     si,3
        jmp     nextext
startexpand:
        add     si,1
        cmp     word ptr cs:[si],0
        je      readdone
        push    ax
        push    bx
        push    cx
        push    dx
        push    si
        push    di
        push    bp
        push    ds
        call    word ptr cs:[si]
        pop     ds
        pop     bp
        pop     di
        pop     si
        pop     dx
        pop     cx
        pop     bx
        pop     ax
readdone:
        pop     si
        ret
keyread         endp

keytab  db      120
        dw      test
        db      0
```

```
            dw       0

            assume   cs:cseg,ds:cseg

teststring          db        'This is a test',0

test                proc      near
       mov   bx,cs
       mov   ds,bx
       mov   si,offset teststring
       call  dstring
       ret
test                endp

; Displays the string pointed to by DS:SI
dstring             proc      near
       push  si
       push  ax
       cmp   si,0
       je    dsdone
dloop:
       mov   al,[si]
       cmp   al,0
       je    dsdone
       call  dchar
       inc   si
       jmp   dloop
dsdone:
       pop   ax
       pop   si
       ret
dstring             endp

; Display the character contained in AL
dchar               proc      near
       push  ax
       push  bx
       mov   bh,1
       mov   ah,0EH
       int   10H
       pop   bx
       pop   ax
       ret
dchar               endp
```

```
initialize:
        assume  cs:cseg,ds:cseg
        mov     bx,cs
        mov     ds,bx

        mov     al,16H
        mov     ah,35H
        int     21H
        mov     old_keyboard_io,bx
        mov     old_keyboard_io[2],es
        mov     dx,offset new_keyboard_io
        mov     al,16H
        mov     ah,25H
        int     21H

        mov     dx,offset initialize
        int     27H

cseg    ends
        end     start
```

The first part of this code is almost identical to the corresponding parts of the keystroke expander. We intercept the **read-character** subfunction of INT 16H *(keyboard I/O)*. If the character read is an expanded character, then we scan through a table until we find a match. Up to this point, we are using the same code we wrote for the keystroke expander. Here, however, things get a little different. If we find a match in the table, we will have a word that is the starting address of a subroutine. Given that, we save the state of the machine onto the stack and then call the subroutine. The ability to treat pointers to code like data is an important and powerful programming tool. Many sophisticated programs keep tables of subroutines to simplify the coding structures. These tables, one of which is shown in the current example, are known as *dispatch tables*, since they perform a directive function similar to a dispatcher in a train station, or a taxi company. Dispatch tables, and treating pointers to subroutines as data, are a basic concept on which threaded languages, such as FORTH, are based. In some cases, you can dramatically simplify the way a program is written by using this technique. In other cases, of course, you can make a simple program almost impossible to read or debug with exactly the same set of tools.

The basic program we have built will detect one particular keystroke, ALT-1. When that key is typed, the **test** subroutine will be run. For the purposes of this experiment, **test** will simply cause a letter to appear on the screen. At first glance, this seems similar to the keystroke expander. This is misleading, because the character, though it has appeared on the screen, can never be read by DOS. We are not transmitting it back through the return mechanism as we did for the keystroke expander. We are sending back the character that was read and acted on, in this case, the `ALT-1`.

9.2 The State of the Serial Ports

One of the first steps toward correctly changing something is to understand it as it is now. While DOS provides a ROM system call to set the state of the serial ports, it does not provide a call to examine what that state is. But since we are in the machine anyway, perhaps we can write one.

We now have a skeleton through which we can run little snippets of code, to examine or change the state of the machine as we wish. To add functions, we simply need add a character, a pointer, and a subroutine to this skeleton and we can call the code with a single keystroke. Now we just need to figure out what to put in that subroutine, and we are all set.

Several of the IBM PC peripheral devices are connected to *I/O ports*. Many people quite understandably confuse these ports with *communication ports*, the devices that speak to the modem or a serial line. The two are quite similar ideas at different layers of complexity. A communications port is a high-level concept for an IBM PC. It is a device that permits the communication of information from your computer to another computer or device. It is a way to get information in and out of the box. The low-level I/O ports we are speaking of here are devices that allow one component of your IBM PC to communicate with other components. They are ways of passing information back and forth *within* the box. In fact, it takes quite a few low-level I/O ports to perform the higher-level function of a single communications port.

One reads an I/O port by using the `IN` opcode. Writing to an I/O port is done with the corresponding `OUT` opcode. The 8086/8088 permits a system to have as many as sixty-four thousand I/O ports, as many as a 16-bit word can address. To allow a sort of compatibility with programs from 8-bit machines, the architecture provides for two kinds of I/O port addresses: those less than a full byte and those that require a full word. To use a port whose number is less than 256, you simply use the number directly:

```
in      ax,80H          ; Read a word from port 80H
in      al,90H          ; Read a byte from port 90H
```

All input and output calls must use the AX register. To read a word, use AX. To read a byte, use AL. For ports whose number is greater than or equal to 256, the DX register is used:

```
mov     dx,180H
in      ax,dx            ; Read a word from port 180H
mov     dx,190H
in      al,dx            ; Read a byte from port 190H
```

A single communications port requires seven I/O ports to operate. Full details of the operations can be painfully extracted from the *IBM Technical Reference Manual.* Luckily for us, full details are rarely necessary. One can set the state of a communications port by using INT 14H function OH *(initialize communications port).* To read the state, one has to use just three of the seven ports.

DOS permits the IBM PC to have up to four communications ports. Typically, IBM PCs have just two: COM1: and COM2:. Each communications port requires seven I/O ports. The I/O port addresses are not random, but follow a pattern. Each address is a full word. The low-order byte indicates which I/O port of the seven to use. The available ports are: F8H, F9H, FAH, FBH, FCH, FDH, and FEH. The ports we are interested in are F8H and F9H, which contain a value that we can use to determine the baud rate, and FBH, which contains the line control register (LCR). The LCR contains the rest of the information about line status that we need.

The high-order byte of the I/O port address indicates the communications port, with COM1: = 3 and COM2: = 2. Thus, if we wanted to read the LCR of COM1:, we would use this code:

```
mov     dx,3FBH          ; Read Line Control Register for COM1:
in      al,dx            ;   into AL
```

Baud rate is determined by a number that the communications hardware uses as a divisor. The divisor is a single word, whose low byte can be found at port F8H and whose high byte can be found at port F9H – sometimes. A special bit, called the divisor latch access bit (DLAB) (bit 7) of the LCR determines what can be found on ports F8H and F9H. If the DLAB is one, then the divisor we want will be there. Other information will be present if the DLAB is zero. We can get the divisor (in BX) with this code:

```
        mov     dx,3FBH         ; Read Line Control Register for COM1:
        in      al,dx           ;   into al
        push    ax              ; Save old LCR on stack
        or      al,80H          ; Set the DLAB to 1
        out     dx,al           ; and set the new LCR
        mov     dx,3F8H         ; Get the divisor low byte
        in      al,dx
        mov     bl,al           ; Save it in BX
        mov     dx,3F9H         ; Get the divisor high byte
        in      al,dx
        mov     bh,al           ; Save it in BX
        pop     ax
        mov     dx,3FBH         ; Restore Line Control Register for COM1:
        out     dx,al
```

The divisor is meaningless to us directly, but it can be translated into baud rate information. Here are the most common baud rates and their corresponding divisors:

Divisor	Baud Rate
1047	110
384	300
96	1200
48	2400
24	4800
12	9600

Looking into the LCR, we can determine the other useful parameters of a port.

Bits 1 and 0 are a two-bit number that represents the number of bits in a character. The interesting values here are 2, which means 7 bits per character, and 3, which means 8 bits per character.

Bit 2 represents the number of stop bits. If it is 0, only one stop bit will be generated. If it is 1, two stop bits will be used.

Bits 4 and 3 represent a two-bit number that can be used to determine parity. If the number is 0 or 2, no parity will be used. If the number is 1, odd parity will be generated. If the number is 3, even parity will be generated.

With this information, we can find out what we want to know from any serial port on the system. Now all that remains is to write some code that does so.

9.3   A Port Status Display

Once we have determined the information about the state of a communications port, how should we display it, and where should we put it? The DOS `MODE` command uses expressions of the form `COM1:1200,N,8,1` to represent the information that communications port 1 is to be set to 1200 baud, no parity, eight bits per character, one stop bit. This is a compact form and has the advantage that it can be typed directly to the `MODE` command; however, it has few other positive aspects. A better representation might be the one that we used in the second half of the descriptive sentence. That is the form we understand and the form we mentally translate the cryptic expression into.

As for location, one possibility is simply to display the data at the current cursor location. This is almost always wrong, however, since the cursor location is where our attention is focused at the moment we issue the command. Also, it is almost certainly where our telecommunications work is focused as well. Thus, the current cursor location is probably the worst place to display status info. A better choice might be the lower right corner, since it is a fixed location and out of the way of most normal screen usage. However, many telecom programs use the bottom line for status information, and so this display might interfere with that. In addition, if we are to place any information on the bottom line, we must take greater pains to restore the screen contents. If we leave any characters on the screen, they will scroll upward as the rest of the screen does and thus will remain on screen for quite a while.

Probably the least offensive place would be the upper right corner, but many programs, desk clocks in particular, use that corner for precisely that reason. The information we want to display is marginally transient. We want to see it and we may want to keep it around for a little while, but when we go back to our work via the telecom program, it can safely vanish. One solution is to put it in the upper left corner of the screen, and let it disappear as the screen scrolls up. This is essentially the same solution we used for the resident interrupt-vector display.

We know that we will need the cursor functions written for the interrupt-vector display and the same basic save-reposition-restore algorithm for the display routine here. If we flush the test routine from our earlier skeleton program, we can add some code that will rough out the basic shape of this application:

```
keytab  db      120             ; ALT-1
        dw      port1status
```

```
        db      121                     ; ALT-2
        dw      port2status
        db      0
        dw      0

        assume  cs:cseg,ds:cseg

; Display the status of COM1
port1status     proc    near
        mov     bx,cs
        mov     ds,bx

        mov     dh,3                    ; Port offset for COM1
        call    portstatus

        ret
port1status     endp

; Display the status of COM1
port2status     proc    near
        mov     bx,cs
        mov     ds,bx

        mov     dh,2                    ; Port offset for COM2
        call    portstatus

        ret
port2status     endp

; Display the status of any comm port
; Call with
;       DH contains the I/O port offset for the comm port
portstatus      proc    near
        push    bx
        call    getpos                  ; Get the current cursor position
        push    bx                      ;    and save it on the stack.
        mov     bx,0                    ; Move to the upper left corner (0,0)
        call    setpos
        call    showcom                 ; Show the current comm port name
        call    showbaud                ; Show the current baud rate
        call    showlen                 ; Show the bits per character
        call    showstop                ; Show the number of stop bits
        call    showparity              ; Show the parity
        pop     bx                      ; Retrieve the old cursor position
        call    setpos                  ;    and restore the cursor to there.
```

```
        pop     bx
        ret
portstatus      endp

com1            db      'COM1: ',0
com2            db      'COM2: ',0
comtab          dw      com1
                dw      com2
                dw      0

; Call with
;       DH = I/O port offset for the communications port
showcom         proc    near
        push    bx
        push    dx
        push    si
        mov     bh,0            ; Zero the high byte of the index
        mov     bl,3            ; Compute the index = 3-port offset
        sub     bl,dh
        shl     bx,1            ; Multiply by two to get a word index
        mov     si,comtab[bx]   ; And get the appropriate string
        call    dstring         ; Print the string
        pop     si
        pop     dx
        pop     bx
        ret
showcom         endp

showbaud        proc    near
        ret
showbaud        endp

showparity      proc    near
        ret
showparity      endp

showstop        proc    near
        ret
showstop        endp

showlen         proc    near
        ret
showlen         endp

; Get the current cursor position and return it in BX
```

```
getpos              proc     near
        push    ax
        push    cx                   ; Since this function modifies CX
        push    dx

        mov     ah,03H
        mov     bh,0                 ; Page zero
        int     10H
        mov     bx,dx                ; Return the position in BX

        pop     dx
        pop     cx
        pop     ax
        ret
getpos              endp

; Set the current cursor position to the value in BX
setpos              proc     near
        push    ax
        push    bx
        push    dx

        mov     ah,02H
        mov     dx,bx
        mov     bh,0
        int     10H

        pop     dx
        pop     bx
        pop     ax
        ret
setpos              endp
```

This basic skeleton should display the label for COM1: when ALT-1 is pressed, and the label for COM2: when ALT-2 is pressed. We do this by indexing into a table based on the port offset number. Another approach might be to pass some direct representation of the communications port number, such as 1 for COM1:, 2 for COM2:, and so on. We don't really need to do that for two reasons. First, any set of sequential numbers we might choose will contain the same information. Many of the system calls use 0 for COM1:, 1 for COM2:, and so on. Other programs use the direct mapping as demonstrated earlier. These representations contain essentially the same information. In the jargon of the field, they are *isomorphic* representations. Second, since these numbers cannot be entered directly by users of the program, they are purely internal representations. Once we get the code working, they can never change and thus become invalid, because nobody can type in an incorrect value. Therefore, we can choose a convenient set of numbers just as easily as we could choose an inconvenient set.

The display routines for each of the various parameters have been left as stubs. As we expand each one, we can replace the stub and try out the program to see if it works.

9.3.1 Displaying the Baud Rate

We have seen a table of divisors and corresponding baud rates. Given a divisor, you can find the baud rate by looking it up in that table. There is no reason to approach this programming problem in a different fashion. One slight modification might be how you interpret the baud rate. You are given the divisor as a number. Should you derive the baud rate as a number, also? Well, since the goal of this routine is to print the baud rate on the screen, you'll need to write a routine to convert numbers to the correct base-10 string. This is not difficult, but if you had the answer as a string, you would already have a routine to print strings. There is another reason for using strings, which will be discussed later.

The code for our baud-display routine must do three things, then. First, it should retrieve the baud-rate divisor from the correct communications port. Second, it should use that divisor to select a string that contains the ASCII description of the baud rate. Finally, it should print that string.

```
b110       db      ' 110 baud, ',0
b300       db      ' 300 baud, ',0
b1200      db      '1200 baud, ',0
b2400      db      '2400 baud, ',0
b4800      db      '4800 baud, ',0
b9600      db      '9600 baud, ',0

divtab     dw      1047
           dw      384
           dw      96
           dw      48
           dw      24
           dw      12
           dw      0
```

```
baudtab         dw      b110
                dw      b300
                dw      b1200
                dw      b2400
                dw      b4800
                dw      b9600
                dw      0

showbaud        proc    near
        push    di
        push    si
        push    bx
        call    getbaud         ; Get the baud rate divisor
baudloop:
        cmp     divtab[di],0    ; Scan through the divisor table
        je      bldone          ;  till you reach the end
        cmp     bx,divtab[di]
        je      dbaud           ;  or till you find the divisor
        add     di,2
        jmp     baudloop
dbaud:
        mov     si,baudtab[di]  ; Print the corresponding baud rate
        call    dstring
bldone:
        pop     bx
        pop     si
        pop     di
        ret
showbaud        endp

; Call with
;       DH containing modem port offset (COM1 = 3, COM2 = 2)
; Returns
;       BX = baudrate divisor
getbaud         proc    near
        push    ax
        push    dx
        mov     dl,0FBH
        in      al,dx
        push    ax
        or      al,80H
        out     dx,al
        mov     dl,0F8H
        in      al,dx
        mov     bl,al
```

```
        mov     dl,OF9H
        in      al,dx
        mov     bh,al
        pop     ax
        mov     dl,OFBH
        out     dx,al
        pop     dx
        pop     ax
        ret
getbaud         endp
```

9.3.2 Displaying the Character Length

Next, we need to determine how many bits make up a single character in the
current communications state. We already know how to do this, and we know
that the number will be less than or equal to 8. For numbers less than 10,
conversion to ASCII is easy. One approach would be simply to convert and
display the number of bits, followed by a label string. Nevertheless, we are
going to stick with the method of a string table used in the previous routine
with one slight difference. When your indices to a table can be any number
and you know that the table will be sparsely filled, you may not want to store
all the empty entries. In that case, you must explicitly include the index along
with the entry in a table. When your index is sequential, as are the numbers 7
and 8, you don't need to include an index. If you subtract the base value of the
table (in this case, 7), you can use your adjusted number to index directly into
a table of bytes. Since we want to index into a table of words, we must multiply
the index by two. This can be done in a single instruction simply by shifting
the number one bit to the left.

You may be curious as to why we are going to stick with the string rather
than the number representation of our display. Well, for two reasons. The first
is consistency. If there is no pressing reason to do something different each time,
then keeping your methodology the same has some advantages. In many cases
you can reduce the total amount of code by noticing duplication of code among
instances of the same types of operation. If you optimize each little case, you
can win in the short run, but lose in the long run. By being consistent in the first
pass, you can take advantage of these larger-scale optimizations in the second
pass and possibly save more space or speed up the code.

The second, and by far the more important, reason has to do with the ulti-
mate goal of this program. We are not interested in simply reading the state of

communications ports, we want to be able to change that state. To do this, we
need some way of specifying the new state of a port, a simple application-specific
language for telling the machine what to do. As we discussed earlier, the MODE
command provides one example of how to do this, but it is unpleasant. We
chose to display the state in a pleasant, readable fashion. Surely we will want
to design our input to be just as pleasant to use. We know what all the possible
values of each parameter will be. If we have already declared string equivalents
of those values, we can put them to good use later when we are designing the
input section.

```
char7           db      '7 bits/char, ',0
char8           db      '8 bits/char, ',0
chartab         dw      char7
                dw      char8
                dw      0


showlen         proc    near
        push    ax
        push    bx
        push    si
        call    getlen
        shl     bx,1                    ; Multiply index by 2 for words
        mov     si,chartab[bx]          ; Get the correct label string
        call    dstring                 ;    and display it.
        pop     si
        pop     bx
        pop     ax
        ret
showlen         endp

; Call with
;       DH = modem port offset (COM1 = 3, COM2 = 2)
; Returns
;       BX = the number of bits - 7 (i.e. 0 = 7 bits, 1 = 8 bits)
getlen          proc    near
        push    ax
        push    dx
        mov     dl,0FBH
        in      al,dx
        and     al,03H
        mov     bh,0
        mov     bl,al
        sub     bx,2
        pop     dx
```

```
        pop    ax
        ret
getlen         endp
```

9.3.3   Displaying the Stop Bits and Parity

This code is similar to the bits-per-character code. You may have noticed two
things about our string tables thus far. First, all the entries in a given table are exactly the same length. The reason for this is simple. Since we are
designing the program, we are allowed to choose exactly how things will be displayed. Some representations, for example "7 bits/char" and "seven bits
per character," are equal in information, despite quite different sizes. If we
can find a good representation that will cover all cases and still let us display the
information in a fixed-length field, we can avoid problems later. If values of a
given field were different lengths, the display string would expand and contract
as the values changed. Then we would have to worry about what happens at
the edge of the string.

In two cases, the parity and the baud rate, we cannot easily justify changing
the format just to even up the length. In the case of baud, we could demand
that 300 baud be represented as 0300 baud, but this is unsightly as well as
distracting. By judiciously padding with a single leading blank, the result is
better looking and still correct. For parity, we could represent "none", "even"
and "odd" with the single characters N, E and O, but this would lose information,
in that the letters must be explained somewhere before they can be useful.
Instead, by placing this field last on the line and padding out the *end* of the
strings with blanks to be even, we ensure that the parity information is distinctly
separate from the rest of screen, and no flickering occurs.

```
stop1          db     '1 stop, ',0
stop2          db     '2 stop, ',0
stoptab        dw     stop1
               dw     stop2
               dw     0

showstop       proc   near
        push   bx
        push   si
        call   getstop
        dec    bx
        shl    bx,1
```

```
        mov     si,stoptab[bx]
        call    dstring
        pop     si
        pop     bx
        ret
showstop        endp

; Call with modem port offset (COM1 = 3, COM2 = 2) in DH
; Returns the number of stop bits (1 or 2) in BX
getstop         proc    near
        push    ax
        push    dx
        mov     bx,1
        mov     dl,0FBH
        in      al,dx
        and     al,04H
        cmp     al,0            ; One stop bit
        je      gsdone
        inc     bx              ; Two stop bits
gsdone:
        pop     dx
        pop     ax
        ret
getstop         endp

pnone           db      'no parity  ',0
podd            db      'odd parity ',0
peven           db      'even parity',0
partab          dw      pnone
                dw      podd
                dw      peven
                dw      0

showparity      proc    near
        push    bx
        push    si
        call    getparity
        shl     bx,1
        mov     si,partab[bx]
        call    dstring
        pop     si
        pop     bx
        ret
showparity      endp
```

```
; Call with modem port offset (COM1 = 3, COM2 = 2) in DH
; Returns parity in BX (0 means none, 1 means odd, 2 means even)
getparity           proc    near
        push    ax
        push    cx
        push    dx
        mov     bx,0
        mov     dl,0FBH
        in      al,dx
        and     al,18H
        cmp     al,00H          ; No parity    (00)
        je      gpdone
        cmp     al,10H          ; No parity    (10)
        je      gpdone
        inc     bx              ; Odd parity   (01)
        cmp     al,18H
        jne     gpdone
        inc     bx              ; Even parity (11)
gpdone:
        pop     dx
        pop     cx
        pop     ax
        ret
getparity           endp
```

9.4   The Virtues of Consistency

You may have noticed that all the string tables in this code are terminated with
a zero field. There is good reason for this, a reason that harkens back to the
earlier discussion of consistency. These tables are data structures. They take the
form they have because the designer has something in mind for them. A good
design should be robust and capable of extensions. Therefore, a good designer
should always take the long view in the design of code.

What information must be known to use a table such as stoptab from the
previous example? First, of course, is the location of that table in memory. Like
your car ignition key, if you can't find it, you can't use it. Second is the shape
of the elements. In the case of stoptab, the elements are single words, pointers
to strings. But they may have been double-precision floating-point numbers –
there is no easy way to tell. Finally, the last characteristic we must know is the
length of the table. If we don't know how long it is, we cannot know whether an

element is real data or simply random bytes pulled from the end of the array. This is especially important in resident applications, where the code and data must live in the same segment. Writing off the end of an array could imply writing over the program segment prefix of the currently running application or, worse, over your own code.

How can an arbitrary extension to this program know these facts about the tables in this code? It can easily know the location of a table, at the time of assembly, by defining a symbol for it. The shape of an element is a much harder problem, because tables are shaped to match their use; for many shapes, there is no simple representation. One approach might be to store, in the beginning of a table, a count indicating the number of bytes per element. This is common in some high-level languages. For this discussion and the code in this book, we will simply beg the question and say that the knowledge of the shape of a table must reside in the code that uses that table. Finally, as to the length, it cannot be determined from a simple table, one not terminated with a zero field. It may be implicit in some of the code that uses it. But it can be determined easily, precisely, and simply, if we add that final zero. By doing that we can greatly generalize the types of things we can do with an "arbitrary" table or structure in memory.

You may have noticed that various structures in this book have been "regularized" by explicit termination. A good example of this is the table used to convert bytes to ASCII hexadecimal strings. It looks like this:

```
hextab   db      '0123456789ABCDEF',0
```

The addition of the zero at the end lets a program determine how long that table is. It also puts it in exactly the same form as a string that can be printed by **dstring**. You may never want to print this string, but you could, and it costs only one byte of memory for that potential.

Blind adherance to an arbitrary standard is silly. Diverging from a standard for a good enough reason and realizing that certain structures are similar, even if the uses they are put to are different, is good programming practice.

9.5   SEEMODE.ASM – Show Communications Mode

This program displays the state of a communications port in the upper left corner of the screen.

```
cseg    segment
        assume  cs:cseg,ds:cseg
        org     100H
start:
        jmp     initialize


old_keyboard_io dd

        assume  ds:nothing
new_keyboard_io         proc    far
        sti
        cmp     ah,0                ; Is this call a READ request?
        je      ksread
        jmp     old_keyboard_io ; handle remaining subfunction.
ksread:
        call    keyread             ; Get next character to return
        iret
new_keyboard_io         endp

; Read a character from keyboard input queue, if not expanding
; or expansion string, if expansion is in progress.
keyread         proc    near
        push    si
readchar:
        pushf                       ; Let original routine
        call    old_keyboard_io ; determine keyboard status.
        cmp     al,0
        je      extended
        jmp     readdone
extended:
        mov     si,offset keytab
nextext:
        cmp     byte ptr cs:[si],0  ; Is this end of table?
        je      readdone
        cmp     ah,cs:[si]
        je      startexpand
        add     si,3
        jmp     nextext
startexpand:
        add     si,1
        cmp     word ptr cs:[si],0
        je      readdone
        push    ax
        push    bx
        push    cx
```

```
          push      dx
          push      si
          push      di
          push      bp
          push      ds
          call      word ptr cs:[si]
          pop       ds
          pop       bp
          pop       di
          pop       si
          pop       dx
          pop       cx
          pop       bx
          pop       ax
readdone:
          pop       si
          ret
keyread           endp

keytab   db        120               ; ALT-1
         dw        port1status
         db        121               ; ALT-2
         dw        port2status
         db        0
         dw        0


         assume    cs:cseg,ds:cseg

; Display status of COM1
port1status       proc      near
         mov       bx,cs
         mov       ds,bx
         mov       dh,3              ; Port offset for COM1
         call      portstatus
         ret
port1status       endp

; Display status of COM1
port2status       proc      near
         mov       bx,cs
         mov       ds,bx

         mov       dh,2             ; Port offset for COM2
         call      portstatus
```

```
        ret
port2status       endp

; Display status of any comm port
; Call with
;       DH contains I/O port offset for comm port
portstatus        proc    near
        push    bx
        call    getpos              ; Get current cursor position
        push    bx                  ;   and save it on stack.
        mov     bx,0                ; Move to upper left corner (0,0)
        call    setpos
        call    showcom             ; Show current comm port name
        call    showbaud            ; Show current baud rate
        call    showlen             ; Show bits per character
        call    showstop            ; Show number of stop bits
        call    showparity          ; Show parity
        pop     bx                  ; Retrieve old cursor position
        call    setpos              ;   and restore cursor to there.
        pop     bx
        ret
portstatus        endp

com1              db      'COM1: ',0
com2              db      'COM2: ',0
comtab            dw      com1
                  dw      com2
                  dw      0

; Call with
;       DH = I/O port offset for communications port
showcom           proc    near
        push    bx
        push    dx
        push    si
        mov     bh,0    ; Zero high byte of index
        mov     bl,3    ; Compute index = 3-port offset
        sub     bl,dh
        shl     bx,1    ; Multiply by two to get a word index
        mov     si,comtab[bx]; And get appropriate string
        call    dstring ; Print string
        pop     si
        pop     dx
        pop     bx
        ret
```

```
showcom         endp

b110            db      ' 110 baud, ',0
b300            db      ' 300 baud, ',0
b1200           db      '1200 baud, ',0
b2400           db      '2400 baud, ',0
b4800           db      '4800 baud, ',0
b9600           db      '9600 baud, ',0

divtab          dw      1047
                dw      384
                dw      96
                dw      48
                dw      24
                dw      12
                dw      0

baudtab         dw      b110
                dw      b300
                dw      b1200
                dw      b2400
                dw      b4800
                dw      b9600
                dw      0

showbaud        proc    near
        push    di
        push    si
        push    bx
        call    getbaud  ; Get baud rate divisor
        mov     di,0
baudloop:
        cmp     divtab[di],0; Scan through divisor table
        je      bldone   ; till you reach end
        cmp     bx,divtab[di]
        je      dbaud    ; or till you find divisor
        add     di,2
        jmp     baudloop
dbaud:
        mov     si,baudtab[di]  ; Print corresponding baud rate
        call    dstring
bldone:
        pop     bx
        pop     si
        pop     di
```

```
        ret
showbaud        endp

; Call with
;       DH containing modem port offset (COM1 = 3, COM2 = 2)
; Returns
;       BX = baudrate divisor
getbaud         proc    near
        push    ax
        push    dx
        mov     dl,0FBH
        in      al,dx
        push    ax
        or      al,80H
        out     dx,al
        mov     dl,0F8H
        in      al,dx
        mov     bl,al
        mov     dl,0F9H
        in      al,dx
        mov     bh,al
        pop     ax
        mov     dl,0FBH
        out     dx,al
        pop     dx
        pop     ax
        ret
getbaud         endp


char7           db      '7 bits/char, ',0
char8           db      '8 bits/char, ',0
chartab         dw      char7
                dw      char8
                dw      0

showlen         proc    near
        push    ax
        push    bx
        push    si
        call    getlen
        shl     bx,1            ; Multiply index by 2 for words
        mov     si,chartab[bx]  ; Get correct label string
        call    dstring         ;   and display it.
        pop     si
```

```
        pop     bx
        pop     ax
        ret
showlen         endp

; Call with
;       DH = modem port offset (COM1 = 3, COM2 = 2)
; Returns
;       BX = number of bits - 7 (i.e. 0 = 7 bits, 1 = 8 bits)
getlen          proc    near
        push    ax
        push    dx
        mov     dl,0FBH
        in      al,dx
        and     al,03H
        mov     bh,0
        mov     bl,al
        sub     bx,2
        pop     dx
        pop     ax
        ret
getlen          endp


stop1           db      '1 stop, ',0
stop2           db      '2 stop, ',0
stoptab         dw      stop1
                dw      stop2
                dw      0

showstop        proc    near
        push    bx
        push    si
        call    getstop
        dec     bx
        shl     bx,1
        mov     si,stoptab[bx]
        call    dstring
        pop     si
        pop     bx
        ret
showstop        endp

; Call with modem port offset (COM1 = 3, COM2 = 2) in DH
; Returns number of stop bits (1 or 2) in BX
```

```
getstop         proc    near
        push    ax
        push    dx
        mov     bx,1
        mov     dl,0FBH
        in      al,dx
        and     al,04H
        cmp     al,0      ; One stop bit
        je      gsdone
        inc     bx        ; Two stop bits
gsdone:
        pop     dx
        pop     ax
        ret
getstop         endp

pnone           db      'no parity  ',0
podd            db      'odd parity ',0
peven           db      'even parity',0
partab          dw      pnone
                dw      podd
                dw      peven
                dw      0

showparity      proc    near
        push    bx
        push    si
        call    getparity
        shl     bx,1
        mov     si,partab[bx]
        call    dstring
        pop     si
        pop     bx
        ret
showparity      endp

; Call with modem port offset (COM1 = 3, COM2 = 2) in DH
; Returns parity in BX (0 means none, 1 means odd, 2 means even)
getparity       proc    near
        push    ax
        push    cx
        push    dx
        mov     bx,0
        mov     dl,0FBH
        in      al,dx
```

```
        and     al,18H
        cmp     al,00H   ; No parity   (00)
        je      gpdone
        cmp     al,10H   ; No parity   (10)
        je      gpdone
        inc     bx       ; Odd parity  (01)
        cmp     al,18H
        jne     gpdone
        inc     bx       ; Even parity (11)
gpdone:
        pop     dx
        pop     cx
        pop     ax
        ret
getparity       endp

; Get current cursor position and return it in BX
getpos          proc    near
        push    ax
        push    cx       ; Since this function modifies CX
        push    dx

        mov     ah,03H
        mov     bh,0     ; Page zero
        int     10H
        mov     bx,dx    ; Return position in BX

        pop     dx
        pop     cx
        pop     ax
        ret
getpos          endp

; Set current cursor position to value in BX
setpos          proc    near
        push    ax
        push    bx
        push    dx

        mov     ah,02H
        mov     dx,bx
        mov     bh,0
        int     10H

        pop     dx
```

```
        pop     bx
        pop     ax
        ret
setpos          endp


; Displays string pointed to by DS:SI
dstring         proc    near
        push    si
        push    ax
        cmp     si,0
        je      dsdone
dloop:
        mov     al,[si]
        cmp     al,0
        je      dsdone
        call    dchar
        inc     si
        jmp     dloop
dsdone:
        pop     ax
        pop     si
        ret
dstring         endp

; Display character contained in AL
dchar           proc    near
        push    ax
        push    bx
        mov     bh,1
        mov     ah,0EH
        int     10H
        pop     bx
        pop     ax
        ret
dchar           endp

initialize:
        assume  cs:cseg,ds:cseg
        mov     bx,cs
        mov     ds,bx

        mov     al,16H
        mov     ah,35H
        int     21H
```

```
        mov     old_keyboard_io,bx
        mov     old_keyboard_io[2],es
        mov     dx,offset new_keyboard_io
        mov     al,16H
        mov     ah,25H
        int     21H

        mov     dx,offset initialize
        int     27H

cseg    ends
        end     start
```

Chapter 10

Setting the Mode

So far, we've built a program to look at the configuration of a given serial port. The next step is to learn to modify that configuration. And we'll do that by taking our display code and sort of rewriting it backward.

In chapter 9, we wrote code to find the value of each parameter of the communications port configurations. First, we called a routine that translated the arcane machine-state information into a number of some kind. Using that number, we displayed a portion of the status string that reflected the correct setting.

Here, we will add to that same program code that does exactly the reverse. We will display a series of strings representing all the possible choices for a given parameter. One of those strings will be selected. Based on that, we can come up with a number that will be given to a routine that translates it into the arcane procedure that must be used to set a given parameter.

There is a ROM system call to set the communications port configuration INT 14H function OH *(initialize communications port)*, which we won't use here. We know how to read the values of the parameters for the ports and have built a structure to do so. We should be able to reverse that structure to set those values. This involves duplicating a function that is already built into the ROM. Duplicating code is something that should normally be avoided, but from time to time it can be useful.

The first question you should ask when faced with doing something as foolish as rewriting operating system calls is: What don't I understand about this call?

For DOS, that may be difficult to determine. The inner workings of DOS are sometimes mysterious beyond human ken. However, if you are willing to take

167

a stab at it, there are some very good public-domain disassemblers available from bulletin boards. A disassembler is a program that performs, as you might guess, the opposite function of an assembler. It takes the binary code that the machine can execute and writes an assembly-language source program that can be assembled into that code.

This is not quite as wonderful as it sounds. A program is not just executable code. It is a representation of a complex thought. Disassemblers can create a program that will work correctly, but they cannot provide the thought that went into creating the source. A disassembled program has no comments, no variable names, no subroutine names, no segment names. It may work, but you'll have to put the thought back into it before it becomes a readable program. It is possible to deduce the inner workings of a disassembled program, but it ain't easy.

ROM calls are much easier. The *DOS Technical Reference Manual* provides a full listing of the ROM sources. This makes them much more readable and understandable than disassembled code, but they are still somewhat cryptic. Nevertheless, there is a surprising amount of useful information buried in these listings. By examining them, you can determine if your proposed changes will conflict with the expectations of the operating system. Fortunately, setting the communications-port parameters is straightforward and duplicating that code should cause no real problems. Knowing that something is possible is a big step toward being able to do it.

10.1   Designing the Code

First, to the matter of user interface. We have already defined a system for displaying the state of a port. We should be able to use that same system to set the state of a port. We have a series of tokens in an ordered list for each parameter and we have routines to position the cursor. We should be able to turn these ingredients into a pleasant concoction of some sort.

You may have noticed that this book stresses the design details of user interface more than any other design issues. This is not accidental. One of the first things you notice about people you've just met is they way they speak – in a very crude sense, their "user interface." It is the same with computer programs. A clumsy user interface is like a thick accent. No matter that the intentions are good, if the presentation is poor, it is difficult to get the message across.

The details of an interface often take the lion's share of the code. Attention to detail is an important facet of the design process, but an obsession with those details can prevent a perfectly good program from seeing the light of day. Designers should aim for a good balance. The programs in this book may not have perfect interfaces, but they are usable, and the code is not too complex to be understood.

For this program, we need to set four parameters for a given communications port: baud rate, number of bits in a character, number of stop bits, and parity. We also need some way to select which communications port we are setting.

One approach would be to print a menu for each parameter, perhaps with numbers to select between individual values. This is a classical approach and one that is used with great effect in other programs. It could take up a great deal of screen real estate, however, and would require some sort of very simple parser to determine if the number entered was valid and, if so, to cause the appropriate action.

What are we looking for in an input mechanism? First, it should be clear what is being selected. When we select a baud rate, we don't want to select baud rate 4 or baud rate D – we want to select 9600 baud. That is the meaning of the parameter, and the further our interface forces us to be removed from that, the more difficult it will seem to be to use.

Second comes the question of illegal input. A maxim among those devoted to the scientific method maintains that *how* you ask a question is sometimes as important as the question itself. This issue raises one of those cases. If we ask ourselves how to design a user interface that minimizes bad input, we may come up with a parser, or a menu system, or something along those lines. If we rephrase the question to be one of how to design a system that *always produces correct input*, we may come up with something different.

One way to guarantee that your input is correct is to make all the choices ahead of time. We already know every possible value of all the parameters. If we write a routine that lets us select from only that set, we can take a good step toward being foolproof. Typing an index to a menu item, on the other hand, would still have a potential for bad input. After all, even if valid input goes from 1 to 6, you still need to handle the case of a typed 8.

Look at the design of machinery. Some stereos have a selector knob that allows you to switch among the phono, the tape, and the tuner inputs. With those three selections, it is impossible to select an illegal input; it is only possible to select an inappropriate one. There is no way to specify anything other than phono/tape/tuner in the language of stereo controls. Surely, if a manufacturer can build something so simple from a few bits of metal and plastic, we should be able to do something similar with our expensive personal computer.

We have a valid format for displaying port information. The name of the port, followed by a baud rate, followed by the number of bits in a character, the number of stop bits, and the parity, all displayed in the upper left corner of the screen. If we start with the first field and write code to cycle through all the possible variations, with a method for saying that the currently displayed field should be used, and move to every field in turn, we will have an input system that cannot be used to enter illegal information.

Since the mechanism for entering this information can be separated from the mechanism for setting each parameter, we can build the input routines first. Since these functions are an addition to the `SEEMODE.ASM`, we have to add an entry to the key table, so that we can call our setup routine. Since we typically want to reset the baud rate, we might use the `ALT-B` key to call the setup routine.

```
keytab  db      120                     ; ALT-1
        dw      port1status
        db      121                     ; ALT-2
        dw      port2status
        db      48                      ; ALT-B
        dw      setport
        db      0
        dw      0
```

The `setport` routine needs to do several things. It needs to set up the data segment. It must save the old cursor position and then move the cursor to the upper left corner. Then, each parameter must be set up in turn. Finally, the cursor must be returned to its original position.

The selector routine, which we can call `dmenu`, since it displays all the possible choices, should be general enough to accept a pointer to any array of strings. It should then display the first string in the array and wait for a keystroke. If that keystroke is anything but the selector character, the routine should cycle to the next value in the list. When the end of the list is reached, we should start again at the beginning. Since we are moving from right to left, a reasonable character might be the Right Arrow, extended character code 77. In addition, to achieve the cycling effect, we want to reposition the cursor to the beginning of the field and redisplay on top of the previous value.

By building simple routines that just display the appropriate menus we can try out the interface.

```
setport         proc    near
```

```
        push    bx
        mov     bx,cs
        mov     ds,bx
        call    getpos          ; Get the current cursor position
        push    bx              ;   and save it on the stack.
        mov     bx,0            ; Move to the upper left corner (0,0)
        call    setpos
        call    setcom          ; Set the current comm port name
        call    setbaud         ; Set the current baud rate
        call    setlen          ; Set the bits per character
        call    setstop         ; Set the number of stop bits
        call    setparity       ; Set the parity
        pop     bx              ; Retrieve the old cursor position
        call    setpos          ;   and restore the cursor to there.
        pop     bx
        ret
setport         endp

; Returns
;       DH = I/O port offset
setcom          proc    near
        push    di
        mov     di,offset comtab
        call    dmenu
        mov     dh,3    ; Convert the table index into port offset
        sub     dh,bl
        call    showcom
        pop     di
        ret
setcom          endp

setbaud         proc    near
        push    di
        mov     di,offset baudtab
        call    dmenu
        call    showbaud
        pop     di
        ret
setbaud         endp

setlen          proc    near
        push    di
        mov     di,offset chartab
        call    dmenu
        call    showlen
```

```
        pop     di
        ret
setlen          endp

setstop         proc    near
        push    di
        mov     di,offset stoptab
        call    dmenu
        call    showstop
        pop     di
        ret
setstop         endp

setparity       proc    near
        push    di
        mov     di,offset partab
        call    dmenu
        call    showparity
        pop     di
        ret
setparity       endp

; Call with
;       DI = pointer to the table to display
; Returns
;       BX = index into table divided by 2
dmenu           proc    near
        push    ax
        push    cx
        push    dx
        push    si
        push    bp
mstart:
        mov     bp,0
mloop:
        call    getpos  ; Save the cursor position
        push    bx      ;   on the stack
        mov     si,word ptr ds:[di+bp]
        call    dstring ; Display the current menu entry
        pop     bx      ; Move the cursor back to the beginning
        call    setpos  ;   of the field
        call    cycle   ; Get a command
        cmp     cx,0    ; If CX=0 then use this entry
        je      mdone
        add     bp,2    ; If CX not 0 then go to nex entry
```

```
            cmp     word ptr ds:[di+bp],0   ; Unless we've reached end of table
            je      mstart  ; If at end, start at beginning
            jmp     mloop
mdone:
            mov     bx,bp    ; Move the index to BX
            shr     bx,1     ; Divide the index by 2
            pop     bp
            pop     si
            pop     dx
            pop     cx
            pop     ax
            ret
dmenu           endp

cycle           proc    near
            mov     cx,1
            mov     ah,0
            pushf
            assume  cs:nothing
            call    old_keyboard_io
            assume  cs:cseg
            cmp     al,0
            je      cxchar
cdone:
            ret
cxchar:
            cmp     ah,77    ; Right Arrow
            jne     cdone
            mov     cx,0
            jmp     cdone
cycle           endp
```

10.2 Setting up the Communications Ports

With the user interface in place, we can flesh it out to set the parameters. First, of course, must be the port itself. As with the display part of this program, the most convenient choice for representing the port is by the high-order-byte communication-port offset. The menu routine will return a 0 for COM1: and a 1 for COM2:. A little basic arithmetic and we can convert these values to offset 3 for COM1: and offset 2 for COM2:. Then we can pass that value along in DH exactly as we did in the earlier portion of the program.

```
; Returns
```

```
;       DH = I/O port offset
setcom          proc    near
        push    di
        mov     di,offset comtab
        call    dmenu
        mov     dh,3    ; Convert the table index into port offset
        sub     dh,bl
        call    showcom
        pop     di
        ret
setcom          endp
```

Next, we want to set up the baud rate. This is a bit more complicated. In the display code, we separated the processes of divisor-information acquisition, divisor-to-baud-rate conversion, and baud rate into separate routines. In fact, all the parameter routines were divided into these three parts. The processes here are similar to those three, but in reverse order. We want to display the menu, convert the resulting number into a baud rate, and then set that baud rate. These three parts once again apply to all the parameters, so there is no reason that the structure of these input routines should not reflect the structure of the display routines.

One minor point not mentioned thus far is the mechanism for moving from one field to another. There are two approaches we could use for this. In the first, we simply do not move the cursor to the beginning of the field until we know it is necessary to do so, which would be when any character but the selector character is typed. This is a perfectly reasonable thing to do, but there is another, better alternative.

That alternative is to set each parameter as it is selected. This is a little more work for the computer, but less for us. We could have chosen to build one value and then set the line control register all at once. That would mean more code to pass the value along, but fewer I/O port calls. In the long run, that doesn't really matter. However, the fact that we have chosen this route lets us do something interesting.

In the code, we leave the cursor at the beginning of the field. That means when the right value has been selected and the value set, we need to move the cursor to the end of the current field to be ready to display the next field. We could calculate the next cursor position, or we could simply redisplay the string. Rather than redisplay a string that we believe to be the value of the parameter we can show the actual value of the parameter, by calling the display routine we wrote for the first part of this program. When we finish the setup line, what we have left is exactly what we would have by doing a display command. We don't have to accept that on faith. We know, because we have checked it.

```
; Call with
;        DH = I/O port offset
setbaud         proc    near
        push    di
        mov     di,offset baudtab
        call    dmenu
        shl     bx,1    ; Multiply by two to get word index
        mov     bx,divtab[bx]
        call    putbaud
        call    showbaud
        pop     di
        ret
setbaud         endp

;Call with
;        BX = baudrate divisor
putbaud         proc    near
        push    ax
        push    dx
        mov     dl,0FBH
        in      al,dx
        push    ax
        or      al,80H
        out     dx,al
        mov     dl,0F8H
        mov     al,bl
        out     dx,al
        mov     dl,0F9H
        mov     al,bh
        out     dx,al
        pop     ax
        mov     dl,0FBH
        out     dx,al
        pop     dx
        pop     ax
        ret
putbaud         endp

; Call with
;        DH = I/O port offset
setlen          proc    near
```

```
        push    di
        mov     di,offset chartab
        call    dmenu
        call    putlen
        call    showlen
        pop     di
        ret
setlen          endp

; Call with
;       DH = modem port offset (COM1 = 3, COM2 = 2)
;       BX = the number of bits - 7 (i.e. 0 = 7 bits, 1 = 8 bits)
putlen          proc    near
        push    ax
        push    dx
        mov     dl,0FBH
        in      al,dx
        and     al,11111100B; Mask out original value, leaving the rest
        or      al,00000010B; Set to 7 bits (10)
        cmp     bx,1    ; Should it be 8 bits?
        jne     pldone
        or      al,00000001B; Set it to 8 bits (11)
pldone:
        out     dx,al
        pop     dx
        pop     ax
        ret
putlen          endp

; Call with
;       DH = I/O port offset
setstop         proc    near
        push    di
        mov     di,offset stoptab
        call    dmenu
        call    putstop
        call    showstop
        pop     di
        ret
setstop         endp

; Call with
;       DH = modem port offset (COM1 = 3, COM2 = 2)
;       BX = the number of stop bits - 1 (0 = 1 stop or 1 = 2 stop)
putstop         proc    near
```

```
        push    ax
        push    cx
        push    dx
        mov     dl,0FBH
        in      al,dx
        and     al,11111011B; Mask out bit 2
        cmp     bx,0
        je      psdone
        or      al,00000100B; Set bit 2
psdone:
        out     dx,al
        pop     dx
        pop     cx
        pop     ax
        ret
putstop         endp

; Call with
;       DH = I/O port offset
setparity       proc    near
        push    di
        mov     di,offset partab
        call    dmenu
        call    putparity
        call    showparity
        pop     di
        ret
setparity       endp

; Call with
;       DH = modem port offset (COM1 = 3, COM2 = 2)
;       BX = parity (0 means none, 1 means odd, 2 means even)
putparity       proc    near
        push    ax
        push    cx
        push    dx
        mov     dl,0FBH
        in      al,dx
        and     al,11100111B; Mask out the parity bits
        cmp     bx,0    ; No parity (00)
        je      ppdone
        or      al,00001000B; Set odd parity (01)
        cmp     bx,2    ; Check for even parity
        jne     ppdone
        or      al,00010000B; Set even parity (11)
```

```
ppdone:



        out     dx,al
        pop     dx
        pop     cx
        pop     ax
        ret
putparity       endp
```

The advantage of designing a standard interface is that the components you design can be hooked together in interesting ways. By selecting the correct set of components, you can build some interesting applications.

We have written some useful and interesting functions here. There is no reason we cannot do more with them.

10.3   SETMODE.ASM – Set Serial Mode

This program displays or sets the mode of either COM1: or COM2:.

```
cseg    segment
        assume  cs:cseg,ds:cseg
        org     100H
start:
        jmp     initialize


old_keyboard_io dd

        assume  ds:nothing
new_keyboard_io         proc    far
        sti
        cmp     ah,0            ; Is this call a READ request?
        je      ksread
        jmp     old_keyboard_io ; handle remaining subfunction.
ksread:
        call    keyread         ; Get next character to return
        iret
new_keyboard_io         endp



; Read a character from keyboard input queue, if not expanding
```

```
; or expansion string, if expansion is in progress.
keyread         proc    near
        push    si
readchar:
        pushf                           ; Let original routine
        call    old_keyboard_io ; determine keyboard status.
        cmp     al,0
        je      extended
        jmp     readdone
extended:
        mov     si,offset keytab
nextext:
        cmp     byte ptr cs:[si],0  ; Is this end of table?
        je      readdone
        cmp     ah,cs:[si]
        je      startexpand
        add     si,3
        jmp     nextext
startexpand:
        add     si,1
        cmp     word ptr cs:[si],0
        je      readdone
        push    ax
        push    bx
        push    cx
        push    dx
        push    si
        push    di
        push    bp
        push    ds
        call    word ptr cs:[si]
        pop     ds
        pop     bp
        pop     di
        pop     si
        pop     dx
        pop     cx
        pop     bx
        pop     ax
readdone:
        pop     si
        ret
keyread         endp

keytab  db      120                     ; ALT-1
```

```
        dw      port1status
        db      121             ; ALT-2
        dw      port2status
        db      48              ; ALT-B
        dw      setport
        db      0
        dw      0


        assume  cs:cseg,ds:cseg

; Display status of COM1
port1status     proc    near
        mov     bx,cs
        mov     ds,bx
        mov     dh,3            ; Port offset for COM1
        call    portstatus
        ret
port1status     endp

; Display status of COM1
port2status     proc    near
        mov     bx,cs
        mov     ds,bx

        mov     dh,2            ; Port offset for COM2
        call    portstatus

        ret
port2status     endp

; Display status of any comm port
; Call with
;       DH contains I/O port offset for comm port
portstatus      proc    near
        push    bx
        call    getpos          ; Get current cursor position
        push    bx              ;   and save it on stack.
        mov     bx,0            ; Move to upper left corner (0,0)
        call    setpos
        call    showcom         ; Show current comm port name
        call    showbaud        ; Show current baud rate
        call    showlen         ; Show bits per character
        call    showstop        ; Show number of stop bits
        call    showparity      ; Show parity
        pop     bx              ; Retrieve old cursor position
```

```
        call    setpos          ;  and restore cursor to there.
        pop     bx
        ret
portstatus      endp

com1            db      'COM1: ',0
com2            db      'COM2: ',0
comtab          dw      com1
                dw      com2
                dw      0


; Call with
;       DH = I/O port offset for communications port
showcom         proc    near
        push    bx
        push    dx
        push    si
        mov     bh,0    ; Zero high byte of index
        mov     bl,3    ; Compute index = 3-port offset
        sub     bl,dh
        shl     bx,1    ; Multiply by two to get a word index
        mov     si,comtab[bx]   ; And get appropriate string
        call    dstring ; Print string
        pop     si
        pop     dx
        pop     bx
        ret
showcom         endp

b110            db      ' 110 baud, ',0
b300            db      ' 300 baud, ',0
b1200           db      '1200 baud, ',0
b2400           db      '2400 baud, ',0
b4800           db      '4800 baud, ',0
b9600           db      '9600 baud, ',0

divtab          dw      1047
                dw      384
                dw      96
                dw      48
                dw      24
                dw      12
                dw      0

baudtab         dw      b110
```

```
                    dw      b300
                    dw      b1200
                    dw      b2400
                    dw      b4800
                    dw      b9600
                    dw      0


showbaud            proc    near
        push    di
        push    si
        push    bx
        call    getbaud ; Get baud rate divisor
        mov     di,0
baudloop:
        cmp     divtab[di],0; Scan through divisor table
        je      bldone  ;  till you reach end
        cmp     bx,divtab[di]
        je      dbaud   ;  or till you find divisor
        add     di,2
        jmp     baudloop
dbaud:
        mov     si,baudtab[di]  ; Print corresponding baud rate
        call    dstring
bldone:
        pop     bx
        pop     si
        pop     di
        ret
showbaud            endp


; Call with
;       DH containing modem port offset (COM1 = 3, COM2 = 2)
; Returns
;       BX = baudrate divisor
getbaud             proc    near
        push    ax
        push    dx
        mov     dl,0FBH
        in      al,dx
        push    ax
        or      al,80H
        out     dx,al
        mov     dl,0F8H
        in      al,dx
        mov     bl,al
```

```
        mov     dl,0F9H
        in      al,dx
        mov     bh,al
        pop     ax
        mov     dl,0FBH
        out     dx,al
        pop     dx
        pop     ax
        ret
getbaud         endp


char7           db      '7 bits/char, ',0
char8           db      '8 bits/char, ',0
chartab         dw      char7
                dw      char8
                dw      0

showlen         proc    near
        push    ax
        push    bx
        push    si
        call    getlen
        shl     bx,1            ; Multiply index by 2 for words
        mov     si,chartab[bx]  ; Get correct label string
        call    dstring         ;    and display it.
        pop     si
        pop     bx
        pop     ax
        ret
showlen         endp

; Call with
;       DH = modem port offset (COM1 = 3, COM2 = 2)
; Returns
;       BX = number of bits - 7 (i.e. 0 = 7 bits, 1 = 8 bits)
getlen          proc    near
        push    ax
        push    dx
        mov     dl,0FBH
        in      al,dx
        and     al,03H
        mov     bh,0
        mov     bl,al
        sub     bx,2
```

```
            pop     dx
            pop     ax
            ret
getlen              endp

stop1               db      '1 stop, ',0
stop2               db      '2 stop, ',0
stoptab             dw      stop1
                    dw      stop2
                    dw      0

showstop            proc    near
            push    bx
            push    si
            call    getstop
            shl     bx,1
            mov     si,stoptab[bx]
            call    dstring
            pop     si
            pop     bx
            ret
showstop            endp

; Call with
;       DH = modem port offset (COM1 = 3, COM2 = 2)
; Returns
;       BX = number of stop bits - 1 (0 = 1 stop or 1 = 2 stop)
getstop             proc    near
            push    ax
            push    dx
            mov     bx,0
            mov     dl,0FBH
            in      al,dx
            and     al,04H
            cmp     al,0    ; One stop bit
            je      gsdone
            inc     bx      ; Two stop bits
gsdone:
            pop     dx
            pop     ax
            ret
getstop             endp

pnone               db      'no parity  ',0
podd                db      'odd parity ',0
```

```
peven           db      'even parity',0
partab          dw      pnone
                dw      podd
                dw      peven
                dw      0

showparity      proc    near
        push    bx
        push    si
        call    getparity
        shl     bx,1
        mov     si,partab[bx]
        call    dstring
        pop     si
        pop     bx
        ret
showparity      endp

; Call with
;       DH = modem port offset (COM1 = 3, COM2 = 2)
; Returns
;       BX = parity (0 means none, 1 means odd, 2 means even)
getparity       proc    near
        push    ax
        push    cx
        push    dx
        mov     bx,0
        mov     dl,0FBH
        in      al,dx
        and     al,18H
        cmp     al,00H  ; No parity   (00)
        je      gpdone
        cmp     al,10H  ; No parity   (10)
        je      gpdone
        inc     bx      ; Odd parity  (01)
        cmp     al,18H
        jne     gpdone
        inc     bx      ; Even parity (11)
gpdone:
        pop     dx
        pop     cx
        pop     ax
        ret
getparity       endp
```

```
setport         proc    near
        push    bx
        mov     bx,cs
        mov     ds,bx
        call    getpos          ; Get current cursor position
        push    bx              ;   and save it on stack.
        mov     bx,0            ; Move to upper left corner (0,0)
        call    setpos
        call    setcom          ; Set current comm port name
        call    setbaud         ; Set current baud rate
        call    setlen          ; Set bits per character
        call    setstop         ; Set number of stop bits
        call    setparity       ; Set parity
        pop     bx              ; Retrieve old cursor position
        call    setpos          ;   and restore cursor to there.
        pop     bx
        ret
setport         endp


; Returns
;       DH = I/O port offset
setcom          proc    near
        push    di
        mov     di,offset comtab
        call    dmenu
        mov     dh,3    ; Convert table index into port offset
        sub     dh,bl
        call    showcom
        pop     di
        ret
setcom          endp


; Call with
;       DH = I/O port offset
setbaud         proc    near
        push    di
        mov     di,offset baudtab
        call    dmenu
        shl     bx,1    ; Multiply by two to get word index
        mov     bx,divtab[bx]
        call    putbaud
        call    showbaud
        pop     di
        ret
setbaud         endp
```

```
;Call with
;       BX = baudrate divisor
putbaud         proc    near
        push    ax
        push    dx
        mov     dl,0FBH
        in      al,dx
        push    ax
        or      al,80H
        out     dx,al
        mov     dl,0F8H
        mov     al,bl
        out     dx,al
        mov     dl,0F9H
        mov     al,bh
        out     dx,al
        pop     ax
        mov     dl,0FBH
        out     dx,al
        pop     dx
        pop     ax
        ret
putbaud         endp

; Call with
;       DH = I/O port offset
setlen          proc    near
        push    di
        mov     di,offset chartab
        call    dmenu
        call    putlen
        call    showlen
        pop     di
        ret
setlen          endp

; Call with
;       DH = modem port offset (COM1 = 3, COM2 = 2)
;       BX = number of bits - 7 (i.e. 0 = 7 bits, 1 = 8 bits)
putlen          proc    near
        push    ax
        push    dx
        mov     dl,0FBH
        in      al,dx
```

```
        and     al,11111100B; Mask out original value, leaving rest
        or      al,00000010B; Set to 7 bits (10)
        cmp     bx,1     ; Should it be 8 bits?
        jne     pldone
        or      al,00000001B; Set it to 8 bits (11)
pldone:
        out     dx,al
        pop     dx
        pop     ax
        ret
putlen          endp


; Call with
;       DH = I/O port offset
setstop         proc    near
        push    di
        mov     di,offset stoptab
        call    dmenu
        call    putstop
        call    showstop
        pop     di
        ret
setstop         endp


; Call with
;       DH = modem port offset (COM1 = 3, COM2 = 2)
;       BX = number of stop bits - 1 (0 = 1 stop or 1 = 2 stop)
putstop         proc    near
        push    ax
        push    cx
        push    dx
        mov     dl,0FBH
        in      al,dx
        and     al,11111011B; Mask out bit 2
        cmp     bx,0
        je      psdone
        or      al,00000100B; Set bit 2
psdone:
        out     dx,al
        pop     dx
        pop     cx
        pop     ax
        ret
putstop         endp
```

```
; Call with
;       DH = I/O port offset
setparity       proc    near
        push    di
        mov     di,offset partab
        call    dmenu
        call    putparity
        call    showparity
        pop     di
        ret
setparity       endp


; Call with
;       DH = modem port offset (COM1 = 3, COM2 = 2)
;       BX = parity (0 means none, 1 means odd, 2 means even)
putparity       proc    near
        push    ax
        push    cx
        push    dx
        mov     dl,0FBH
        in      al,dx
        and     al,11100111B; Mask out parity bits
        cmp     bx,0    ; No parity (00)
        je      ppdone
        or      al,00001000B; Set odd parity (01)
        cmp     bx,2    ; Check for even parity
        jne     ppdone
        or      al,00010000B; Set even parity (11)
ppdone:
        out     dx,al
        pop     dx
        pop     cx
        pop     ax
        ret
putparity       endp


; Call with
;       DI = pointer to table to display
; Returns
;       BX = index into table divided by 2
dmenu           proc    near
        push    ax
        push    cx
        push    dx
        push    si
```

```
        push    bp
mstart:
        mov     bp,0
mloop:
        call    getpos  ; Save cursor position
        push    bx      ;   on stack
        mov     si,word ptr ds:[di+bp]
        call    dstring ; Display current menu entry
        pop     bx      ; Move cursor back to beginning
        call    setpos  ;   of field
        call    cycle   ; Get a command
        cmp     cx,0    ; If CX=0 then use this entry
        je      mdone
        add     bp,2    ; If CX not 0 then go to nex entry
        cmp     word ptr ds:[di+bp],0    ; Unless we've reached end of table
        je      mstart  ; If at end, start at beginning
        jmp     mloop
mdone:
        mov     bx,bp   ; Move index to BX
        shr     bx,1    ; Divide index by 2
        pop     bp
        pop     si
        pop     dx
        pop     cx
        pop     ax
        ret
dmenu           endp

cycle           proc    near
        mov     cx,1
        mov     ah,0
        pushf
        assume  cs:nothing
        call    old_keyboard_io
        assume  cs:cseg
        cmp     al,0
        je      cxchar
cdone:
        ret
cxchar:
        cmp     ah,77   ; Right Arrow
        jne     cdone
        mov     cx,0
        jmp     cdone
cycle           endp
```

```
; Get current cursor position and return it in BX
getpos          proc    near
        push    ax
        push    cx      ; Since this function modifies CX
        push    dx

        mov     ah,03H
        mov     bh,0    ; Page zero
        int     10H
        mov     bx,dx   ; Return position in BX

        pop     dx
        pop     cx
        pop     ax
        ret
getpos          endp

; Set current cursor position to value in BX
setpos          proc    near
        push    ax
        push    bx
        push    dx

        mov     ah,02H
        mov     dx,bx
        mov     bh,0
        int     10H

        pop     dx
        pop     bx
        pop     ax
        ret
setpos          endp

; Displays string pointed to by DS:SI
dstring         proc    near
        push    si
        push    ax
        cmp     si,0
        je      dsdone
dloop:
        mov     al,[si]
        cmp     al,0
        je      dsdone
```

```
        call    dchar
        inc     si
        jmp     dloop
dsdone:
        pop     ax
        pop     si
        ret
dstring         endp

; Display character contained in AL
dchar           proc    near
        push    ax
        push    bx
        mov     bh,1
        mov     ah,0EH
        int     10H
        pop     bx
        pop     ax
        ret
dchar           endp

initialize:
        assume  cs:cseg,ds:cseg
        mov     bx,cs
        mov     ds,bx

        mov     al,16H
        mov     ah,35H
        int     21H
        mov     old_keyboard_io,bx
        mov     old_keyboard_io[2],es
        mov     dx,offset new_keyboard_io
        mov     al,16H
        mov     ah,25H
        int     21H

        mov     dx,offset initialize
        int     27H

cseg    ends
        end     start
```

Chapter 11

Using the Disk

There was a time when users of small computers entered their code by flipping switches on the front panel of a computer. An experienced programmer could enter almost an entire kilobyte of binary code in only ten or twenty minutes. Of course, there was paper tape, but those readers and punches were *expensive*, and the paper chaff made an awful mess on the carpet. Then came a tremendous breakthrough in mass storage technology, the cassette tape interface. Once that kilobyte had been entered and verified, it could be saved forever on a cassette tape. The next time the software was needed, it could be reloaded from tape. Perhaps it took two or three tries or a bit of tweaking with a screwdriver because the audio filters in the interface had drifted off frequency, but eventually it worked. It wasn't quite as intimate as toggling in code on the front panel, and some programmers probably had mixed feelings the day they noticed that the callouses on their fingers had vanished, but tape was clearly superior.

Then, the first floppy disks came on the scene, and none too soon. Of course, they were very expensive, big (8 inches across), and somewhat fragile, but they did store almost 80 kilobytes, and you could retrieve the contents of a file almost every time. As technology advanced, the disks grew bigger and more reliable. When the IBM PC first came onto the market, disks were in their adolescence. The early PCs were equipped with a cassette interface that almost no one used. Few people even considered buying a PC without at least a single disk, one of the new 5 1over4-inch drives. They weren't as fast as the 8-inch drives, and they weren't as reliable, but they were cheaper and easier to carry about. The early PC disks could store 180 kilobytes on one side of a disk, a capacity that was soon doubled when cheap double-sided disk drives came along. People soon found that a single drive just wasn't enough. Two drives became a necessity, not just a luxury.

Floppies were fine, but there were still those times when the program you wanted to use was on a disk that wasn't in either drive, and both drives were needed for something else. Disk juggling was an unpleasant fact of life. Then, Winchester hard disks began to appear on the market. Again, the first ones were expensive, but they could store five entire megabytes! After a while, when ten megabytes became more the order of business, you could boot off a hard disk. Hard disks became a staple of computing, with floppies used for archival and data transfer between computers.

When computer designers get together, they talk about the architecture of a computer. To many people, this means the operations that the central processor is capable of performing. But a computer architecture is much more than the central processor. It encompasses all the details of how the computer will manage its primary storage; the random access memory (RAM), from which programs execute; and the secondary storage systems, such as disk drives, where programs are kept for execution at a later time.

A great central processor with a lousy mass-storage system has few practical uses. Certainly, there are those applications that require the machine to read in a very small amount of information and produce a very small amount of output, but that take vast amounts of computing power in between. These jobs, which use computer time but very little I/O time, are called *compute-bound* programs. On the other hand, a marginally adequate central processor with a good disk subsystem is much more useful. The Apple II with a single disk and a spreadsheet calculator program revolutionized the way the business world operates. The IBM PC and the business products that run on it have continued and accelerated this trend.

Disks are a key part of how a PC does what it does. As such a vital part of the machine, we must address how disk I/O can be done from within the context of a memory resident program.

11.1   Safety First

DOS was not designed for multi-tasking. In fact, many of the system operations within DOS depend on the fact that there is only a single program executing at any given time. Memory resident programs are, in a sense, a limited violation of that trust. We find ways to safely bend the rules enough to do what must be done, without destroying the system. That, as any revolutionary will tell you, is a hard game to play.

The programs discussed thus far have read from the keyboard or written to the screen. They have activated themselves during interrupts and modified or displayed the contents of memory. These are all fairly harmless activities, and yet we were forced to go to great pains to write that software to be as inoffensive as possible to the programs running normally on the machine. Disk I/O is the most complicated subsystem in the IBM PC. It is here that the decisions of the early DOS designers have the most impact on us. We are trying to achieve limited multi-tasking in a system that does not normally permit such activities. If we succeed, we can expect only a limited victory. If we fail, the consequences are potentially disastrous.

Interfering with DOS disk I/O is dangerous, not in the sense of physical danger, but in the potential threat to the normal operation of the system. If DOS is about to write a buffer to disk and your resident program changes that buffer, you will lose the information you intended to write. If DOS is about to write a buffer to disk and you change the location of that write, even accidentally, you are likely to clobber something. If that something happens to be the file that DOS uses to boot, or a copy-protected program, or an important data file you haven't gotten around to backing up yet, you probably will not be amused by the consequences.

For that reason, there are several guidelines you should keep in mind when developing disk-based resident applications.

- *Never use a critical disk as your development disk.* If you are writing a program that may change the current disk, your current disk should be an empty floppy, rather than the hard disk with your income tax or stock portfolio information on it. By correctly setting the DOS PATH variable, you can still execute normal programs, such as the editor or assembler from your hard disk, but you will not be placing that disk in as much jeopardy. Better still, if you are truly unsure of your code, spin down your hard disk and use only floppies during the critical parts of your development.

- *Paranoids have enemies too.* Be suspicious of your code. You can't possibly know everything that is going on in the system, so if you write your code carefully, and test each part, you stand a much better chance of succeeding. Think up ways to make your code fail. You'd be amazed at the number of programs that have failed because a programmer thought that nobody would be foolish enough to try something, and then somebody did. A corollary of Murphy's law is: *For every foolproof program, there exists a determined fool capable of breaking it.* A good programmer should never be contemptuous of users, just suspicious of them.

- *Fences make good neighbors.* Always try to limit the amount of damage your program can cause. Firewall your code, test it as a normal application rather than a resident one, limiting yourself to the current disk at first rather than solving the general case immediately – you can save yourself quite a lot of grief in testing. Make backup copies, in case the originals are accidentally destroyed.

It is possible to write safe disk-based applications by being careful and always cleaning up after yourself. *Always* save the contents of the registers on entry to your code. *Always* restore them when you are done. And *always* restore the contents to the registers you originally got them from. You may not fully appreciate that last statement until the fourth or fifth time you get the order of POPs almost, but not quite, the same as the order of PUSHs. One trick to getting this ordering correct every time is simple but effective: assign the registers to a sequence (such as the one shown in the MASM manual: AX, BX, CX, DX, BP, SI, DI), then always stick with that sequence for PUSHing and its reverse for POPing. Even if you choose not to save particular registers, keeping the sequence with the remaining set is a good tool for keeping the order correct. Of course, you *must* POP as many registers as you PUSH. Many times when a program causes the machine to halt abruptly, the reason is unbalanced stack operations. After all, if you leave even a single word on the stack, the return address for the current subroutine will never be reached. When the routine returns, it will pull the return address off the top of the stack. If that value is wrong, the machine will try to use it anyway, and crash.

11.2   The Disk Subsystem

There are many different kinds of disks that can be used with a IBM PC. From the earliest single-sided, single-density 180-kilobyte floppy disks, to more modern 80-megabyte SCSI disks and beyond. If you had to know the intimate details of each of these drives to write a program that used the disk, you would probably go into another line of work. Fortunately, DOS provides several layers of software that encompass all these disks and many yet to come. If an interface can be created to mate a new disk to the the underside of the software layer, all programs that behave correctly with the top side can be used with the new equipment without modification.

Early versions of DOS saw each disk as a simple directory that contained files. If the disk held fifty files, the directory had fifty entries. This type of file system, known as a *flat* file system, is common because it is very easy to create and understand.

Flat file systems can become unmanageable as the amount of available disk space grows. When your disks hold just 180 kilobytes, the number of files you can have is small. When you have a 20-megabyte disk, you can create thousands of files. To force someone to sit through a directory listing of thousands of files is cruel, to say nothing of boring. Of course, in the original versions of DOS, it was impossible to create a single directory with thousands of files. The original flat file systems in early DOS versions were capable of storing a few dozen files at most.

Newer versions of DOS solved the problem of overcrowding by adopting a tree-structured file system, like those used in more advanced operating systems. A directory can contain not only files, but subdirectories. A subdirectory looks just like a directory and it can contain files and subdirectories as well. If you imagine the files to be leaves on a tree, with the root directory being the trunk and each subdirectory a branch, you can see where the analogy comes from. A tree has one trunk, that trunk can have many branches, and those branches can have branches. Leaves can grow anywhere.

The root directory is the trunk from which all branches grow. Each volume has one root directory, no more, no less. Usually, a disk is a volume and a volume a disk, but on hard disks you may have more than one volume on a single disk. Volumes are referred to by a letter, followed by a colon, as in `A:`. DOS permits up to 26 volumes, or `A:-Z:`. RAMDisks, which are chunks of RAM with a program to simulate a disk, can be assigned a volume label also. The root directory is named `\`. Thus, the root directory on volume `A:` would be named `A:\`. Under that root directory a subdirectory called `GLOP` would have the full name `A:\GLOP\`. The file `REAMDE.TXT` under that subdirectory would have the full name `A:\GLOP\README.TXT`.

In many books, this one included, you'll find the terms *directory* and *subdirectory* used interchangeably. There is really only a slight difference, and it is not a particularly important point for nonprogrammers. There is really only one directory per volume. That structure is the root directory. For compatibility reasons, it can hold only a limited number of file entries. Subdirectories are directories that are linked in a tree from the root directory. These directories can hold any number of files.

Despite the time we have spent discussing how a tree-structured file system resembles a natural tree, programmers typically picture a tree with the root at the top and each subdirectory a branch descending from that root. Thus, it is common, and very confusing, to find books that sing the virtues of ascending trees, but show diagrams of descending ones. Don't worry too much about this. There is no up or down on the disk. The important fact is the *relationship* among directories, subdirectories, and files. Think of them as trees, or roots, or file folders within file folders, or make up your own analogy. The analogy isn't as important as the concept that it is intended to reflect.

11.2.1   Directories

The first step in learning to use files is learning to find them. It is often said that a directory "contains" files, but what does that mean? Physically, files and directories are magnetized spots on a spinning platter. They are also highly organized *ideas*, thoughts given shape by software. The idea in this case is to allow a program to wander through a world filled with files, in the same way you might walk down the corridors of a library, browsing through the stacks, occasionally selecting a book for further study. In that sense, an organized collection of files is called a *file system* in the same way a library (an organized collection of books) could be called a *book system*.

To permit a program to wander the corridors of our system of files, we must have a *data structure* that tells it where the files are on disk, how big they are, and what they are named. To permit a person to walk through the file system, we must have programs capable of moving through the system and narrating their progress in human terms. The DIR command, which lists the contents of a directory or subdirectory, is just such a program.

DIR displays information about the files in a particular directory or subdirectory. Essentially, the DIR command prints the contents of a machine-readable directory data structure in a way that is people-readable. You can use DIR to find the names of files, their sizes, or the date they were created. The problem with the DIR command is that it is often unavailable when we need it. For example, suppose you are using a telecommunications program and you want to know what files are available in the current directory. Unless the programmer has specifically written a directory command or the equivalent, the only choice is to exit from the telecom program, list the directory, and then try to regain lost ground by restarting the communications program. What we need is the ability to list the entries in the current directory at any time, regardless of the design of the currently running application program. This seems like a good niche for a resident application.

The most common thing to want to see in a directory listing is, of course, the names of the files. For our purposes, that information alone will do for a basic resident directory lister. As we have discussed before, the correct place to display the information is not at the cursor location when the function is invoked. A much better choice is to "overlay" a window at the top of the screen, starting at the upper left corner.

We can build a directory lister from the basic structure of our keystroke-dispatcher program. Using that skeleton, we can construct an empty application that will be the framework for this application:

```
cseg    segment
        assume  cs:cseg,ds:cseg
        org     100H
start:
        jmp     initialize

old_keyboard_io dd

        assume  ds:nothing
new_keyboard_io         proc    far
        sti
        cmp     ah,0                    ; Is this call a READ request?
        je      ksread
        jmp     old_keyboard_io         ; handle the remaining subfunction.
ksread:
        call    keyread                 ; Get the next character to return
        iret
new_keyboard_io         endp


; Read a character from the keyboard input queue, if not expanding
; or the expansion string, if expansion is in progress.
keyread         proc    near
        push    si
readchar:
```

```
        pushf                                      ; Let the original routine
        call    old_keyboard_io                    ; determine keyboard status.
        cmp     al,0
        je      extended
        jmp     readdone
extended:
        mov     si,offset keytab
nextext:
        cmp     byte ptr cs:[si],0                 ; Is this the end of the table?
        je      readdone
        cmp     ah,cs:[si]
        je      startexpand
        add     si,3
        jmp     nextext
startexpand:
        add     si,1
        cmp     word ptr cs:[si],0
        je      readdone
        push    ax
        push    bx
        push    cx
        push    dx
        push    si
        push    di
        push    bp
        push    ds
        call    word ptr cs:[si]
        pop     ds
        pop     bp
        pop     di
        pop     si
        pop     dx
        pop     cx
        pop     bx
        pop     ax
readdone:
        pop     si
        ret
keyread         endp

keytab  db      32
        dw      dirlist
        db      0
        dw      0
```

```
        assume  cs:cseg,ds:cseg

; Keystroke routines go here

dirlist         proc    near
        ret
dirlist         endp

; Displays the string pointed to by DS:SI
dstring         proc    near
        push    si
        push    ax
        cmp     si,0
        je      dsdone
dloop:
        mov     al,[si]
        cmp     al,0
        je      dsdone
        call    dchar
        inc     si
        jmp     dloop
dsdone:
        pop     ax
        pop     si
        ret
dstring         endp

; Display the character contained in AL
dchar           proc    near
        push    ax
        push    bx
        mov     bh,1
        mov     ah,0EH
        int     10H
        pop     bx
        pop     ax
        ret
dchar           endp

initialize:
        assume  cs:cseg,ds:cseg
        mov     bx,cs
        mov     ds,bx

        mov     al,16H
```

```
        mov     ah,35H
        int     21H
        mov     old_keyboard_io,bx
        mov     old_keyboard_io[2],es
        mov     dx,offset new_keyboard_io
        mov     al,16H
        mov     ah,25H
        int     21H

        mov     dx,offset initialize
        int     27H

cseg    ends
        end     start
```

With this skeleton, we can build a resident program that will display a list of all the file names in the current directory when we type an ALT-D on the keyboard.

Listing directories is built on two closely related DOS functions, INT 21H function 4EH *(search for first match)* and INT 21H function 4FH *(search for next match)*. These two functions search in the current directory for a file that matches some criterion. That criterion is an ASCIIZ string that represents a form of file name. For example, if we wanted to get the directory listing for a particular file, say, "CMD.ASM", the match pattern would contain exactly that string. If you wanted to list all the assembly-language source files, the match pattern would be "*.ASM". If we wanted to match all the assembly language source files that had three character names beginning with the letter C, our match pattern would be "C??.ASM". And if we wanted to match all the files on the disk, we would use the match pattern "*.*".

The *search for first match* function also requires an attribute on which to search. This attribute is carried over to all other matches. Possible attributes are:

Attribute bit	Meaning
76543210	
xxxxxxx1	Read-only files
xxxxxx1x	Hidden files
xxxxx1xx	System files
xxxx1xxx	Volume label
xxx1xxxx	Subdirectory
xx1xxxxx	Archive

Adding these attribute bits extends the search. If the attribute byte is zero, only normal files are found. The *search for first match* function returns the file information for the first file in the directory that matches the pattern. The *search for next match* function returns successive matches after that. Both functions return a set CF if they find a match, or a cleared CF if no match is found.

```
dirlist         proc     near
        mov     bx,cs
        mov     ds,bx

        mov     ah,2FH                  ; Get the original DTA value
        int     21H
        push    es                      ; Save the DTA Segment on stack
        push    bx                      ; Save the DTA Offset on stack

        mov     dx,offset mydta         ; Set the DTA to our buffer
        mov     ah,1AH
        int     21H
        mov     dx,offset pattern       ; Set the search pattern
        mov     cx,0H                   ; Search for only normal files
        mov     ah,4EH                  ; Find the first match
        int     21H
        jc      dirdone                 ; If no first match, return
        mov     si,offset crlf
        call    dstring
display:
        mov     si,offset mydta+30      ; Print the file name
        call    dstring
        mov     si,offset crlf          ;    followed by a newline
        call    dstring
nextfile:
        mov     ah,4FH                  ; Search for the next match
        int     21H
        jnc     display                 ; If matched, print it
dirdone:
        pop     dx                      ; Get original DTA from stack
        pop     ds                      ;    but in different registers
        mov     ah,1AH                  ; Reset the DTA to the old value
        int     21H
        ret
dirlist         endp

crlf    db      0dH,0aH,0
```

```
pattern db        '*.*',0
mydta    db        64 dup (0)
```

This is a simple, yet useful function. By slightly changing the parameters, we can cause it to find out many useful pieces of information about the current directory.

One important concept used in this code is the idea of the disk transfer area (DTA). The DTA is a buffer that is used by many disk-oriented system calls as a staging area for disk information. In this case, it is where the information for each file is kept after the file was matched. This program determined the DTA location on entry, saved that location, and restored it before exiting. The DTA was allocated explicitly in this code as a 64-byte buffer. The syntax of the allocation should be explained. The assembler line

```
mydta    db        64 dup (0)
```

results in two separate actions by the assembler. The first is to allocate 64 bytes of memory at the current address, which will be referred to by the label `mydta`. The second involves the peculiar expression "`dup (0)`". This tells the assembler to fill those 64 bytes with zeros. We easily could have filled them with `FFH`, or anything else. In addition, we could have specified a "`dup (?)`", which would have allocated the space but not changed its contents at all.

It is not important where your DTA is located, except that it cannot be in a portion of memory used for some other purpose. It is important that your application create a DTA for itself, rather than use some existing DTA. It would be almost impossible to avoid a conflict between the running application and your resident application if they both used the same transfer area. By creating your own DTA and carefully setting and restoring it every time control passes to your resident application, you can avoid these types of conflicts.

11.3   Making a Useful Directory Display

Listing the contents of the current directory after the prompt is fine as a test, but we should be able to turn this subroutine into something more useful. First, of course, we should get it out of the way of the prompt. As in the past, we will start the display at the upper left corner of the screen. Since we may be displaying quite a few files, more than the number of lines on the screen, we should have some way of using more than the first ten columns of the screen.

DOS has a wide mode for directory listings, which displays a columnar list of files. Since we will be writing variable strings that will be less than or equal to twelve characters in length, we should make provisions for erasing the underlying screen contents.

It is likely that the screen will contain some information already. We would prefer not to mix our directory listing with extraneous information already on the screen. One way around this would be to cause the listing to pop up, blanking part of the screen, and then, at some signal from the user, vanish, restoring the original contents. Pop-up listings require you to remember information, however, while simple displays require you simply to copy information. For our purposes, we shall create a display that blanks each line it is about to touch, and thus "disambiguate" our directory listing from the other information on display.

```
dirlist         proc    near
        mov     bx,cs
        mov     ds,bx

        call    get_pos
        push    dx
        mov     dx,0
        call    set_pos
        call    blankline

        mov     ah,2FH                  ; Get the original DTA value
        int     21H
        push    es                      ; Save the DTA Segment on stack
        push    bx                      ; Save the DTA Offset on stack

        mov     dx,offset mydta         ; Set the DTA to our buffer
        mov     ah,1AH
        int     21H
        mov     dx,offset pattern       ; Set the search pattern
        mov     cx,0H                   ; Search for only normal files
        mov     ah,4EH                  ; Find the first match
        int     21H
        jc      dirdone                 ; If no first match, return
        mov     bp,0
display:
        mov     si,offset mydta+30      ; Print the file name
        call    fillstring
        inc     bp
        cmp     bp,4
        jne     nextfile
```

```
            mov     bp,0
            call    blankline
nextfile:
            mov     ah,4FH                  ; Search for the next match
            int     21H
            jnc     display                 ; If matched, print it
dirdone:
            pop     dx                      ; Get original DTA from stack
            pop     ds                      ;   but in different registers
            mov     ah,1AH                  ; Reset the DTA to the old value
            int     21H


            pop     dx
            call    set_pos
            ret
dirlist         endp
tab     db      09H,0
crlf    db      0dH,0aH,0
pattern db      '*.*',0
mydta   db      64 dup (0)

; Position in DX
get_pos         proc    near
            push    ax
            push    bx
            push    cx
            mov     ah,03H
            mov     bh,0
            int     10H
            pop     cx
            pop     bx
            pop     ax
            ret
get_pos         endp

; Position in DX
set_pos         proc    near
            push    ax
            push    bx
            mov     ah,02H
            mov     bh,0
            int     10H
            pop     bx
            pop     ax
            ret
```

```
set_pos         endp

blankline       proc    near
        push    ax
        push    bx
        push    cx
        mov     ah,09H
        mov     al,' '
        mov     bh,0
        mov     bl,7
        mov     cx,80
        int     10H
        pop     cx
        pop     bx
        pop     ax
        ret
blankline       endp

;DS:SI points to ASCIIZ string to print
fillstring      proc    near
        push    cx
        call    dstring
fillchar:
        cmp     cx,20
        je      filldone
        mov     al,' '
        call    dchar
        inc     cx
        jmp     fillchar
filldone:
        pop     cx
        ret
fillstring      endp
```

Organizing the display into columns is usually not difficult. There are many ways to do this, and many work under different sets of circumstances. In this case, we are exploiting a feature of the ROM character I/O calls. We know that a file name will be a maximum of twelve characters long. Files can have up to eight characters of name, followed by a period (.), followed by up to three characters of extension. Thus, FILENAME.EXT is as long as any pathless filename can be under DOS.

We know that there are two types of text displays on the IBM PC. Some have 80 character lines, others have 40 character lines. Twelve does not divide cleanly into either of these numbers. Besides that, we must have some amount of blank space between each file name as separation. By being just a little clever and realizing that INT 10H function 0EH *(write character in TTY mode)* will wrap around when it reaches the last column of the screen, we can provide a columnar directory listing by simply adding one small routine fillstring. This routine displays each file name, left justified, in a 20-character fixed width field, padded with blanks. Since 20 divides evenly into both 80 and 40, this display will work correctly in both cases, simply by printing the characters in a single line and letting the cursor wrap-around do the work for us. Since this function is supported under all versions of the IBM ROM and is likely to be in any clone ROMs, portability is not an issue.

11.4   LD.ASM – **List a directory**

After running this program, typing an ALT-D will cause a reasonably neat directory listing to be displayed in the upper part of the screen.

```
cseg    segment
        assume  cs:cseg,ds:cseg
        org     100H
start:
        jmp     initialize


old_keyboard_io dd

        assume  ds:nothing
new_keyboard_io         proc    far
        sti
        cmp     ah,0                    ; Is this call a READ request?
        je      ksread
        jmp     old_keyboard_io         ; handle the remaining subfunction.
ksread:
        call    keyread                 ; Get the next character to return
        iret
new_keyboard_io         endp


; Read a character from the keyboard input queue, if not expanding
; or the expansion string, if expansion is in progress.
keyread         proc    near
        push    si
```

```
readchar:
        pushf                                   ; Let the original routine
        call    old_keyboard_io                 ; determine keyboard status.
        cmp     al,0
        je      extended
        jmp     readdone
extended:
        mov     si,offset keytab
nextext:
        cmp     byte ptr cs:[si],0              ; Is this the end of the table?
        je      readdone
        cmp     ah,cs:[si]
        je      startexpand
        add     si,3
        jmp     nextext
startexpand:
        add     si,1
        cmp     word ptr cs:[si],0
        je      readdone
        push    ax
        push    bx
        push    cx
        push    dx
        push    si
        push    di
        push    bp
        push    ds
        call    word ptr cs:[si]
        pop     ds
        pop     bp
        pop     di
        pop     si
        pop     dx
        pop     cx
        pop     bx
        pop     ax
readdone:
        pop     si
        ret
keyread         endp

keytab  db      32
        dw      dirlist
        db      0
        dw      0
```

```
        assume  cs:cseg,ds:cseg

; Keystroke routines go here

dirlist         proc    near
        mov     bx,cs
        mov     ds,bx

        call    get_pos
        push    dx
        mov     dx,0
        call    set_pos
        call    blankline

        mov     ah,2FH              ; Get the original DTA value
        int     21H
        push    es                  ; Save the DTA Segment on stack
        push    bx                  ; Save the DTA Offset on stack

        mov     dx,offset mydta     ; Set the DTA to our buffer
        mov     ah,1AH
        int     21H
        mov     dx,offset pattern   ; Set the search pattern
        mov     cx,0H               ; Search for only normal files
        mov     ah,4EH              ; Find the first match
        int     21H
        jc      dirdone             ; If no first match, return
        mov     bp,0
display:
        mov     si,offset mydta+30  ; Print the file name
        call    fillstring
        inc     bp
        cmp     bp,4
        jne     nextfile
        mov     bp,0
        call    blankline
nextfile:
        mov     ah,4FH              ; Search for the next match
        int     21H
        jnc     display             ; If matched, print it
dirdone:
        pop     dx                  ; Get original DTA from stack
        pop     ds                  ;   but in different registers
        mov     ah,1AH              ; Reset the DTA to the old value
```

```
        int     21H

        pop     dx
        call    set_pos
        ret
dirlist         endp

tab     db      09H,0
crlf    db      0dH,0aH,0
pattern db      '*.*',0
mydta   db      64 dup (0)

; Position in DX
get_pos         proc    near
        push    ax
        push    bx
        push    cx
        mov     ah,03H
        mov     bh,0
        int     10H
        pop     cx
        pop     bx
        pop     ax
        ret
get_pos         endp

; Position in DX
set_pos         proc    near
        push    ax
        push    bx
        mov     ah,02H
        mov     bh,0
        int     10H
        pop     bx
        pop     ax
        ret
set_pos         endp

blankline       proc    near
        push    ax
        push    bx
        push    cx
        mov     ah,09H
        mov     al,' '
        mov     bh,0
```

```
        mov     bl,7
        mov     cx,80
        int     10H
        pop     cx
        pop     bx
        pop     ax
        ret
blankline       endp

;DS:SI points to ASCIIZ string to print
fillstring      proc    near
        push    cx
        call    dstring
fillchar:
        cmp     cx,20
        je      filldone
        mov     al,' '
        call    dchar
        inc     cx
        jmp     fillchar
filldone:
        pop     cx
        ret
fillstring      endp

; Displays the string pointed to by DS:SI
dstring         proc    near
        push    si
        push    ax
        mov     cx,0
        cmp     si,0
        je      dsdone
dloop:
        mov     al,[si]
        cmp     al,0
        je      dsdone
        call    dchar
        inc     si
        inc     cx
        jmp     dloop
dsdone:
        pop     ax
        pop     si
        ret
dstring         endp
```

```
; Display the character contained in AL
dchar           proc    near
        push    ax
        push    bx
        mov     bh,1
        mov     ah,0EH
        int     10H
        pop     bx
        pop     ax
        ret
dchar           endp

initialize:
        assume  cs:cseg,ds:cseg
        mov     bx,cs
        mov     ds,bx

        mov     al,16H
        mov     ah,35H
        int     21H
        mov     old_keyboard_io,bx
        mov     old_keyboard_io[2],es
        mov     dx,offset new_keyboard_io
        mov     al,16H
        mov     ah,25H
        int     21H

        mov     dx,offset initialize
        int     27H

cseg    ends
        end     start
```

Chapter 12

Strolling the Corridors

The directory for a disk is something like a telephone directory. It tells you whether certain files are present and, if so, where they are located on the disk. But there is a big difference between finding the name of a restaurant in the phonebook and going to that restaurant for dinner. The second part of using the file system from within memory resident programs is knowing how to use the files you have located in the directory.

DOS has two different types of functions for file I/O. The first type is the file control block (FCB) operations. These are the file operations that were written for the earliest versions of DOS. In many ways they are reminiscent of some file operations from CP/M (an early disk operating system that was very popular for 8-bit computers and the inspiration for much of MS-DOS). The FCB is a structure in memory that contains many useful pieces of information about a particular stream of file operations. You can have any number of file control blocks and thus any number of file operations in progress at a given time.

The other type of file operations are *handle* operations, which are strongly flavored by similar operations in the UNIX operating system. These routines are more flexible and easier to use and require somewhat less memory in your programs, because all the file state information is kept by DOS in memory allocated by the operating system. They are called handle operations because the first call one uses, *"open file"* or *"create file"*, returns an integer that is a token DOS uses to find the internal file status structure. Early versions of DOS may be missing these functions.

For writing general applications, the handle functions are the better choice. They are much more pleasant to use and require less work than the FCB functions to accomplish the same task. Unfortunately, one of the ways they accomplish this flexibility limits them for use in an resident application. Handle functions are easy to use because they abstract the file information into a single token, and that token can be used to represent a particular file throughout the life of a program. DOS keeps track of the details, and the file operations just work right. Because DOS has internal tables for file state, a resident application that uses handle operations is likely to become noticeable.

Suppose a normal application program wants to open several files at the same time. DOS will allocate a handle for each file that is opened. The maximum number of files that can be open at once is set by the FILES command in your CONFIG.SYS. Suppose the default value of eight files is being used. The application has opened seven files and is about to open an eighth, when a resident application (a pop-up notepad, for example) is run. The notepad opens a file and leaves it open, even after it has completed, and control returns to the application. Because of that open file, the application will fail where it should have succeeded.

There are two solutions to this problem. The first is administrative. Simply set the value of FILES to be larger than eight. This doesn't really solve the problem, though. It simply pushes it into the future. The second choice is to fix the resident application to work without interfering. This is harder, but it means that your code is more likely to work on a variety of machines. The FCB calls are a little more useful to us, though they are more painful to use. The file control block is a structure that is located somewhere in memory. We can decide where it should go, so is no reason it cannot be located within the memory space of a resident application. With no disk state to be managed by the system, the resident application becomes less noticeable, but not entirely invisible. Remember that the disk code will change the position of the disk heads and the low-level state of the disk hardware.

The handle functions are not a complete loss, however. We would prefer to use them, because they are simpler to use and thus make our resident code that much smaller. One way to accomplish this involves the notion of a *session*. An application program loads from disk, runs, and then exits. It has only one session. A resident application loads from disk, installs itself, and then waits to be called. It may be invoked many times and thus has any number of sessions. A session is the time in which a given program has control over the machine. Once a resident application is activated, its session begins. The resident application can do whatever it likes and retains control over the machine until it chooses to give it up. When the resident application gives up control, that particular session has ended.

By guaranteeing that a set of disk operations (open file/use file/close file) remains within a single session, you improve the likelihood of your resident application working correctly. If you open a file, read or write it, and close it all within the space of a single session, you stand a much better chance of keeping everything working correctly. In addition, since the handle operation would remain in a single session, they can be used from within a memory resident program.

For devices such as the screen, the idea of a session is interesting and sometimes useful, but not critical. If a resident application writes to the screen, the worst thing you might have is a messy screen. That will not crash the program in progress, nor will it turn good results into bad. Disk operations have a much greater potential for disaster and so should be taken very seriously in the design of your code. Imagine the problems you would have when you realized that the resident application you just ran accidentally changed a *single byte* somewhere on the disk containing your income tax spreadsheet information. Then imagine trying to explain that to your auditor.

12.1 Browsing in the Stacks

A good example of using disk I/O from within a resident application, and also a fairly useful one, is a disk browsing program. How many times have you been working within a program and realized that you needed to load a file. You know the file is on your disk. You've displayed a directory listing, using that nifty little directory lister we wrote in the last chapter. But you can't remember whether the file you want is GLOP.ASM or PLOP.ASM. If you could see the contents of either file, you would know. What you need to be able to do is stroll around through the file system at will, looking at the files you find there.

Once again, we will begin with the basic skeleton of our keystroke dispatcher. It is probably worthwhile to mention that even though this skeleton has reappeared several times, it is not always necessary to duplicate the skeleton for each function you want to dispatch. If you want to cut each function into a separate program, by all means do so. But if you prefer to use one dispatcher and create a single large program containing the routines for each keystroke, there is no reason not to do so.

```
cseg    segment
        assume  cs:cseg,ds:cseg
        org     100H
start:
        jmp     initialize


old_keyboard_io dd

        assume  ds:nothing
new_keyboard_io         proc    far
        sti
        cmp     ah,0                    ; Is this call a READ request?
        je      ksread
        jmp     old_keyboard_io         ; handle the remaining subfunction.
ksread:
        call    keyread                 ; Get the next character to return
        iret
new_keyboard_io         endp


; Read a character from the keyboard input queue, if not expanding
; or the expansion string, if expansion is in progress.
keyread         proc    near
        push    si
readchar:
        pushf                           ; Let the original routine
        call    old_keyboard_io         ; determine keyboard status.
        cmp     al,0
        je      extended
        jmp     readdone
extended:
        mov     si,offset keytab
nextext:
        cmp     byte ptr cs:[si],0      ; Is this the end of the table?
        je      readdone
        cmp     ah,cs:[si]
        je      startexpand
        add     si,3
        jmp     nextext
startexpand:
        add     si,1
        cmp     word ptr cs:[si],0
        je      readdone
        push    ax
        push    bx
```

```
                push    cx
                push    dx
                push    si
                push    di
                push    bp
                push    ds
                call    word ptr cs:[si]
                pop     ds
                pop     bp
                pop     di
                pop     si
                pop     dx
                pop     cx
                pop     bx
                pop     ax
readdone:
                pop     si
                ret
keyread         endp

keytab  db      48                      ; ALT-B
        dw      browse
        db      0
        dw      0

        assume  cs:cseg,ds:cseg

; Keystroke routines go here

browse          proc    near
        ret
browse          endp

; Displays the string pointed to by DS:SI
dstring         proc    near
                push    si
                push    ax
                cmp     si,0
                je      dsdone
dloop:
                mov     al,[si]
                cmp     al,0
                je      dsdone
                call    dchar
                inc     si
```

```
        jmp     dloop
dsdone:
        pop     ax
        pop     si
        ret
dstring         endp

; Display the character contained in AL
dchar           proc    near
        push    ax
        push    bx
        mov     bh,1
        mov     ah,0EH
        int     10H
        pop     bx
        pop     ax
        ret
dchar           endp

initialize:
        assume  cs:cseg,ds:cseg
        mov     bx,cs
        mov     ds,bx

        mov     al,16H
        mov     ah,35H
        int     21H
        mov     old_keyboard_io,bx
        mov     old_keyboard_io[2],es
        mov     dx,offset new_keyboard_io
        mov     al,16H
        mov     ah,25H
        int     21H

        mov     dx,offset initialize
        int     27H

cseg    ends
        end     start
```

We have bound the browse function to the **ALT-B** key. Now, with the skeleton
built, we can begin to think about the user interface. In the resident application
we created for setting the mode on the communications port, we developed a
nice cyclic system for selecting a particular option from a known set of options.

This case is similar to that. We know that there are a fixed number of files in the current directory. We may not know how many there are, but we know that INT 21H function 4EH *(search for first match)* will give us the name of the first, and continued application of INT 21H function 4FH *(search for next match)* will scan through all the files until we reach the last. Given these facts, there is no reason not to use the same method of allowing the user to confirm selection of the currently displayed file or pass to the next file. As with many of these applications, the display should take place in the upper left corner of the screen for the same reasons given elsewhere.

When ALT-B is typed, the cursor is moved to the upper left corner of the screen and the first file name displayed. If the RightArrow key is hit, that file is accepted and displayed. If the End key is hit, the browser will quit and control will return to wherever it came from. If any other key is hit, the display will cycle on to the next file in the directory. When the end of the list of files is reached, the display starts again at the beginning. This is an extremely simple interface, but it is also quite powerful. It can be applied to any situation where all the choices are known. One addition, which was not done here to keep the program as simple and clear as possible, would be to allow another key, the UpArrow perhaps, to cycle the choices in the opposite direction. This would permit you to recover quickly from hitting a key and realizing that you passed the correct choice. It is important to note that this simple addition would add a great deal of complexity to this application. We have, through DOS, an easy means of scanning *forward* through the files in a directory. We do not have any similar means of scanning *backward*. For the sake of adding a little polish, we would increase the complexity of our application.

12.2 Prototyping the Selector

We know how we want to select files. Before we move on to the design of the file-display mechanism, a reasonable thing to do would be to create a prototype of the selection mechanism.

In chapter 11, we chose to blank an entire line before we wrote anything on it. This serves two purposes. First, it draws attention to the display on that line, and second, it prevents that display from seeming cluttered. This is important when you consider that the display of a file name on top of what may have been a directory listing could be very confusing indeed. By blanking the line, we can be sure that what we seem to be reading is really what was meant to be read.

These same reasons apply here, for both selection and display. For that reason, we will blank the background behind our file selector. To do this, we require the `blankline` routine from chapter 11.

Since we intend to cycle through a series of file names, we need some method of keeping them from overlapping. We could blank the entire line each time, but we already have a routine that will print a string within a fixed-width string, filled out by spaces. The execution time for each is quite small, so a choice cannot be made on that basis. If we wanted to display a series of things, we would need to make different arrangements other than blanking the entire line, however. For that reason – upward mobility – we should choose the `fillstring` routine.

Another routine we need is the `dirlist` function from chapter 11. This routine was designed to scan through an entire directory, displaying fixed-width file names. In this case, we don't want to scan through all at once. We want to show one file at at time. When the end of the list is reached, we want to start over again at the beginning. The `dirlist` routine could be modified to be called `nextfile`, meaning "Display the next file in sequence." It would look like this:

```
nextfile        proc    near
        call    get_pos
        push    dx
firstmatch:
        cmp     si,0
        jne     nextmatch
        mov     si,1
        mov     dx,offset pattern; Set the search pattern
        mov     cx,0H           ; Search for normal files
        mov     ah,4EH          ; Find the first match
        int     21H
        jnc     showmatch
        mov     si,0
        jmp     matchdone
nextmatch:
        mov     ah,4FH          ; Search for next match
        int     21H
        jnc     showmatch       ; Display match
        mov     si,0
        jmp     firstmatch
showmatch:
        mov     si,offset mydta+30 ; Print the file name
        call    fillstring
```

```
matchdone:
        pop     dx
        call    set_pos
        ret
nextfile        endp
```

This routine takes in one state variable. The value in SI determines whether the directory listing starts from the beginning (SI is 0) or somewhere in the middle (SI not 0). Each time this routine is called it displays the next value in the "circular" list of files – circular, because when the end of the directory is reached, the next file is the first file in the list.

By wrapping a little cursor-positioning code around this routine, we can create the cyclic effect used in the modem program, SETMODE.ASM. We must also take the same precautions as before, saving the old disk transfer area (DTA) and setting our own.

```
browse          proc    near
        mov     bx,cs
        mov     ds,bx

        call    get_pos         ;Save current position
        push    dx
        mov     dx,0            ;Move to Upper Left Corner
        call    set_pos
        call    blankline       ;Blank entire line

        mov     ah,2FH          ;Get original DTA
        int     21H
        push    es              ;Save DTA Segment
        push    bx              ;Save DTA Offset

        mov     dx,offset mydta ;Set our DTA
        mov     ah,1AH
        int     21H

        mov     si,0            ;Set FIRST for nextfile
cycle:
        call    nextfile        ;Display next file
        call    getchar         ;Get a character
        cmp     al,0            ;Is it extended?
        jne     cycle           ;If so, loop
        cmp     ah,79           ;Is it an END
        je      bdone           ;If so, quit
```

```
                cmp     ah,77           ;Is it a Right Arrow
                jne     cycle           ;If not, loop
                call    showfile        ;If so, display the file
        bdone:
                pop     dx              ;Get original DTA from stack
                pop     ds              ;  but in different registers
                mov     ah,1AH          ;Reset DTA to old value
                int     21H

                pop     dx              ;Get old position
                call    set_pos         ;And restore cursor position
                ret
        browse          endp

        showfile        proc    near
                ret
        showfile        endp
```

12.3   Displaying the File

Once a file has been selected, it must be displayed. There are many ways to accomplish this – we'll choose the easiest and most straightforward. Once the file has been chosen, we want to move the cursor again to the upper left corner and begin displaying the file. As with the directory display, we should never mix old and new screen information. Once we choose to write anything on a line, that entire line should be blanked first.

Displaying any part of the file is just as hard, from the resident application point of view, as displaying the entire file. For the purposes of this book and for many cases when simply browsing through files, we need display only the first few lines of a file. For simplicity, we will display the first 512 bytes. Adding a simple user interface to scan through the entire file is not difficult, but it adds nothing to the theme of this book. The additional code is left (as they said in those books that you found so annoying in school) as an exercise for the reader. One possibility for this interface would be to move along the same lines as the rest of this program. Display a page of the file. The **End** key stops the display and drops out of the browser. Any other key advances a page. A few frills might be to allow the browser to move forward or backward through the files, binding those functions to the **PgDn** and **PgUp** keys.

The simplest **showfile** routine, displaying only the first 512 bytes of the file, would look like this:

```
showfile        proc    near
        call    blankline       ;Blank the first line
        mov     ah,3DH          ;Open the file
        mov     al,0            ;Access is Read-Only
                                ;File name is in DTA+30
        mov     dx,offset mydta+30
        int     21H             ;Handle returned in BX

        mov     si,offset mydta ;Clear the DTA to all zeros
        mov     cx,512
cleardta:
        mov     byte ptr [si],0
        inc     si
        loop    cleardta

        mov     bx,ax           ;Read a block from the file
        mov     ah,3FH
        mov     cx,512          ;First 512 bytes or less
        mov     dx,offset mydta
        int     21H
        mov     si,offset mydta ;Print the block
        call    dstring

        mov     ah,3EH          ;Close the file
        int     21H
        ret
showfile        endp

mydta   db      512 dup (0)
        db      0
```

Because we have enclosed the file I/O within a single routine and thus within a single session, we can use the handle functions. You should take note of two parts of this function, one code, one data. The first operation this code performs is to open the file. The file name is known to be thirty bytes from the beginning of the disk transfer area used by the search operations. After the file is open, we no longer need the file name; therefore, we can reuse the DTA as a staging area for the block of data we want to read. We know that the data placed into the DTA will be less than or equal to 512 bytes in length. If we want to print that information, we must either be concerned with its length, or take steps to ensure

that the end of the data can be detected. After we open the file, the next step
we take here is to fill the DTA with zeroes. This means that a block of less than
512 bytes will be terminated by a zero byte. If we have read in a binary file,
it may have zero bytes in it. This means that the display will stop sooner, but
that is acceptable, since we will not be getting much information from looking
at the character representation of a binary file. For the case of a data block
that is exactly 512 bytes long, we have placed an extra zero byte immediately
after the DTA. This will never be overwritten by the disk routines, so the block
will be zero-terminated in that case as well. Since we know the starting length
and can detect the end of the block, we can simply use the `dstring` routine to
display the block as though it were an ASCIIZ string.

12.4 BROWSE.ASM – Examine File Contents

After this program is installed an **ALT-B** will display a filename in the upper left
corner of the screen. A **RightArrow** will select the displayed filename and print
the top of the file on the screen. An **End** will quit. Any other key will display
the next filename in the directory.

```
cseg    segment
        assume  cs:cseg,ds:cseg
        org     100H
start:
        jmp     initialize

old_keyboard_io dd

        assume  ds:nothing
new_keyboard_io         proc    far
        sti
        cmp     ah,0                    ; Is this call a READ request?
        je      ksread
        jmp     old_keyboard_io         ; handle the remaining subfunction.
ksread:
        call    keyread                 ; Get the next character to return
        iret
new_keyboard_io         endp


; Read a character from the keyboard input queue, if not expanding
; or the expansion string, if expansion is in progress.
```

```
keyread         proc    near
        push    si
readchar:
        pushf                                   ; Let the original routine
        call    old_keyboard_io                 ; determine keyboard status.
        cmp     al,0
        je      extended
        jmp     readdone
extended:
        mov     si,offset keytab
nextext:
        cmp     byte ptr cs:[si],0      ; Is this the end of the table?
        je      readdone
        cmp     ah,cs:[si]
        je      startexpand
        add     si,3
        jmp     nextext
startexpand:
        add     si,1
        cmp     word ptr cs:[si],0
        je      readdone
        push    ax
        push    bx
        push    cx
        push    dx
        push    si
        push    di
        push    bp
        push    ds
        call    word ptr cs:[si]
        pop     ds
        pop     bp
        pop     di
        pop     si
        pop     dx
        pop     cx
        pop     bx
        pop     ax
readdone:
        pop     si
        ret
keyread         endp

keytab  db      48
        dw      browse
```

```
        db      0
        dw      0

        assume  cs:cseg,ds:cseg

; Keystroke routines go here

browse          proc    near
        mov     bx,cs
        mov     ds,bx

        call    get_pos
        push    dx
        mov     dx,0
        call    set_pos
        call    blankline

        mov     ah,19H
        int     21H
        push    ax

        mov     ah,2FH                  ; Get the original DTA value
        int     21H
        push    es                      ; Save the DTA Segment on stack
        push    bx                      ; Save the DTA Offset on stack

        mov     dx,offset mydta         ; Set the DTA to our buffer
        mov     ah,1AH
        int     21H
        mov     si,0
cycle:
        call    nextfile
        call    getchar                 ; Get a character
        cmp     al,0                    ; Is it extended?
        jne     cycle                   ; If so, loop
        cmp     ah,79                   ; Is it an END
        je      bdone
        cmp     ah,77                   ; Is it a Right Arrow
        jne     cycle
        call    showfile
bdone:
        mov     ah,0DH
        int     21H

        pop     dx                      ; Get original DTA from stack
```

```
        pop     ds                      ;   but in different registers
        mov     ah,1AH                  ; Reset the DTA to the old value
        int     21H

        mov     ah,0EH
        pop     dx
        int     21H

        pop     dx
        call    set_pos
        ret
browse          endp

tab     db      09H,0
crlf    db      0dH,0aH,0
pattern db      '*.*',0
mydta   db      512 dup (0)
        db      0

showfile        proc    near
        call    blankline
        mov     ah,3DH                  ; Open the file
        mov     al,0
        mov     dx,offset mydta+30
        int     21H
        mov     si,offset mydta
        mov     cx,512
cleardta:
        mov     byte ptr [si],0
        inc     si
        loop    cleardta

        mov     bx,ax
        mov     ah,3FH
        mov     cx,512
        mov     dx,offset mydta
        int     21H
        mov     si,offset mydta
        call    dstring

        mov     ah,3EH
        int     21H
        ret
showfile        endp
```

```
nextfile        proc    near
        call    get_pos
        push    dx
firstmatch:
        cmp     si,0
        jne     nextmatch
        mov     si,1
        mov     dx,offset pattern       ; Set the search pattern
        mov     cx,0H                   ; Search for only normal files
        mov     ah,4EH                  ; Find the first match
        int     21H
        jnc     showmatch
        mov     si,0
        jmp     matchdone
nextmatch:
        mov     ah,4FH                  ; Search for the next match
        int     21H
        jnc     showmatch               ; Display match
        mov     si,0
        jmp     firstmatch
showmatch:
        mov     si,offset mydta+30      ; Print the file name
        call    fillstring
matchdone:
        pop     dx
        call    set_pos
        ret
nextfile        endp

getchar proc    near
        pushf
        mov     ah,0
        assume  cs:nothing
        call    old_keyboard_io
        assume  cs:cseg
        ret
getchar endp

; Position in DX
get_pos         proc    near
        push    ax
        push    bx
        push    cx
        mov     ah,03H
        mov     bh,0
```

```
        int     10H
        pop     cx
        pop     bx
        pop     ax
        ret
get_pos         endp

; Position in DX
set_pos         proc    near
        push    ax
        push    bx
        mov     ah,02H
        mov     bh,0
        int     10H
        pop     bx
        pop     ax
        ret
set_pos         endp

blankline       proc    near
        push    ax
        push    bx
        push    cx
        mov     ah,09H
        mov     al,' '
        mov     bh,0
        mov     bl,7
        mov     cx,80
        int     10H
        pop     cx
        pop     bx
        pop     ax
        ret
blankline       endp

;DS:SI points to ASCIIZ string to print
fillstring      proc    near
        push    cx
        call    dstring
fillchar:
        cmp     cx,20
        je      filldone
        mov     al,' '
        call    dchar
        inc     cx
```

```
        jmp     fillchar
filldone:
        pop     cx
        ret
fillstring      endp

; Displays the string pointed to by DS:SI
dstring         proc    near
        push    si
        push    ax
        mov     cx,0
        cmp     si,0
        je      dsdone
dloop:
        mov     al,[si]
        cmp     al,0
        je      dsdone
        call    dchar
        cmp     al,0AH
        jne     endloop
        call    blankline
endloop:
        inc     si
        inc     cx
        jmp     dloop
dsdone:
        pop     ax
        pop     si
        ret
dstring         endp

; Display the character contained in AL
dchar           proc    near
        push    ax
        push    bx
        mov     bh,1
        mov     ah,0EH
        int     10H
        pop     bx
        pop     ax
        ret
dchar           endp

initialize:
        assume  cs:cseg,ds:cseg
```

```
        mov     bx,cs
        mov     ds,bx

        mov     al,16H
        mov     ah,35H
        int     21H
        mov     old_keyboard_io,bx
        mov     old_keyboard_io[2],es
        mov     dx,offset new_keyboard_io
        mov     al,16H
        mov     ah,25H
        int     21H

        mov     dx,offset initialize
        int     27H

cseg    ends
        end     start
```

Chapter 13

The Roads Not Taken

Design, as we have discussed before, is a matter of trade-offs. Each choice you make leads you toward some other decisions and away from others. There is more than one path from start to finish, but each path stresses some aspects and leaves some things undone. Knowing why a path was *not* taken is as important as knowing which paths were chosen.

Writing memory resident programs is not always easy. Many people have stayed up late, cursing their computers, trying to dig a little deeper into the operating system and the reasons why things fail. By the nature of the task, you are trying to make the machine do useful work in areas where the designers of the operating system believed you'd never venture.

For any subject stressed in this book, there are others that were avoided or only briefly touched. Some topics were inappropriate, others too risky to recommend, still others could have been expanded indefinitely. Unfortunately, books have deadlines and space constraints, and authors have to get some sleep, now and again. Nevertheless, there are some topics that should have some mention, even if only to explain their absence.

13.1 Emerging Standards

In 1986, proposals for a standardization of memory resident programs began to emerge. As these words are being written, few facts are available on the standards, but they are firming and gathering support in some quarters. Standards, someone once said, are wonderful because there are always so many to choose from. The final words are far from spoken on the concept of a standard for resident applications programming. Borland International, one of the first companies with a commercial set of resident applications, has proposed a standard that has been well received in some places. But as of this writing, no programs have been marketed that conform to this standard.

If you plan to write commercial resident applications, following an existing standard is vitally important. As the IBM PC architecture matures with the AT and subsequent generations, the rules necessary to make a well-behaved resident application will become less of a suggestion and more of a requirement. If your memory resident program is a maverick and does not follow the standard, you will simply be creating a market for a similar product that does adhere to the standard.

13.2   Compatibility

In lieu of an existing, well-defined standard, there is an ad hoc standard of a sort, used by many resident application programmers. This "standard" is quite simple: will it run with Sidekick? Borland's resident desk accessory package pushes a regular PC to its limits in some cases. If your program works correctly with Sidekick also loaded and Sidekick works with your program loaded, there is a good chance that your program is safe for distribution.

One point should be made about testing resident applications with Sidekick or any other memory resident program. The order of installation is often important. It would be easy to write a program that can be loaded before Sidekick and still work, but would not work when loaded after Sidekick. A program that does not pass through the call on an interrupt vector to the previous vector will not permit earlier programs on that same vector to work correctly.

Some programs will not work correctly if other resident applications are loaded on top of them. One example is FPANEL (see Chapter 7). Because of the design of the program, FPANEL must be the last application installed on the timer interrupt. If another application is loaded, FPANEL will not crash, but it will display a constant and fairly meaningless number.

13.3   Video Modes

For the sake of clarity and simplicity, the programs in this book have been written to work in 80x25 monochrome text mode. This is a common mode for the IBM PC and easy to use, since the largely irrelevant (for the theme of this book) issues of color and display attributes can be ignored. Though these programs may work correctly for other video modes, they have not been proven to do so; thus, some displays may not be correct, especially for low-resolution color modes.

13.4 Disabling Interrupts

One technique that is quite useful, but not covered elsewhere in this book, is a method of disabling interrupts. Suppose you chose to redirect the timer interrupt. The timer is occurring at approximately 18.2 times per second, which gives each interrupt a maximum of about 55 milliseconds to execute. Under some circumstances, you may want to use a routine that will take more than 55 milliseconds to execute. If the timer interrupt occurs during your timer-interrupt service routine any number of things, all bad, can happen. But disabling the interrupts is a poor solution to this problem.

A better solution is to have the timer-interrupt handler redirect the timer interrupt to a null routine, one that looks like this:

```
nullint         proc    far
        sti
        iret
nullint         endp
```

If this routine is used for the duration of the extended timer interrupt, a few time ticks can occur and not be noticed. The interrupt handler should correctly reset the timer vector before it exits, of course.

The trade-off in this case is in accuracy of the system clock. If a few timer ticks are missed on a regular basis, the system clock will begin to drift, because the system timer-interrupt handler is used to advance the clock tick counter. In that case, a slightly better solution would be to have the long-duration timer interrupt first call the old handler as a subroutine and then replace the vector with the address of the old routine. That order of operations is important, because simply replacing the handler with an older address would cause the system to miss a tick. When the long handler has completed, it can reset the vector with a pointer to itself.

When resetting interrupt vectors from within interrupt handlers, be sure to disable interrupts (with CLI), modify the vector, and then reenable interrupts (with STI).

13.5   Rolling Your Own

Throughout this book, there have been a set of useful subroutines that have shown up again and again. Good examples of these would be the **dchar** routine, which displays a character on the screen, and **dstring**, which displays an ASCIIZ string on the screen. If you were to load all the programs in this book at once, there would be several duplicated copies of these routines scattered about in the address space of your computer.

There are two basic solutions to that problem. One would be to write a master resident application that encompassed all the functions in this book without duplicating the low-level routines. There is nothing fundamentally wrong with this approach, except that it takes some time to assemble such a program, and it does put all your eggs, as they say, in a single basket.

The other approach is the same one taken by DOS. Write all your utility routines as soft interrupt handlers, and then write a single loader that will load the interrupt handlers and install them. DOS permits up to 256 interrupt vectors. Many of these are reserved, but many of the ones in the range of 40H-7FH are available. Some of the vectors in the range of 40H-49H are used by the IBM PCjr. Vector 67H is used for the extended memory-management packages.

Using a soft interrupt as a vehicle for managing utilities is a good idea, but it comes at a price. If your utilities are not installed, your resident applications will fail immediately. If you make one change to the utility package, every resident application that uses that package can be affected. If you intend to sell these packages individually, you may prefer to keep them self-contained. For your own use, though, commandeering a soft interrupt as a personal utility package is not at all unreasonable.

13.6   Undocumented Functions

Many authors of memory resident programs make use of a special function, INT 21H function 34H *(get pointer to INDOS flag)*, that returns a pointer in ES:BX. This flag indicates whether a DOS function is currently operating at any given time. Since many DOS functions are not reentrant, this can be an important piece of information for running simple multi-tasking under the timer interrupt, for example.

The INDOS function was found by taking apart PRINT.COM with a disassembler. This program is a background print spooler included with many versions of DOS. A print spooler is a resident application that accepts a print job from the operating system and continues to print it on the printer, even though other DOS operations are going on in the foreground. This program permits a person to run DOS normally, executing commands while simultaneously printing. Since this program works adequately and is available with DOS or on many computer bulletin boards, it was not duplicated here.

None of the programs shown in this book use the INDOS call, and for good reason. INDOS is "undocumented," a term that has two meanings. The first is, of course, that you cannot look it up in the DOS manual. The second is that Microsoft, the vendors of DOS, reserve the right to change or delete this function from subsequent versions of DOS. In fact, the INDOS call as shown here is useful only under DOS version 2.x (where x is any of the minor version numbers). In DOS version 3.x the call still exists, but has changed quite a bit from the older versions. In DOS 4.0, this function does something quite different; thus, calls to the INDOS function will fail miserably.

For that reason, use of the INDOS function call or any undocumented DOS function is not recommended.

13.7 Designing Programs

You may have noticed, as we go about the business of building new programs, that many of the programs in this book were not written in the traditional "top-down" design style found in programming textbooks. Top-down design would have us create a high-level plan and then work downward in a series of refinements, until the last thing we do is write all the little low-level routines that are combined to do the high-level task. Instead, we have been inclined to plunk down a skeleton and some low-level utilities and then build, and sometimes throw away, code until it works.

There are several good reasons for programming as we have done in this book. First, and most important, is that very few programmers actually use the top-down style as it is written in the textbooks. All have learned it. Many claim it to be a good and valid way of writing programs, but also sheepishly admit that they don't do it that way. Many may also claim that they *do* design from the top down, but if you watch them, they seem to be doing something quite different.

In fact, what is happening *is* a sort of top-down design, but not the sort that one finds in a textbook for introductory programming. It is a mixed mode, where a programmer's experience and judgment allow the programming process to be accelerated while still keeping the virtues of top-down design in mind. A programmer thinks about a goal for a while and, from experience, sees a pattern for an approach to that goal. This pattern determines roughly how the program will be structured, and how it might be separated into subgoals. By juggling these subgoals around a bit, some common characteristics might fall out, such as the need to read characters from the console or set the position of the cursor. Many times, these common low-level routines are the first ones that a programmer will type in, apparently in violation of the rules of top-down design.

Pure top-down design sees each problem with a fresh perspective. Yet all good programmers will tell you that they reuse code like mad. This reflects two schools of programming philosophy. Imagine, if you will, two car designers. One chooses to design a car in which every part and indeed the arrangements of the parts themselves are tuned to perfection. Every unnecessary part is eliminated. Each and every part is optimized for the highest possible performance in this car. The other designer chooses to build from standard parts. The fits may be poor, the carburetor may not provide exactly the right mixture for high-power combustion, but if the car breaks, it can be fixed easily.

Tuning for performance takes time and costs money. Hand-crafting of parts takes time and costs money. The special-purpose car will be expensive, but for some applications, like the Indianapolis 500, it will be the correct way to go. Off-the-shelf parts cannot provide that level of performance, but they do provide security and speed of development. By building general-purpose components or reusing components designed for another application, you can build a car that might not win the Indy 500, but it will be adequate for everyday use.

For many programmers, the lure of shaving just another millisecond or making a program 10 bytes smaller has evaporated with the emergence of sufficient memory and processors of reasonable power. When memory and cycles become cheap, fewer and fewer people will be stingy with them. The coin of the realm now is development time. The ability to create prototypes quickly and then turn those prototypes into production code is far more valuable than a few cycles or bytes.

In this book the code was written with the idea that it was to be modular. The components of these programs should be thought of as tools, not hand-crafted special-purpose parts. By reusing the concepts and modules in these packages, you should be able to create many packages for your own purposes.

Appendix A

IBM ROM BIOS Services

The ROM services are extremely low-level services provided by a Read-Only Memory device built into the PC. These services are intended to be extremely basic and reliable, so they rarely change. Changing the ROM services would require a disassembly of your machine and the replacement of a particular chip. Several versions of ROMs have been included in different models and versions of PCs. The date of a particular ROM can be found by examining the 8 bytes at memory location F000:FFF5H to F000:FFFCH. These 8 bytes contain ASCII characters describing the release date of the ROM. The release dates can be interpreted as follows:

Release Date	Machine Type
04/24/81	Original PC
10/19/81	Revised PC with some bugs fixed
08/16/82	Original XT
10/27/82	Upgrade for PC ROMs to XT level
11/08/82	Original Portable PC
06/01/83	Original PCjr
01/10/84	Original AT

The *IBM Technical Reference Manual* contains a listing of the entire contents of the ROM and comments about the various ways in which each ROM service operates.

INT 05H (5)   *Print screen*

Prints the contents of the screen on the printer

Input
   None

Output
   None

Notes

The print screen service is a special-purpose routine that copies the contents of the current video display to the printer port, in such a way that the screen is reproduced on the printed page.

This service is typically invoked when the user types the keyboard sequence `CONTROL-PrtSc`. Since it is a software interrupt service like any other, it can be invoked from within a program, however.

INT 010H (16) *Video*

These services manage access to the video displays available on the PC. They provide a set of routines to display text and/or graphics, manage scrolling on the entire screen or in a region of the screen, position the cursor, and select the current display mode.

Using the video services from within a memory resident program is quite reasonable. It is important to remember to clean up after yourself, however. Many applications can become confused if the cursor changes position unexpectedly. It is also possible that some applications actually read from display memory for input. These programs are rare, but a memory resident program that does not completely restore the contents of the screen is sure to confuse them.

Video Function Codes

AH	Function
00H (0)	Set video mode
01H (1)	Set cursor size
02H (2)	Set cursor position
03H (3)	Read cursor position
04H (4)	Read light-pen position
06H (6)	Scroll window up
07H (7)	Scroll window down
08H (8)	Read character and attribute
09H (9)	Write character and attribute
0AH (10)	Write character
0BH (11)	Set color palette
0CH (12)	Write pixel
0DH (13)	Read pixel
0EH (14)	Write character in TTY mode
0FH (15)	Get current video mode

AH = 00H (0)   *Set video mode*
INT 010H (16)   *Video*

Select the current video display and mode

Input
   AL = video mode

Output
   None

Notes

Most IBM PCs have either a monochrome or color graphics display. The monochrome display is fixed at a 25 line, 80 characters per line text-only display. The color graphics adapter (CGA) has several modes for text and graphics.

Video Mode	Meaning
00H	40x25 monochrome text, color adapter
01H	40x25 color text
02H	80x25 monochrome text
03H	80x25 color text
04H	320x200 four-color graphics
05H	320x200 four-color graphics (no color burst)
06H	640x200 two-color graphics
07H	Monochrome Adapter text

AH = 01H (1)
INT 010H (16)

Set cursor size

Video

Set the bounds of the blinking hardware cursor

Input
    CH = starting scan line
    CL = ending scan line

Output
    None

Notes
The scan-line value must be less than 32, so that it occupies only the first 5 bits of the CH or CL register. Setting any bits other than the first 5 can have strange and unpredictable effects.

AH = 02H (2)   *Set cursor position*
INT 010H (16)   *Video*

Move the cursor to a new position on the screen

Input
BH = display page number
DH = row (y-coordinate)
DL = column (x-coordinate)

Output
None

Notes
(0,0) is at the upper left corner of the screen.

In 80x25 text mode, (79,24) is at the lower right corner.

In 40x25 text mode, (39,24) is at the lower right corner.

You can turn off the cursor by moving to a location offscreen, such as (0,25). Moving the cursor very far outside the limits of the screen can have unpredictable results.

AH = 03H (3)   *Read cursor position*
INT 010H (16)   *Video*

Determine the cursor location on the screen

Input
    BH = display page number

Output
    CH = starting scan line
    CL = ending scan line
    DH = row (y-coordinate)
    DL = column (x-coordinate)

Notes

The Color Graphics Adapter has eight display pages (for 40x25 mode) or four display pages (40x25 mode). Use INT 10H function 5H *(set active display page)* to switch between display pages.

AH = 04H (4)   *Read light-pen position*
INT 010H (16)   *Video*

Determine where the light pen is pointing on the screen

Input

   None

Output

   AH = pen trigger signal
   BX = pixel column (x-coordinate)
   CH = pixel row (y-coordinate)
   DH = character row (y-coordinate)
   DL = character column (x-coordinate)

AH = 05H (5)
INT 010H (16)

Set active display page

Video

Input
    AL = page number

Output
    None

Notes
This function is valid only for text modes on the Color Graphics Adapter (CGA.) You can switch between pages without affecting the contents of the starting or ending page. Text can be written via functions 02H, 09H, and 10H to any page, regardless of which page is active.

Display mode	Display type	Valid Page Numbers
00H	CGA	0-7
01H	CGA	0-7
02H	CGA	0-3
03H	CGA	0-3
02H	EGA	0-7
03H	EGA	0-7
0DH	EGA	0-7
0EH	EGA	0-3
0FH	EGA	0-1
10H	EGA	0-1

AH = 06H (6)   *Scroll window up*
INT 010H (16)   *Video*

Scroll a rectangular region up, inserting blank lines at the bottom

Input
    AL = lines to scroll up
    BH = filler attribute
    CH = upper row (y-coordinate)
    CL = left column (x-coordinate)
    DH = lower row (y-coordinate)
    DL = right column (x-coordinate)

Output
    None

Notes
Text scrolled beyond the top of a window is lost. New lines appear at the bottom of the window, filled with blanks that have the attributes specified in BH.

By setting AL to zero, you can use this function to initialize a window. This blanks the region specified by the coordinates. The blanks have the attribute specified in BH.

AH = 07H (7)
INT 010H (16)

Scroll window down

Video

Scroll a rectangular region down, inserting blank lines at the top

Input

AL = lines to scroll down
BH = filler attribute
CH = upper row (y-coordinate)
CL = left column (x-coordinate)
DH = lower row (y-coordinate)
DL = right column (x-coordinate)

Output

None

Notes

Text scrolled beyond the bottom of a window is lost. New lines appear at the top of the window, filled with blanks that have the attributes specified in BH.

By setting AL to zero, you can use this function to initialize a window. This blanks the region specified by the coordinates. The blanks have the attribute specified in BH.

AH = 08H (8)   *Read character and attribute*
INT 010H (16)   *Video*

Read the character at the cursor location, along with the display characteristics of that character

Input
    BH = display page number

Output
    AH = character
    AL = attribute

Notes

By specifying the display page number, you can read a character from any valid display page, not just the currently active one.

AH = 09H (9) *Write character and attribute*
INT 010H (16) *Video*

Write character at the cursor location, along with the display characteristics of that character

Input
AL = character
BH = page number
BL = attribute
CX = number of characters to repeat

Output
None

Notes
This function does not reposition the cursor. When the function returns, the cursor will be at the position it was at when the function was called.

The repetition code in CX should not be used to write past the end of a line.

In graphics mode, bit 7 (mask 80H) causes the character to be exclusive-ORed with the background.

In graphics modes, the bitmaps used for ASCII characters 80H-FFH are located in a table that starts at 0000:007CH. This value is stored in the vector for INT 1FH. By resetting this vector, you can change the location of the bitmap table.

AH = OAH (10)
INT 010H (16)

Write character

Video

Write a character at the cursor location

Input
AL = character
BH = page number
BL = color in graphics mode
CX = count of characters

Output
None

Notes

This function does not reposition the cursor. When the function returns, the cursor will be at the position it was at when the function was called.

The repetition code in CX should not be used to write past the end of a line.

In graphics mode, bit 7 (mask 80H) causes the character to be exclusive-ORed with the background.

In graphics modes, the bitmaps used for ASCII characters 80H-FFH are located in a table that starts at 0000:007CH. This value is stored in the vector for INT 1FH. By resetting this vector, you can change the location of the bitmap table.

AH = OBH (11)
INT 010H (16)

Set color palette

Video

Make a range of colors available for display

Input

BH = palette color id
BL = color to be used with palette

Output

None

Notes

Palette	Value	Color
BH	BL	
0	0	Background
0	1	Green
0	2	Red
0	3	Brown
1	0	Background
1	1	Cyan
1	2	Magenta
1	3	White

If BH=00H, BL should contain the background and border color for graphics modes from the full color palette (0-15). In text modes, BL should contain the border color selected from the full color palette (0-15). The background color of text is determined by the high-order four bits (mask F0H) of the attribute byte for each character.

AH = 0CH (12)   *Write pixel*
INT 010H (16)   *Video*

Set the value of a single point on the graphics display

Input
AL = color
CX = pixel column (x-coordinate)
DL = pixel row (y-coordinate)

Output
None

Notes

In display modes 04H and 05H (four-color graphics modes), pixel values are in the range (0-3). In mode 06H (two-color graphics mode), pixel values are in the range (0-1).

If bit 7 of AL is set, the pixel value are exclusive-ORed with the background.

AH = 0DH (13)
INT 010H (16)

Read pixel

Video

Read the value of a single point on the graphics display

Input
    CX = pixel column (x-coordinate)
    DL = pixel row (y-coordinate)

Output
    AL = pixel color read

Notes

Display Mode	Valid Pixel Values
04H	0-3
05H	0-3
06H	0-1

AH = OEH (14)   *Write char in TTY mode*
INT 010H (16)   *Video*

Write a character and then advance one cursor position

Input
AL = character
BL = color for graphics mode

Output
None

Notes

This function prints a character at the current cursor position, then advances the cursor to the right. Moving the cursor past the end of a line wraps it around to the next line. Moving the cursor past the lower right corner scrolls the screen up one line.

This function is used by the DOS console driver to write operating system text and messages to the screen.

AH = OFH (15)
INT 010H (16)

Get current video mode

Video

Get the display mode of the active display

Input
  None

Output
  AH = width in characters
  AL = video mode
  BH = page number

Notes

Video Mode	Meaning
00H	40x25 monochrome text, color adapter
01H	40x25 color text
02H	80x25 monochrome text
03H	80x25 color text
04H	320x200 four-color graphics
05H	320x200 four-color graphics (no color burst)
06H	640x200 two-color graphics
07H	Monochrome Adapter text

This function can be used to determine the current screen width, since it can be inferred from the video mode.

INT 011H (17)   *Equipment*

Determines what equipment is available on the PC when it is turned on

Input
None

Output
AX = bit-coded equipment list

Notes

AX	Equipment Present at Power On
FEDCBA9876543210	
PPxxxxxxxxxxxxxx	Number of printers (0-3)
xxSxxxxxxxxxxxxx	Serial printer on PCjr (0-1)
xxxGxxxxxxxxxxxx	Game adapter (0-1)
xxxxPPPxxxxxxxxx	Number of serial ports (0-7)
xxxxxxxDxxxxxxxx	DMA chip (0 means installed)
xxxxxxxxDDxxxxxx	Number of diskette drives minus 1 (0-3)
xxxxxxxxxxVVxxxx	Initial video mode (01, 10, 11)
xxxxxxxxxxxxRRxx	RAM on system board (11=64K)
xxxxxxxxxxxxxxxP	Any disks present (0-1).

Initial Video Mode	Display Used
01B	40x25 color
10B	80x25 color
11B	Monochrome

The value for the number of disks in the equipment list are one less than the actual number of disks present on the system. If no disks are present, this number will be zero, and the ANY-DISKS-PRESENT bit will also be zero. If one disk is present, the ANY-DISKS-PRESENT bit are one, but the number of disks will still be zero. Each additional disk increases the number of disks by one, so it remains one less than the actual number (if the number of disks is not zero).

This list should only be read, never written.

INT 012H (18)   *Memory Size*

This function returns the actual amount of memory that the PC has available. It does not return the value from the equipment list, which may be somewhat smaller than the normal value. It returns the correct size of memory in kilobytes.

Input
  None

Output
  AX = memory size in kilobytes

INT 013H (19)   *Disk*

These functions provide low-level access to the disk system. You should avoid calling them and use the DOS functions whenever possible, to maintain compatibility across versions of DOS and workalikes. The DOS functions also provide a much more comprehensive set of routines for disk access.

Disk Function Codes

AH	Function
00H (0)	Reset disk system
01H (1)	Get disk status
02H (2)	Read disk sectors
03H (3)	Write disk sectors
04H (4)	Verify disk sectors
05H (5)	Format disk track

AH = 00H (0)
INT 013H (19)

Reset disk system

Disk

Send a RESET signal to the disk controller and prepare for disk I/O

Input

None

Output

None

AH = 01H (1)
INT 013H (19)

Get disk status

Disk

Determine the status of the disk controller

Input
> *None*

Output
> AL = status code

Notes

Status Code	Meaning
01H	Bad command
02H	Disk is write-protected
04H	Sector not found
08H	DMA overrun
10H	Data error on disk read
20H	Controller error
40H	Seek failure
80H	Disk timed-out

AH = 02H (2)
INT 013H (19)

Read disk sectors

Disk

Read a physical sector from disk into a memory buffer

Input

    AL = number of sectors
    CH = track number
    CL = sector number
    DH = head number
    DL = drive number
    ES:BX = pointer to buffer

Output

    CF = success/failure
    AH = status code
    AL = number of sectors read

Notes

Status Code	Meaning
01H	Bad command
02H	Disk is write-protected
04H	Sector not found
08H	DMA overrun
10H	Data error on disk read
20H	Controller error
40H	Seek failure
80H	Disk timed-out

AH = 03H (3)   *Write disk sectors*
INT 013H (19)   *Disk*

Write a physical sector to disk from a memory buffer

Input
>   AL = number of sectors
>   CH = track number
>   CL = sector number
>   DH = head number
>   DL = drive number
>   ES:BX = pointer to buffer

Output
>   CF = success/failure
>   AH = status code
>   AL = number of sectors written

Notes

Status Code	Meaning
01H	Bad command
02H	Disk is write-protected
04H	Sector not found
08H	DMA overrun
10H	Data error on disk read
20H	Controller error
40H	Seek failure
80H	Disk timed-out

AH = 04H (4)   *Verify disk sectors*
INT 013H (19)   *Disk*

Check the address fields of sectors on the disk

Input
AL = number of sectors
CH = track number
CL = sector number
DH = head number
DL = drive number

Output
CF = success/failure
AH = status code
AL = number of sectors verified

Notes
This function can be used as a test for a readable disk in the drive. It returns successfully if a properly formatted disk is present and fails otherwise.

Status Code	Meaning
01H	Bad command
02H	Disk is write-protected
04H	Sector not found
08H	DMA overrun
10H	Data error on disk read
20H	Controller error
40H	Seek failure
80H	Disk timed-out

AH = 05H (5)   *Format disk track*
INT 013H (19)   *Disk*

Input

    AL = number of sectors
    CH = track number
    CL = sector number
    DH = head number
    DL = drive number
    ES:BX = pointer to list of 4-byte address fields

Output

    CF = success/failure
    AH = status code

Notes

This is a hairy and dangerous function, well beyond the subject of this book. See the *DOS Technical Reference Manual* for a barely readable explanation.

INT 014H (20) *Communications*

These routines manage the communications services. They control access into and out of the PC for telecommunications and possibly printing services. Although often referred to as *ports*, they should not be confused with the low-level I/O ports available elsewhere in the PC. The services referred to in this section are used to move information to and from other devices outside the PC itself. The addressable ports are used within the PC to communicate with various devices attached directly to the processor, such as the video display or sound generators.

Serial ports are addressed by their port number. Typically there are no more than two serial ports on a PC, though the PC architecture provides support for up to four.

Serial Port Number	DOS Device
0	COM1:
1	COM2:
2	COM3:
3	COM4:

Communications Function Codes

AH	Function
00H (0)	Initialize serial port params
01H (1)	Send one character
02H (2)	Receive one character
03H (3)	Get serial port status

AH = 00H (0)   *Initialize serial port params*
INT 014H (20)   *Communications*

Set the speed, parity, word length, and stop bits of a particular communications port

Input
DX = serial port number

Output
AH = port status
AL = modem status

Notes

Port Status	Meaning	Modem Status	Meaning
80H	Timeout	80H	Receive line signal
40H	XMIT shift register empty	40H	Ring indicator
20H	XMIT hold register empty	20H	Data set ready
10H	Break detected	10H	Clear to send
08H	Framing error	08H	RCV line signal changed
04H	Parity error	04H	Ring indicator
02H	Overrun error	02H	Data set ready changed
01H	Data ready	01H	Clear to send changed

AH	Baud	AH	Parameter
76543210		76543210	
000xxxxx	110	xxx00xxx	no parity
001xxxxx	150	xxx01xxx	odd parity
010xxxxx	300	xxx10xxx	no parity
011xxxxx	600	xxx11xxx	even parity
100xxxxx	1200	xxxxx0xx	1 stop bit
101xxxxx	2400	xxxxx1xx	2 stop bits
110xxxxx	4800	xxxxxx10	7 bit words
111xxxxx	9600	xxxxxx11	8 bit words

AH = 01H (1)
INT 014H (20)

Send one character
Communications

Write a character to the specified communications line

Input

AL = character
DX = serial port number

Output

AH = success/failure status code
AL = port status

Notes

Modem Status	Meaning
80H	Timeout
40H	XMIT shift register empty
20H	XMIT hold register empty
10H	Break detected
08H	Framing error
04H	Parity error
02H	Overrun error
01H	Data ready

AH = 02H (2)
INT 014H (20)

Receive one character
Communications

Read a character from the communications line

Input
    DX = serial port number

Output
    AH = success/failure status code
    AL = port status

Notes

Modem Status	Meaning
80H	Timeout
40H	XMIT shift register empty
20H	XMIT hold register empty
10H	Break detected
08H	Framing error
04H	Parity error
02H	Overrun error
01H	Data ready

AH = 03H (3)
INT 014H (20)

Get serial port status
Communications

Determine the status of the communications line

Input
None

Output
AH = port status
AL = modem status

Notes

Port Status	Meaning	Modem Status	Meaning
80H	Timeout	80H	Receive line signal
40H	XMIT shift register empty	40H	Ring indicator
20H	XMIT hold register empty	20H	Data set ready
10H	Break detected	10H	Clear to send
08H	Framing error	08H	RCV line signal changed
04H	Parity error	04H	Ring indicator
02H	Overrun error	02H	Data set ready changed
01H	Data ready	01H	Clear to send changed

INT 015H (21)   *Cassette*

Due to the drop in disk-drive prices shortly after the IBM PC was introduced, few people used the cassette services, which nevertheless remain in some of the ROMs for compatibility reasons. In older PCs, the cassette hardware still exists and can be used. The cassette logic and ROM services can be used to control a relay within the machine. Some people have used that relay as a physical device controller or signalling device. This relay is useful for low-voltage/low-current applications only, however, and rewiring should be attempted only if you know what you are doing.

Cassette Function Codes

AH	Function
00H (0)	Turn on cassette motor
01H (1)	Turn off cassette motor
02H (2)	Read data block
03H (3)	Write data block

AH = 00H (0) *Turn on cassette motor*
INT 015H (21) *Cassette*

Activate the relay in older PCs that turns on the cassette motor

Input
None

Output
None

Notes

To determine whether you have cassette hardware on your machine, call this service. If you have cassette ports on your machine, you'll hear a small click from within the system unit. This is the relay engaging. It will not disengage until you call cassette function 01H to turn it off, or until you turn off or reboot your machine with `CONTROL-ALT-DEL`. A cheaper, easier, and quicker way, but not nearly as much fun, would be to look on the back of your PC, near the keyboard connector, for a cassette connector. Machines without cassette hardware lack this feature.

AH = 01H (1) *Turn off cassette motor*
INT 015H (21) *Cassette*

Deactivate the relay in older PCs that controls the cassette motor

Input
> *None*

Output
> *None*

Notes

Probably the only truly useful function in the cassette interface – the one that stops the use of it.

AH = 02H (2)
INT 015H (21)

Read data block

Cassette

Read a block of data from the cassette interface

Input

CX = count of bytes
ES:BX = pointer to data area

Output

CF = error signal
DX = count of bytes read
ES:BX = pointer past last byte read

AH = 03H (3)   *Write data blocks*
INT 015H (21)   *Cassette*

Write a block of data to the cassette interface

Input

CX = count of bytes
ES:BX = pointer to data area

Output

ES:BX = pointer past last byte written

INT 016H (22) *Keyboard*

For quite a few memory resident applications, these routines are the key (pun intended). A lot of useful things can be done by intercepting the keyboard interrupts. The assembly-language sources for the keyboard services can be found in the *IBM Technical Reference Manual* for your version of DOS. A familiarity with the way the keyboard is handled is an invaluable tool for writing resident applications.

A common term in memory resident programming is "hot key." This refers to the ability of a memory resident program to be accessible at the touch of a particular key, no matter what other applications the machine might be running at the time.

Keyboard Function Codes

AH	Function
00H (0)	Read next keyboard character
01H (1)	Test for character ready
02H (2)	Get shift status

AH = 00H (0)   *Read next keyboard character*
INT 016H (22)   *Keyboard*

Read a character from the keyboard input queue

Input
  None

Output
  AH = scan code (auxiliary byte)
  AL = character code

Notes

This function is the one most likely to be subverted by a memory resident program. Controlling this function is the key to writing "hot key" macro expansion programs.

AH = 01H (1)
INT 016H (22)

Test for character ready
Keyboard

Determine if the keyboard input queue is empty, or if a character is available to be read

Input
None

Output
ZF = queue empty (set means empty/clear means char available)
AH = scan code (auxiliary byte)
AL = character code

Notes
This function does not return via IRET, because it must pass back ZF as an indicator. It uses the optional parameter of RET to specify the number of bytes to flush from the stack. These bytes are additional information necessary for IRET to return successfully.

AH = 02H (2)   *Get shift status*
INT 016H (22)   *Keyboard*

Find out which shift keys are depressed on the keyboard

Input
None

Output
AL = shift status bits

Notes
Several of these shift keys may be depressed simultaneously. The shift status will be all bits for each active shift key, ORed together.

Shift Status	Meaning
80H	Insert on
40H	Caps Lock on
20H	Num Lock on
10H	Scroll Lock on
08H	ALT key down
04H	CTRL key down
02H	LEFT-SHIFT key down
01H	RIGHT-SHIFT key down

INT 017H (23)   *Printer*

Printer services provide a means of creating hardcopy output from the PC. These services are simple and straightforward. You can initialize the printer, send characters to the it, and get the status of the printer.

DOS typically assumes that you have only one printer device (PRN:) connected to your system.

Printer Function Codes

AH	Function
00H (0)	Send character to printer
01H (1)	Initialize printer
02H (2)	Get printer status

AH = 00H (0)   *Send character to printer*
INT 017H (23)   *Printer*

Write a character to the printer interface and return the status of the port

Input

AL = character

Output

AH = printer status

Notes

Printer Status	Meaning
80H	Printer not busy
40H	Acknowledge
20H	Out of paper
10H	Printer selected
08H	I/O error
04H	Not used
02H	Not used
01H	Timeout

AH = 01H (1)
INT 017H (23)

Initialize printer
Printer

Initialize a printer port and return the status of the port

Input
None

Output
AH = printer status

Notes

Printer Status	Meaning
80H	Printer not busy
40H	Acknowledge
20H	Out of paper
10H	Printer selected
08H	I/O error
04H	Not used
02H	Not used
01H	Timeout

AH = 02H (2)
INT 017H (23)

Get printer status
Printer

Get the status of the printer port

Input

·*None*

Output

AH = printer status

Notes

Printer Status	Meaning
80H	Printer not busy
40H	Acknowledge
20H	Out of paper
10H	Printer selected
08H	I/O error
04H	Not used
02H	Not used
01H	Timeout

INT 018H (24) *BASIC*

IBM PCs have a rudimentary BASIC interpreter in ROM that runs if the machine is booted without a disk. It is designed to run in conjunction with the cassette-storage device; as such it is seldom used directly. The ROM BASIC is essential to running `BASICA`, the IBM Disk BASIC interpreter.

Calling this service is essentially equivalent to turning off the machine and rebooting it without inserting a disk in the boot drive. You should have a good reason for calling this function.

Input
None

Output
None

INT 019H (25)   *Reboot*

This service causes the machine to be rebooted in a similar, but not identical, fashion to the reboot caused by typing CONTROL-ALT-DEL or by turning the machine off and then on again. Power-cycling, however, causes the entire state of the machine to be reset from scratch and a memory check performed. CONTROL-ALT-DEL does not cause the memory test to run, but does reset the state of the machine and the memory allocations. By using this service, you can reset DOS without destroying the contents of memory.

Input
> *None*

Output
> *None*

INT 01AH (26) *Clock*

The ROM provides a very low level time-of-day service. The clock is based on the number of system clock-ticks since midnight. These clock ticks occur roughly 18.2 times per second. When the count exceeds 1,573,040 ticks, another day has gone by. When you ask DOS to display the time, it reads this counter and computes the time from the clock count. You can compute components of the time of day by using the following formulas:

```
          Hour = Clock / 65543
Hour-remainder = Clock MODULO 65543
        Minute = Hour-remainder / 1092
 Min-remainder = Hour-remainder MODULO 1092
        Second = Min-remainder / 18.21
```

If you know the time of day, you can compute the current tick count by using this formula:

```
Clock = (Hour*65543.33)+(Minute*1092.38)+(Second*18.21)
```

Clock Function Codes

AH	Function
00H (0)	Read current clock count
01H (1)	Set current clock count

AH = OOH (O)   *Read current clock count*
INT O1AH (26)   *Clock*

Get the current internal DOS tick count, from which the time can be computed

Input
> *None*

Output
> AL = midnight signal
> CX = tick count, high word
> DX = tick count, low word

Notes

This function returns a double word containing the number of clock ticks since midnight. It also returns a byte indicating whether the count has been reset by DOS yet. If this byte is not zero, then the counter has counted out more than 24 hours worth of clock ticks, but the counter has not yet been reset to zero for the new day.

You can compute the time of day by using the following formulas:

$$
\begin{aligned}
\text{Hour} &= \text{Clock} / 65543 \\
\text{Hour-remainder} &= \text{Clock MODULO } 65543 \\
\text{Minute} &= \text{Hour-remainder} / 1092 \\
\text{Min-remainder} &= \text{Hour-remainder MODULO } 1092 \\
\text{Second} &= \text{Min-remainder} / 18.21
\end{aligned}
$$

AH = 01H (1)
INT 01AH (26)

Set current clock count

Clock

Set the current internal DOS tick count to a particular time of day

Input

CX = tick count, high word
DX = tick count, low word

Output

None

Notes

You can compute the current tick count by using this formula:

    Clock = (Hour*65543.33)+(Minute*1092.38)+(Second*18.21)

Appendix B

Hardware Interrupts

The IBM PC uses hardware interrupts to manage hardware and respond to error conditions. They resemble the software interrupts used by DOS or in the ROM as a system-call facility, but for the most part, these interrupts are not generated by software. They are called as a result of some condition in the hardware. Some of these vectors are not pointers to code, but pointers to a table of some kind.

There are 256 possible interrupt vectors in the IBM PC. Of these, some are unused and thus available for programs to use as soft interrupts. The available vectors are 40H-7FH and F1H-FFH.

INT 00H (0) *Divide by zero*

An error interrupt generated when a division by zero is attempted

Notes

Dividing any number by zero is a mathematical mistake. This interrupt allows you to detect that mistake and recover gracefully, if possible. Many programs that work with numbers replace this interrupt, at least on a temporary basis.

INT 01H (1)   *Single step*

Called after each instruction when TF, the trap flag, is set

Notes

When debugging a program, you often want to execute a single instruction and then stop the machine to observe the results. This involves a sort of a contradiction, since it is a running machine that lets you see the results. This interrupt provides the magic for that operation. If the trap flag is set, an interrupt to this routine is generated after each individual instruction has executed. Since an interrupt first turns off the interrupt flag, the interrupt handler indicated here can run unmolested.

Great care should be taken with the STI instruction during the execution of this interrupt.

INT 02H (2)   *Non-maskable (NMI)*

Responds to a major hardware fault

Notes

Not of much use to an applications programmer, since any calls to this interrupt usually signal a major system fault. It can be used to take some emergency action just before a system crash.

INT 03H (3) *Breakpoint*

Used to set breakpoints for program debugging

Notes

When debugging, a programmer may want to let many instructions run, but halt on a particular one. This interrupt permits that.

INT 04H (4)   *Overflow*

An error interrupt generated when an arithmetic overflow occurs

Notes

When an arithmetic operation results in an operation that is too big to be contained in its destination, this interrupt signals the error condition.

INT 08H (8) *Timer Tick*

The system metronome; occurs 18.2 times per second

Notes

A very useful interrupt for the memory resident programmer. The system uses this interrupt to advance the time-of-day counter. 18.2 ticks per second is 91 ticks every 5 seconds, or 1092 ticks per minute.

INT 09H (9)   *Keystroke*

Generated every time a key is pressed

Notes

This interrupt allows a certain amount of type-ahead. When a key is pressed, this interrupt handler reads it and places the character on an input queue. The keyboard interrupts in ROM actually examine that queue, rather than the keyboard. This decoupling permits a much greater flexibility of interface between the keyboard and the application.

INT 0BH (11)   *Serial port 1*

Used for control of communications port COM2:

Notes

It is common to replace this interrupt so that a telecommunications program can run at a reasonable speed. Direct system calls reach their limit at about 1200 baud. By replacing the DOS serial I/O code with a more sophisticated interrupt-management scheme, higher communications speeds can be used.

INT 0CH (12)   *Serial port 0*

Used for control of communications port `COM1`:

Notes

It is common to replace this interrupt so that a telecommunications program can run at a reasonable speed. Direct system calls reach their limit at about 1200 baud. By replacing the DOS serial I/O code with a more sophisticated interrupt-management scheme, higher communications speeds can be used.

INT 0DH (13) *Fixed disk*

Used by the hard-disk controller for disk management

Notes

This interrupt may not be available on older IBM PCs. A newer ROM is required.

INT OEH (14)   *Floppy disk*

Used by the floppy disk controller for diskette management

Notes

The diskette management software in the IBM PC uses this interrupt in esoteric ways to detect various disk transfer completion conditions.

INT OFH (15) *Printer*

Used by the printer controller for printer management

Notes

This low-level printer interrupt detects a printer error or completion condition.

INT 01DH (29)   *Video init table*

Points to a table of video-initialization parameters

Notes

This vector is a pointer to a data table used for the initialization of the video controller for the displays. It should never be be executed as a pointer to code.

INT 01EH (30) *Diskette parameter table*

Points to a table of disk-initialization parameters

Notes

This vector points to a data table used for the initialization of the disk controller. Some of this data may be changed to tune the performance of the disk, but *extreme* care is advised. It should never be be executed as a pointer to code.

INT 01FH (31) *Graphics table*

Points to a bitmap table of characters for graphics display

Notes

This table contains bitmap representations of characters 128-255, as they are displayed in graphics mode on the CGA. At powerup, the system sets this pointer to zero, indicating that no such table is present. Altering that value will permit custom tables to be used.

The table is 1 kilobyte long and contains 128 8-byte entries. Each entry contains a "picture" of what the character will look like in an 8x8 bit matrix.

The vector should never be be executed as a pointer to code.

Appendix C

IBM DOS Services

The functions listed in this appendix are loaded when DOS boots on your machine. Each version of DOS may have slight or dramatic differences in the way these functions work. The functions listed here are valid for DOS major version 2. If you are using an earlier version, many of these functions will not be available. If you are using a later version, you may have additional functions at your disposal. The final arbiter of how these functions operate is the *DOS Reference Manual*.

INT 020H (32)   *Terminate program*

Ends execution of a program and returns control to DOS

Input
None

Output
None

Notes
DOS terminates the program, releases the memory used by that program, and then performs the following operations:

- Restores the termination-handler vector from 000AH in the program segment prefix

- Restores the CONTROL-C handler from 000EH in the program segment prefix

- Restores the critical-error handler from 0012H in the program segment prefix

- Flushes all pending file buffers

Finally, control is transferred to the termination-handler address, which then returns to DOS.

INT 021H (33)   *Universal function*

DOS operating system service request

Input

AH = function number
Other parameters depend on individual functions

Output

Return values depend on individual functions

Notes

This is the portal between the operating system and the application programs. This function is used as a general-purpose dispatcher for different kinds of system functions and I/O requests.

The desired function is invoked by placing a function number in the AH register and setting the other registers to values appropriate for the function being called. Then a soft-interrupt INT 21H is issued, and control transfers to the operating system. When the system service routine has completed, it issues an IRET and returns control to the application.

AH = 00H (0)   *Terminate program*
INT 021H (33)   *Universal function*

Complete execution of a program and return control to DOS

Input

CS = Segment address of program segment prefix

Output

None

Notes

DOS terminates the program, releases the memory used by that program, and then performs the following operations:

- Restores the termination-handler vector from 000AH in the program segment prefix

- Restores the CONTROL-C handler from 000EH in the program segment prefix

- Restores the critical-error handler from 0012H in the program segment prefix

- Flushes all pending file buffers

Finally, control is transferred to the termination-handler address, which then returns to DOS.

CS should contain the segment address of the program segment prefix. For .COM files, this happens automatically, since .COM programs are, by definition, contained within a single code segment. For .EXE files, care should be taken to ensure that the correct value of CS is present. DOS needs to be able to find the program segment prefix in order to correctly execute the Termination Handler.

AH = 01H (1)

Character input with echo

INT 021H (33)

Universal function

Read a character from the keyboard and echo it to the display

Input

None

Output

AL = character read in

Notes

If this function encounters a CONTROL-C, the CONTROL-C handler (located at the INT 23H vector) is executed.

Extended characters, such as the function keys, or keys shifted with ALT, require two calls to this function. The first call returns a zero byte, the second returns the extended key code.

AH = 02H (2)   *Character output*
INT 021H (33)   *Universal function*

Write a character to the current video display

Input
   DL = character to write

Output
   None

Notes

If this function encounters a CONTROL-C, the CONTROL-C handler (located at the INT 23H vector) is executed.

If this function encounters a CONTROL-H, the cursor moves left by one character position.

AH = 03H (3)
INT 021H (33)

Serial input
Universal function

Read a character from AUX:, the standard auxiliary device

Input
None

Output
AL = character read in

Notes
This function reads a character from the standard auxiliary device. Unless redirected with the MODE command, this will be COM1:.

DOS serial I/O is not interrupt driven. This limits the speed at which serial communications can take place.

DOS initializes COM1: to 2400 baud, no parity, 1 stop bit, 8 data bits at boot. COM2: is not initialized.

DOS serial I/O calls cannot be used to determine the status of the serial devices.

AH = 04H (4)   *Serial output*
INT 021H (33)   *Universal function*

Write a character to `AUX:`, the standard auxiliary device

Input

DL = character to write

Output

None

Notes

This function writes a character to the standard auxiliary device. Unless redirected with the `MODE` command, this will be `COM1:`.

DOS serial I/O is not interrupt driven. This limits the speed at which serial communications can take place.

DOS initializes `COM1:` to 2400 baud, no parity, 1 stop bit, 8 data bits at boot. `COM2:` is not initialized.

DOS serial I/O calls cannot be used to determine the status of the serial devices.

AH = 05H (5)
INT 021H (33)

Printer output

Universal function

Write a character to PRN:, the standard printer device

Input

DL = character to write

Output

None

Notes

This function writes a character to the standard printer device. Unless redirected with the MODE command, this will be the parallel line printer port.

DOS does not provide a standard mechanism for determining printer status. This function waits until the printer is ready before writing the character.

AH = 06H (6)   *Direct console I/O*
INT 021H (33)   *Universal function*

Raw character input or output

Notes

Raw I/O is used when you want to send byte data rather than just character data to and from an I/O device. A good example of this would be with a text editor. Text editors and word processing programs are often designed to use control characters as commands. Under normal circumstances DOS would interpret these control characters (such as `CONTROL-H`) as input editing commands directly. Text editor applications want to read those characters and process them on their own. Raw I/O permits this.

It is common to refer to the opposite case of raw I/O (where character interpretation is done by DOS), as *cooked* I/O.

Subfunction Codes

DL	Function
OOH (0) - OFEH (254)	Raw console output
OFFH (255)	Raw console input

DL = 00H-0FEH
AH = 06H (6)
INT 021H (33)

Raw console output
Direct console I/O
Universal function

Display character codes (0-254) on the standard output device

Input
None

Output
None

Notes
This function writes a character to the standard output device. Unless redirected with the MODE command or from the command processor, this will be the console device, CON:.

The character to be written is in DL. Obviously, this cannot be used to write OFFH to the console.

DL = OFFH   *Raw console input*
AH = O6H (6)   *Direct console I/O*
INT 021H (33)   *Universal function*

Read a character from the standard input device

Input

None

Output

AL = character read in

ZF = set if no character ready

Notes

This function reads a character from the standard input device. Unless redirected with the MODE command or from the command processor, this will be the console device, CON:.

This function does not react to CONTROL-C or CONTROL-BREAK.

If no character is queued for input, this function will return with ZF set.

If AL returns zero, this signals that the character read in is an extended ASCII character. In this case, the next read will return the character code.

AH = 07H (7)
INT 021H (33)

Raw input (no echo)
Universal function

Read a character from the standard input device without echo

Input
None

Output
AL = character read in

Notes

This function reads a character from the standard input device. Unless redirected with the MODE command or from the command processor, this will be the console device, CON:.

This function does not react to CONTROL-C or CONTROL-BREAK.

If AL returns zero, this signals that the character read in is an extended ASCII character. In this case, the next read will return the character code.

`AH = 08H (8)`   *Console input (no echo)*
`INT 021H (33)`   *Universal function*

Read a character from the standard input device without echo

Input
None

Output
`AL` = character read in

Notes

This function reads a character from the standard input device. Unless redirected with the `MODE` command or from the command processor, this will be the console device, `CON:`.

If `CONTROL-C` or `CONTROL-BREAK` is read, the `CONTROL-C` handler (located at the `INT 23H` vector) is executed.

If `AL` returns zero, this signals that the character read in is an extended ASCII character. In this case, the next read will return the character code.

AH = 09H (9)   *Display string*
INT 021H (33)   *Universal function*

Write a dollar-sign terminated string to standard output

Input

DS:DX = pointer to output string

Output

None

Notes

This function writes a string to the standard output device. Unless redirected with the MODE command or from the command processor, this will be the console device, CON:.

The string must be terminated with an ASCII "$" character (24H). The dollar sign is not transmitted. Other ASCII control characters can be embedded in the output string. To display a dollar sign, use one of the single character functions.

AH = OAH (10)   *Buffered keyboard input*
INT 021H (33)   *Universal function*

Read a line of characters from standard input

Input
DS:DX = pointer to input buffer

Output
None

Notes
This function reads a string from the standard input device. Unless redirected with the MODE command or from the command processor, this will be the console device, CON:.

If CONTROL-C or CONTROL-BREAK is read, the CONTROL-C handler (located at the INT 23H vector) is executed.

Characters are read until an ASCII carriage return (ODH) is detected. The length of the buffer is contained in the first byte. This limits the possible size of input buffers to 255 characters (since a zero length buffer would be unreasonable). The buffer fills to one less than the size (not counting the final <CR>); subsequent input is ignored until the buffer begins to empty.

Extended ASCII codes occupy two bytes in the input buffer, with the first byte being zero. This is an important point for using C string functions, since language terminates strings with a zero byte.

AH = 0BH (11)   *Get keyboard input status*
INT 021H (33)   *Universal function*

Determine if a character is available to be read from the standard input device

Input
None

Output
AL = 0FFH if available, 00H if not

Notes
This function will continue to return a **CHARACTER-READY** until the input queue has been emptied by one of the character-input functions.

If **CONTROL-C** or **CONTROL-BREAK** is read, the **CONTROL-C** handler (located at the **INT 23H** vector) is executed. If any other character is waiting, it remains in the input queue until it is read by one of the character-input functions.

AH = OCH (12)   *Reset input/execute*
INT 021H (33)   *Universal function*

Clear the type-ahead buffer and invoke one of the keyboard input functions

Input

AL = INT 21H function number (01H, 06H, 07H, 08H, 0AH)
See the appropriate INT 21H *function for other parameters.*

Output

See the appropriate INT 21H *function for output specifications.*

Notes

If CONTROL-C or CONTROL-BREAK is read, the CONTROL-C handler (located at the INT 23H vector) is executed.

All typed but unread characters are flushed. The DOS character-input function whose number is contained in AL is then called. This function then returns exactly as that DOS input function would if it had been called separately.

AH = 0DH (13)
INT 021H (33)

Reset disk I/O

Universal function

Flush all pending file buffers by writing outstanding data to the disk

Input
None

Output
None

Notes

A reset causes all pending, buffered disk I/O to be written to the disk. It does *not* update the directory to reflect changes in the files. Directory updates are done by the CLOSE operation.

AH = OEH (14)   *Select current drive*
INT 021H (33)   *Universal function*

Set the default drive and return the total number of logical drives available
on the system

Input
DL = drive ID

Output
AL = Number of available logical drives

Notes

Drive IDs are numeric, following the drive letters (drive A: has a drive ID of
0, drive B:=1, drive C:=2, and so on).

Be aware that some disk-related functions use drive ID 1 as drive A: with
drive ID 0 indicating the default drive.

Logical drives include all the disk-like devices, such as RAM Disks, floppy
disks, hard disks. For upward compatibility, new applications should not be
expected to be able to use more than 26 drives (A:-Z:).

On a single floppy-disk system, the number of logical drives is returned as
2. A system with a single physical disk drive actually has two logical drives
present, A: and B:.

AH = OFH (15)
INT 021H (33)

Open file with FCB
Universal function

Open a file for subsequent read or write operations

Input
DS:DX = pointer to file control block

Output
AL = return code

Notes

Return Code	Meaning
00H	Successful
0FFH	Unsuccessful

Any changes from the default methods of reading or writing, such as changing the size of block transfers, should be done *after* the file is opened, but *before* any file I/O is done.

FCBs are used for file I/O operations. These functions are not as flexible as the later handle-based functions, and remain primarily for compatibility with earlier versions of DOS. They are useful for extended memory resident file operations.

Offset	FCB Field	Offset	FCB Field
00H	Drive ID	10H	File size
01H	Filename	14H	Date
09H	Extension	16H	Time
0CH	Current block	20H	Current record
0EH	Record size	21H	Random record

AH = 010H (16)   *Close file with FCB*
INT 021H (33)   *Universal function*

End access to a file and update disk and directory information

Input
DS:DX = pointer to file control block

Output
AL = return code

Notes

Return Code	Meaning
00H	Successful
0FFH	Unsuccessful

Any unwritten buffers are written to disk, and the directory information for the file is updated to reflect the changes.

FCBs are used for file I/O operations. These functions are not as flexible as the later handle-based functions, and remain primarily for compatibility with earlier versions of DOS. They are useful for extended memory resident file operations.

Offset	FCB Field	Offset	FCB Field
00H	Drive ID	10H	File size
01H	Filename	14H	Date
09H	Extension	16H	Time
0CH	Current block	20H	Current record
0EH	Record size	21H	Random record

AH = 011H (17)
INT 021H (33)

Search for first match

Universal function

Search for a matching filename with file control block in the current directory

Input
DS:DX = pointer to file control block

Output
AL = return code

Notes

Return Code	Meaning
00H	Successful
0FFH	Unsuccessful

The disk transfer area must be set before this function is called.

Question marks can be used as wildcard matches for filenames. The first filename found that matches the search criterion will be returned.

FCBs are used for file I/O operations. These functions are not as flexible as the later handle-based functions, and remain primarily for compatibility with earlier versions of DOS. They are useful for extended memory resident file operations.

Offset	FCB Field	Offset	FCB Field
00H	Drive ID	10H	File size
01H	Filename	14H	Date
09H	Extension	16H	Time
0CH	Current block	20H	Current record
0EH	Record size	21H	Random record

AH = 012H (18)
INT 021H (33)

Search for next match
Universal function

Continue the search for the next matching filename with a valid file control block

Input

DS:DX = pointer to file control block

Output

AL = return code

Notes

Return Code	Meaning
00H	Successful
0FFH	Unsuccessful

INT 21H function 11H *(search for first match)* must have been called with the same file control block before this function can be called.

FCBs are used for file I/O operations. These functions are not as flexible as the later handle-based functions, and remain primarily for compatibility with earlier versions of DOS. They are useful for extended memory resident file operations.

Offset	FCB Field	Offset	FCB Field
00H	Drive ID	10H	File size
01H	Filename	14H	Date
09H	Extension	16H	Time
0CH	Current block	20H	Current record
0EH	Record size	21H	Random record

AH = 013H (19)
INT 021H (33)

Delete file with FCB
Universal function

Delete all matching files from the current directory

Input

DS:DX = pointer to file control block

Output

AL = return code

Notes

Return Code	Meaning
00H	Successful
0FFH	Unsuccessful

Question marks can be used as wildcard matches in the filename. All matching files are deleted.

A deleted file is not scrubbed from the disk. Deletion occurs by marking the directory entry and the used blocks as free. It may be possible to recover all or part of a deleted file if no subsequent disk activity has taken place.

This function permits the deletion of files only in the current working directory. For full access to the file system, use INT 21H function 41H.

FCBs are used for file I/O operations. These functions are not as flexible as the later handle-based functions, and remain primarily for compatibility with earlier versions of DOS. They are useful for extended memory resident file operations.

Offset	FCB Field	Offset	FCB Field
00H	Drive ID	10H	File size
01H	Filename	14H	Date
09H	Extension	16H	Time
0CH	Current block	20H	Current record
0EH	Record size	21H	Random record

AH = 014H (20)
INT 021H (33)

Sequential FCB read

Universal function

Read the next data block from a file, advancing the file pointer

Input

DS:DX = pointer to file control block

Output

AL = return code

Notes

Return Code	Meaning
00H	Read was successful
01H	End of file
02H	Segment overflow or wraparound
03H	Partial record was read at the end of file

The file control block (FCB) must have been prepared with a **CREATE** or an **OPEN** call before this function can be used.

The record size for the read is set by modifying the record size field in the file control block.

The location of the block within the file to be read is determined by the current block field and the current record field of the file control block.

FCBs are used for file I/O operations. These functions are not as flexible as the later handle-based functions, and remain primarily for compatibility with earlier versions of DOS. They are useful for extended memory resident file operations.

Offset	FCB Field	Offset	FCB Field
00H	Drive ID	10H	File size
01H	Filename	14H	Date
09H	Extension	16H	Time
0CH	Current block	20H	Current record
0EH	Record size	21H	Random record

AH = 015H (21)
INT 021H (33)

Sequential FCB write
Universal function

Write the next data block to a file, advancing the file pointer

Input
  DS:DX = pointer to file control block

Output
  AL = return code

Notes

Return Code	Meaning
00H	Write was successful
01H	Disk is full
02H	Segment overflow or wraparound

The file control block (FCB) must have been prepared with a **CREATE** or an **OPEN** call before this function can be used.

The record size for the write is set by modifying the record size field in the file control block.

The location of the block within the file to be written is determined by the current block field and the current record field of the FCB.

Partial records are padded with zeros.

FCBs are used for file I/O operations. These functions are not as flexible as the later handle-based functions, and remain primarily for compatibility with earlier versions of DOS. They are useful for extended memory resident file operations.

Offset	FCB Field	Offset	FCB Field
00H	Drive ID	10H	File size
01H	Filename	14H	Date
09H	Extension	16H	Time
0CH	Current block	20H	Current record
0EH	Record size	21H	Random record

AH = 016H (22)　　　*Create file with FCB*
INT 021H (33)　　　　　　*Universal function*

Create a new directory entry, or make an existing file zero bytes in length, opening that file for access

Input
DS:DX = pointer to file control block

Output
AL = return code

Notes

Return Code	Meaning
00H	File was created successfully
0FFH	File was not created (no directory space available)

This function truncates an existing file to zero length. The disk blocks occupied by the file is not scrubbed, so it is sometimes possible to recover an accidentally truncated file.

FCBs are used for file I/O operations. These functions are not as flexible as the later handle-based functions, and remain primarily for compatibility with earlier versions of DOS. They are useful for extended memory resident file operations.

Offset	FCB Field	Offset	FCB Field
00H	Drive ID	10H	File size
01H	Filename	14H	Date
09H	Extension	16H	Time
0CH	Current block	20H	Current record
0EH	Record size	21H	Random record

AH = 017H (23)
INT 021H (33)

Rename file with FCB
Universal function

Change the name of all matching files, using a special file control block

Input
DS:DX = pointer to special file control block

Output
AL = return code

Notes
The file control block (FCB) for this function should have a drive ID, a filename, and an extension in the usual locations. The new filename is located 6 bytes after the first filename.

Question marks in the second file name cause the corresponding letters in the first file name to remain unchanged.

AL	Return Code
00H	File was renamed successfully
0FFH	No match or the new name was already in use

The FCB used for the RENAME operation is different from a normal FCB. It contains two filenames, with the second filename being the new name for the file. Note that a drive for the second filename cannot be specified. Renaming can be done only on the current disk.

Offset	FCB Field	Offset	FCB Field
00H	Drive ID	10H	File size
01H	Filename	11H	New Filename
09H	Extension	19H	New Extension
0CH	Current block	20H	Current record
0EH	Record size	21H	Random record

018H (24)
INT 021H (33)

Not Used
Universal function

AH = 019H (25)
INT 021H (33)

Get current drive

Universal function

Get the drive ID of the current disk

Input
None

Output
AL = drive ID

Notes
Drive IDs are numeric, following the drive letters (drive A: has a drive ID of 0, drive B:=1, drive C:=2, and so on).

Be aware that some disk-related functions use drive ID 1 as drive A: with drive ID 0 indicating the default drive.

This function does not specify the path to the current directory. If subdirectories are in use, this function must be used in conjunction with INT 21H function 47H *(get current directory)*. Since that function also returns the same drive ID information, it may be more appropriate for general use.

AH = 01AH (26)
INT 021H (33)

Set disk transfer area
Universal function

Set the location of the disk transfer area

Input
DS:DX = pointer to disk transfer area

Output
None

Notes
The default disk transfer area is located at offset 0080H in the program segment prefix. The default DTA size is 128 bytes.

A correct disk transfer area is vital to the operation of the file control block (FCB) disk functions.

AH = 01BH (27)
INT 021H (33)

Get current drive info

Universal function

Return allocation and identification information about the current drive

Input

None

Output

AL = sectors per allocation unit
CX = bytes per sector
DX = number of allocation units
DS:BX = pointer to file allocation table ID byte

Notes

The first byte of the FAT contains a type identifier. These codes are valid:

Code	Meaning
0F8H	Fixed disk.
0F9H	Floppy disk. Double-sided, 15 sectors per track
0FCH	Floppy disk. Single-sided, 9 sectors per track
0FDH	Floppy disk. Double-sided, 9 sectors per track
0FEH	Floppy disk. Single-sided, 8 sectors per track
0FFH	Floppy disk. Double-sided, 8 sectors per track

The pointer to the FAT ID byte points to a *copy* of that byte. It does not necessarily point to a valid file allocation table.

AH = 01CH (28)

Get drive info

INT 021H (33)

Universal function

Return allocation and identification information about any drive

Input
DL = drive ID

Output
AL = sectors per allocation unit
CX = bytes per sector
DX = number of allocation units
DS:DX = pointer to file allocation table ID byte

Notes
The first byte of the FAT contains a type identifier. These codes are valid:

Code	Meaning
0F8H	Fixed disk.
0F9H	Floppy disk. Double-sided, 15 sectors per track
0FCH	Floppy disk. Single-sided, 9 sectors per track
0FDH	Floppy disk. Double-sided, 9 sectors per track
0FEH	Floppy disk. Single-sided, 8 sectors per track
0FFH	Floppy disk. Double-sided, 8 sectors per track

The pointer to the FAT ID byte points to a *copy* of that byte. It does not necessarily point to a valid file allocation table.

Drive IDs are numeric, following the drive letters (drive A: has a drive ID of 1, drive B:=2, drive C:=3, and so on). A drive ID of zero indicates that the default drive is to be used.

Be aware that some disk-related functions use drive ID 0 as drive A: in those cases when the concept of a default drive is not supported.

| 01DH (29) | *Not Used* |
| INT 021H (33) | *Universal function* |

| 01EH (30) | *Not Used* |
| INT 021H (33) | *Universal function* |

| 01FH (31) | *Not Used* |
| INT 021H (33) | *Universal function* |

| 020H (32) | *Not Used* |
| INT 021H (33) | *Universal function* |

AH = 021H (33)
INT 021H (33)

Random read with FCB

Universal function

Read a data block from an arbitrary location in a file

Input
DS:DX = pointer to file control block

Output
AL = return code

Notes

Return Code	Meaning
00H	Read was successful
01H	End of file
02H	Segment overflow or wraparound
03H	Partial record was read at the end of file

The file control block (FCB) must have been prepared with a **CREATE** or an **OPEN** call before this function can be used.

The location within the file to be read is determined by the random record field and the record size field in the file control block.

The current file pointers are not modified by this function. This means that repeated calls to the random read function read the same point within the file.

Partial records are padded with zeros.

FCBs are used for file I/O operations. These functions are not as flexible as the later handle-based functions, and remain primarily for compatibility with earlier versions of DOS. They are useful for extended memory resident file operations.

Offset	FCB Field	Offset	FCB Field
00H	Drive ID	10H	File size
01H	Filename	14H	Date
09H	Extension	16H	Time
0CH	Current block	20H	Current record
0EH	Record size	21H	Random record

AH = 022H (34)
INT 021H (33)

Random write with FCB
Universal function

Write a data block to an arbitrary location in a file

Input
DS:DX = pointer to file control block

Output
AL = return code

Notes

Return Code	Meaning
00H	Write was successful
01H	Disk is full
02H	Segment overflow or wraparound

The location of the write is specified in the random-record field of the file control block (FCB). The size of the write is specified by the record-size field.

The FCB must have been prepared with a **CREATE** or an **OPEN** call before this function can be used.

The current file pointers are not modified by this function. This means that repeated calls to the random write function will write to the same location within the file.

AH = 023H (35)
INT 021H (33)

Get file size

Universal function

Update the file control block with size information if a matching file is found

Input

DS:DX = pointer to file control block

Output

AL = return code

Notes

Return Code	Meaning
00H	Match found; FCB offset 21H set to number of records
0FFH	No match found

The file control block (FCB) must have been prepared with a **CREATE** or an **OPEN** call before this function can be used.

FCBs are used for file I/O operations. These functions are not as flexible as the later handle-based functions, and remain primarily for compatibility with earlier versions of DOS. They are useful for extended memory resident file operations.

Offset	FCB Field	Offset	FCB Field
00H	Drive ID	10H	File size
01H	Filename	14H	Date
09H	Extension	16H	Time
0CH	Current block	20H	Current record
0EH	Record size	21H	Random record

AH = 024H (36)
INT 021H (33)

Set random record field
Universal function

Switch from sequential to random (FCB) file I/O by converting the sequential location to a random access file position

Input
DS:DX = pointer to file control block

Output
None

Notes
This function converts the current sequential I/O position to the corresponding random-access position.

The file control block (FCB) must have been prepared with a **CREATE** or an **OPEN** call before this function can be used.

FCBs are used for file I/O operations. These functions are not as flexible as the later handle-based functions, and remain primarily for compatibility with earlier versions of DOS. They are useful for extended memory resident file operations.

Offset	FCB Field	Offset	FCB Field
00H	Drive ID	10H	File size
01H	Filename	14H	Date
09H	Extension	16H	Time
0CH	Current block	20H	Current record
0EH	Record size	21H	Random record

AH = 025H (37)
INT 021H (33)

Set interrupt vector

Universal function

Set the handler location for a hard or a soft interrupt

Input

AL = interrupt number
DS:DX = pointer to interrupt handler

Output

None

Notes

This function takes all precautions to ensure that interrupts do not occur when the vector is only partially changed. For that reason, it is the preferred method of modifying interrupt vectors.

The current contents of an interrupt vector can be obtained with INT 21H function 35H *(get interrupt vector)*. The register conventions used are incompatible between this function and that one.

In a normal application that changes an interrupt vector, the previous interrupt vector should be obtained via INT 21H function 35H and restored before the application terminates. INT 22H *(termination handler)*, INT 23H (CONTROL-C *handler)*, and INT 24H *(critical error handler)* are restored by DOS from the program segment prefix when a program exits.

AH = 026H (38)
INT 021H (33)

Create PSP

Universal function

Make a new program segment prefix by copying from the current one and then updating it for a new program

Input
DX = segment address

Output
None

Notes

Information for the current program segment prefix is taken from the currently executing program (the program calling this function). Values for INT 22H *(termination handler)*, INT 23H *(CONTROL-C handler)*, and INT 24H *(critical error handler)* are copied from their current values.

This function simply prepares a program segment prefix; it neither loads nor executes a program.

The Program Segment Prefix

Offset	Meaning
0000H	Termination Handler Address
0002H	Segment, end of allocation block
0004H	Reserved
0005H	Long call to MS-DOS function dispatcher
000AH	Previous termination handler vector
000EH	Previous CONTROL-C vector
0012H	Previous critical error handler vector
0016H	Reserved
002CH	Segment address of environment block
002EH	Reserved
005CH	Default File Control Block #1
006CH	Default File Control Block #2
0080H	Command tail and default Disk Transfer Area

AH = 027H (39)
INT 021H (33)

Random block FCB read

Universal function

Read one or more sequential records from an arbitrary point in a file

Input

CX = record count
DS:DX = pointer to file control block

Output

AL = return code
CX = actual record count

Notes

Return Code	Meaning
00H	Read was successful
01H	End of file
02H	Segment overflow or wraparound
03H	Partial record was read at the end of file

The file control block (FCB) must have been prepared with a **CREATE** or an **OPEN** call before this function can be used.

Partially read records are padded with zeros.

After the transfer has occurred, the file pointers in the FCB are advanced to point to the next logical record.

AH = 028H (40)
INT 021H (33)

Random block FCB write

Universal function

Write one or more sequential records to an arbitrary point in a file

Input
    CX = record count
    DS:DX = pointer to file control block

Output
    AL = return code
    CX = actual record count

Notes

Return Code	Meaning
00H	Write was successful
01H	Disk is full
02H	Segment overflow or wraparound

The file control block (FCB) must have been prepared with a CREATE or an OPEN call before this function can be used.

If this function is called with CX=0, no data is written, but the file is lengthened or shortened to match the length in the FCB.

After the transfer has occurred, the file pointers in the FCB are advanced to point to the next logical record.

AH = 029H (41)   *Parse filename*
INT 021H (33)   *Universal function*

Crack a text string into the components of a file name

Input
    AL = parsing control bits
    DS:SI = pointer to command line
    ES:DI = pointer to file control block

Output
    AL = return code
    DS:SI = pointer to following place in command line
    ES:DI = pointer to file control block

Notes
If no valid filename can be derived from the information present, ES:DI+1 will point to an ASCII blank.

An asterisk (∗) in a filename or extension causes all the remaining characters in that component to be set to question marks (?).

A question mark (?) matches any single character.

Parsing control bits

76543210	Meaning
xxxx0xxx	Extension field changed only if extension present
xxxx1xxx	Extension field blanked if no extension entered
xxxxx0xx	Filename field changed only if filename present
xxxxx1xx	Filename field blanked if no filename entered
xxxxxx0x	Drive field changed only if filename present
xxxxxx1x	Drive field blanked if no drive entered
xxxxxxx0	Leading separators will be ignored
xxxxxxx1	Leading separators will not be ignored

AH = 02AH (42)
INT 021H (33)

Get system date

Universal function

Ask the system what day it is

Input
None

Output
AL = day of week
CX = year (1980 to 2099)
DH = month
DL = day

Notes
The registers used for output in this function are assigned in the same manner as those used in INT 21H function 2BH *(set system date)*, with the exception of AL, the day of the week.

AH = 02BH (43)
INT 021H (33)

Set system date
Universal function

Tell the system what day it is

Input
    CX = year (1980 to 2099)
    DH = month
    DL = day

Output
    AL = return code

Notes

Return Code	Meaning
00H	Successful
0FFH	Unsuccessful

The registers used for input in this function are assigned in the same manner as those used in INT 21H function 2AH *(get system date)*.

AH = 02CH (44)
INT 021H (33)

Get system time

Universal function

Ask the system what time it is

Input
None

Output
CH = hours
CL = minutes
DL = hundreds of seconds
DH = seconds

Notes
The registers used for output in this function are assigned in the same manner as those used in INT 21H function 2DH *(get system time)*.

AH = 02DH (45)
INT 021H (33)

Set system time

Universal function

Tell the system what time it is

Input
CH = hours
CL = minutes
DL = hundreds of seconds
DH = seconds

Output
AL = return code

Notes

Return Code	Meaning
00H	Successful
0FFH	Unsuccessful

The registers used for input in this function are assigned in the same manner as those used in INT 21H function 2CH *(get system time)*.

The system date is not affected by this function.

AH = 02EH (46)   *Disk write verification*
INT 021H (33)   *Universal function*

Enable or disable automatic read-after-write comparison of data written with data read

Input
AL = 0 to disable, 1 to enable
DL = 0 (for compatibility with DOS 1 and 2)

Output
None

Notes
Verification happens by reading back the data just written and comparing that result with the data that was *supposed* to have been written. Verification slows down access to the file system, but may increase reliability.

Verification can be globally enabled or disabled with the DOS VERIFY command. VERIFY ON enables verification. VERIFY OFF disables verification.

AH = 02FH (47)
INT 021H (33)

Get DTA address
Universal function

Ask the system what disk transfer area is being used

Input

None

Output

ES:BX = pointer to disk transfer area

Notes

The disk transfer area can be set using INT 21H function 1AH *(set disk transfer area)*. The register conventions used by these two functions are not compatible.

If not explicitly set, the default disk transfer area will be a 128-byte buffer located in the program segment prefix at offset 80H.

AH = 030H (48)
INT 021H (33)

Get DOS version number

Universal function

Get the major and minor version numbers of the currently running DOS

Input
None

Output
AL = major version number
AH = minor version number

Notes
The minor version number is returned as a two-significant-digit number. Thus, DOS version 2.1 will be returned as AL=02 AH=0AH (10), rather than AH=01 (which would represent the non-existent DOS version 2.01).

AH = 031H (49)   *Keep process*
INT 021H (33)   *Universal function*

Advanced terminate and stay resident

Input
AL = return code
DX = paragraphs of memory to reserve

Output
None

Notes

Memory is specified in paragraphs, or 16-byte chunks. Because of this, more than 64 kilobytes can be reserved.

Take care in using this function in conjunction with the memory allocation functions. Allocated memory is not included in the preserved code.

Open files are not automatically closed by this function.

032H (50)
INT 021H (33)

Not Used
Universal function

AH = 033H (51)   CONTROL-C *checking*
INT 021H (33)   *Universal function*

Determine or set checking for CONTROL-C or CONTROL-BREAK

Input
AL = 0 to read checking state; 1 to set checking state
DL = state to set (0 off, 1 on)

Output
DL = current state (0 off, 1 on)

Notes
CONTROL-C checking is performed during system I/O operations. On purely compute-bound operations or operations involving no I/O, CONTROL-C does not interrupt the operation.

CONTROL-C checking is a global setting. If checking is disabled in one application and never reenabled before that program terminates, it remains disabled through all subsequent programs.

AH = 034H (52)

INT 021H (33)

Unsupported
Universal function

AH = 035H (53)
INT 021H (33)

Get interrupt vector
Universal function

Determine the address of an interrupt handler

Input

AL = interrupt number

Output

ES:BX = interrupt vector

Notes

An interrupt vector can be modified with INT 21H function 25H *(set interrupt vector)*. The register conventions used are incompatible between this function and that one.

AH = 036H (54)
INT 021H (33)

Get disk capacity

Universal function

Returns parameters from which the total storage capacity and remaining capacity of a drive can be calculated

Input
DL = drive ID

Output
AX = sectors per cluster (SC)
BX = available cluster count (AC)
CX = bytes per sector (BS)
DX = total clusters (TC)

Notes
Drive IDs are numeric, following the drive letters (drive A: has a drive ID of 1, drive B:=2, drive C:=3, and so on). A drive ID of zero indicates that the default drive is to be used.

Be aware that some disk-related functions use drive ID 0 as drive A: in those cases when the concept of a default drive is not supported.

AX is returned as 0FFFFH if the drive specified in DL is invalid.

Total capacity (C) can be calculated with the formula

$$C = TC * SC * BS$$

Remaining capacity (R) can be calculated with the formula

$$R = AC * SC * BS$$

037H (55)   *Not Used*

INT 021H (33)   *Universal function*

AH = 038H (56)
INT 021H (33)

Get country info
Universal function

Get national information such as currency symbol and time or date format

Input

AL = 0 for standard information
AL = country code or
AL = OFFH if country code greater than 255
BX = country code if AL == OFFH
DS:DX = pointer to 32-byte buffer

Output

AX = return code (if CF set)
BX = country code
DS:DX = information

Notes

Byte offset	Meaning
0	Date format (0=(m d y), 1=(d m y), 2=(y m d))
2	ASCIIZ Currency symbol string
7	ASCIIZ Thousands separator string
9	ASCIIZ Decimal separator string
11	ASCIIZ Date separator string
13	ASCIIZ Time separator string
15	Currency format
16	Number of digits after decimal
17	Time format (0=12-hour clock), 1=24-hour clock)
18	Address for case-mapping routine
22	ASCIIZ Data-list separator string
24	Reserved

Currency format	Meaning
76543210	
xxxxxxx0	Currency symbol precedes value
xxxxxx0x	No space between value and symbol
xxxxxx1x	One space between value and symbol

AH = 039H (57)   *Make subdirectory*
INT 021H (33)   *Universal function*

Create a subdirectory at a specified drive and path

Input
DS:DX = pointer to ASCIIZ string

Output
If function was successful:
   CF = cleared

If function was unsuccessful:
   CF = set
   AX = error code

Notes
If the path string begins with a drive or a "\", the operation occurs relative to the root directory; otherwise, the operation occurs relative to the current directory.

Code	Standard Error	Code	Standard Error
00	Successful	16	Removing current directory
01	Invalid function number	17	Not same device
02	File not found	18	No more files to be found
03	Path not found	19	Disk is write-protected
04	No more handles available	20	Unknown disk
05	Access denied	21	Drive is not ready
06	Invalid handle	22	Unknown command
07	Bad memory control blocks	23	Data error (CRC)
08	Insufficient memory	24	Bad request length
09	Invalid memory block address	25	Seek error
10	Invalid environment	26	Unknown media type
11	Invalid format	27	Sector not found
12	Invalid access code	28	Printer out of paper
13	Invalid data	29	Write fault
14	Not used	30	Read fault
15	Invalid drive specification	31	General failure

AH = 03AH (58)
INT 021H (33)

Remove directory
Universal function

Delete an empty subdirectory at a specified drive and path

Input
DS:DX = pointer to ASCIIZ string

Output

If function was successful:
CF = cleared

If function was unsuccessful:
CF = set
AX = return code

Notes

The directory to be deleted must be empty, or this operation will fail.

If the path string begins with a drive or a "\", the operation occurs relative to the root directory; otherwise, the operation occurs relative to the current directory.

Code	Standard Error	Code	Standard Error
00	Successful	16	Removing current directory
01	Invalid function number	17	Not same device
02	File not found	18	No more files to be found
03	Path not found	19	Disk is write-protected
04	No more handles available	20	Unknown disk
05	Access denied	21	Drive is not ready
06	Invalid handle	22	Unknown command
07	Bad memory control blocks	23	Data error (CRC)
08	Insufficient memory	24	Bad request length
09	Invalid memory block address	25	Seek error
10	Invalid environment	26	Unknown media type
11	Invalid format	27	Sector not found
12	Invalid access code	28	Printer out of paper
13	Invalid data	29	Write fault
14	Not used	30	Read fault
15	Invalid drive specification	31	General failure

AH = 03BH (59)
INT 021H (33)

Set current working dir

Universal function

Set the default directory using the specified path

Input
DS:DX = pointer to ASCIIZ string

Output
If function was successful:
CF = cleared

If function was unsuccessful:
CF = set
AX = return code

Notes
If the path string begins with a drive or a "\", the operation occurs relative to the root directory; otherwise, the operation occurs relative to the current directory.

Code	Standard Error	Code	Standard Error
00	Successful	16	Removing current directory
01	Invalid function number	17	Not same device
02	File not found	18	No more files to be found
03	Path not found	19	Disk is write-protected
04	No more handles available	20	Unknown disk
05	Access denied	21	Drive is not ready
06	Invalid handle	22	Unknown command
07	Bad memory control blocks	23	Data error (CRC)
08	Insufficient memory	24	Bad request length
09	Invalid memory block address	25	Seek error
10	Invalid environment	26	Unknown media type
11	Invalid format	27	Sector not found
12	Invalid access code	28	Printer out of paper
13	Invalid data	29	Write fault
14	Not used	30	Read fault
15	Invalid drive specification	31	General failure

AH = 03CH (60)
INT 021H (33)

Create file with handle

Universal function

Create a new directory entry if one does not exist, or set the file length to zero if the entry exists

Input
    CX = file attribute
    DS:DX = pointer to ASCIIZ string

Output
If function was successful:
    CF = cleared
    AX = file handle

If function was unsuccessful:
    CF = set
    AX = return code

Notes
A handle is a 16-bit token, which is used by the operating system to manage the file state information.

If the path string begins with a drive or a "\", the operation occurs relative to the root directory; otherwise, the operation occurs relative to the current directory.

File Attribute	Meaning
00H	Normal
01H	Read-Only
02H	Hidden
04H	System

This function truncates an existing file to zero length. The disk blocks occupied by the file is not scrubbed, so it is sometimes possible to recover an accidentally truncated file.

If this function fails, the return code is one of the standard error codes.

AH = 03DH (61)
INT 021H (33)

Open file with handle

Universal function

Open a file for subsequent read or write access

Input
AL = access code
DS:DX = pointer to ASCIIZ string

Output
If function was successful:
CF = cleared
AX = file handle

If function was unsuccessful:
CF = set
AX = return code

Notes
A handle is a 16-bit token, which is used by the operating system to manage the file state information.

Access code	Meaning
76543210	
xxxxx000	Read access
xxxxx001	Write access
xxxxx010	Read/write access
xxxx0xxx	Reserved (should be zero)
x000xxxx	Compatibility mode (compatible with FCB method)
x001xxxx	Read/Write access denied
x010xxxx	Write access denied
x011xxxx	Read access denied
x100xxxx	Full access permitted
0xxxxxxx	File inherited by child process
1xxxxxxx	File private to current process

If the path string begins with a drive or a "\", the operation occurs relative to the root directory; otherwise, the operation occurs relative to the current directory.

If this function fails, the return code is one of the standard error codes.

AH = 03EH (62)
INT 021H (33)

Close file with handle

Universal function

End access to a file, flush all internal buffers, and update directory information

Input
BX = file handle

Output
If function was successful:
CF = cleared

If function was unsuccessful:
CF = set
AX = return code

Notes
A handle is a 16-bit token, which is used by the operating system to manage the file state information.

Handle 0 is the standard input device, normally the keyboard. Closing this handle accidentally has the unfortunate result of terminating all access to the keyboard until the next reboot.

All internal DOS buffers with pending output for this handle will be flushed by writing that information to disk, before the close has occurred.

If this function fails, the return code is one of the standard error codes.

AH = 03FH (63)   *Read from file or device*
INT 021H (33)   *Universal function*

Read a stream of bytes from a file or device

Input
    BX = file handle
    CX = bytes to read
    DS:DX = pointer to disk transfer area buffer

Output
If function was successful:
    CF = cleared
    AX = number of bytes read

If function was unsuccessful:
    CF = set
    AX = return code

Notes
A handle is a 16-bit token, which is used by the operating system to manage the file state information.

This function requires that the handle be opened by INT 21H function 3CH *(create file)* or INT 21H function 3DH *(open file)*

If CF returns clear but AX is zero, the file pointer is already at the end of file.

If CF returns clear but AX is less than CX, a partial record has been read.

If this function fails, the return code is one of the standard error codes.

AH = 040H (64)

INT 021H (33)

Write to file or device

Universal function

Write a stream of bytes to a file or device

Input

BX = file handle
CX = bytes to write
DS:DX = pointer to disk transfer area buffer

Output

If function was successful:

CF = cleared
AX = number of bytes written

If function was unsuccessful:

CF = set
AX = return code

Notes

A handle is a 16-bit token, which is used by the operating system to manage the file state information.

This function requires that the handle be opened by INT 21H function 3CH *(create file)* or INT 21H function 3DH *(open file)*

If CF returns clear but AX is less than CX, a partial record has been read.

If this function fails, the return code is one of the standard error codes.

AH = 041H (65)   *Delete file*
INT 021H (33)   *Universal function*

Remove a file entry from the specified disk and directory path

Input
DS:DX = pointer to ASCIIZ string

Output
If function was successful:
  CF = cleared

If function was unsuccessful:
  CF = set
  AX = return code

Notes
A deleted file is not scrubbed from the disk. Deletion occurs by marking the directory entry and the used blocks as free. It may be possible to recover all or part of a deleted file if no subsequent disk activity has taken place.

Code	Standard Error	Code	Standard Error
00	Successful	16	Removing current directory
01	Invalid function number	17	Not same device
02	File not found	18	No more files to be found
03	Path not found	19	Disk is write-protected
04	No more handles available	20	Unknown disk
05	Access denied	21	Drive is not ready
06	Invalid handle	22	Unknown command
07	Bad memory control blocks	23	Data error (CRC)
08	Insufficient memory	24	Bad request length
09	Invalid memory block address	25	Seek error
10	Invalid environment	26	Unknown media type
11	Invalid format	27	Sector not found
12	Invalid access code	28	Printer out of paper
13	Invalid data	29	Write fault
14	Not used	30	Read fault
15	Invalid drive specification	31	General failure

AH = 042H (66)
INT 021H (33)

Position file pointer
Universal function

Set the position of subsequent file access within a file

Input

AL = method code
BX = file handle
CX = most significant word of offset
DX = least significant word of offset

Output

If function was successful:

CF = cleared
DX = most significant word of new pointer location
AX = least significant word of new pointer location

If function was unsuccessful:

CF = set
AX = return code

Notes

Method	Meaning
0	Absolute byte offset from beginning of file
1	Relative byte offset from current position
2	Absolute byte offset from end of file

The next record written or read will be at the file position set by this function.

Methods 1 and 2 can be used to set a position before the beginning of the file. Setting this position will not cause an error, but I/O operations on the file will fail.

The returned offset is always an absolute byte offset from the start of the file.

If this function fails, the return code is one of the standard error codes.

AH = 043H (67)
INT 021H (33)

Get/set file attributes

Universal function

Determine or modify the attribute of a file

Input

AL = (0, get attribute; 1, set attribute)
CX = new attribute
DS:DX = pointer to ASCIIZ string

Output

If function was successful:
CF = cleared
CX = old attribute if get

If function was unsuccessful:
CF = set
AX = return code

Notes

File Attribute	Meaning
00H	Normal
01H	Read-Only
02H	Hidden
04H	System

This function cannot be used to set a volume label; that must be done with an extended file control block function.

If this function fails, the return code is one of the standard error codes.

AH = 044H (68)
INT 021H (33)

I/O control for devices
Universal function

Direct I/O management for device access

Input

AL = subfunction code
BL = drive number
BX = file handle
CX = number of bytes to read or write

Output

If function was successful:
CF = cleared
AX = number of bytes transferred
DX = device information

If function was unsuccessful:
CF = set
AX = return code

Notes

Subfunction Code	Meaning
00	Get device information
01	Set device information
02	Read from control channel to buffer
03	Write from buffer to control channel
04	Read from block device to buffer
05	Write from buffer to block device
06	Get input status
07	Get output status

This function is used to manage general I/O to devices.

If performing ordinary file I/O rather than device I/O, only functions 00H, 06H, and 07H are valid. Reading and writing should be done by the appropriate handle functions.

If this function fails, the return code is one of the standard error codes.

AH = 045H (69)   *Duplicate file handle*
INT 021H (33)   *Universal function*

Create a copy of a currently opened file handle

Input
BX = file handle

Output

If function was successful:
CF = cleared
AX = file handle

If function was unsuccessful:
CF = set
AX = return code

Notes
Moving the file position of one of the duplicated handles will cause the position of the other to be changed as well.

This function causes the file information in the directory to be updated. One use might be to duplicate a file descriptor and then close the duplicate, forcing an update to the directory without affecting the originally opened file.

Code	Standard Error	Code	Standard Error
00	Successful	16	Removing current directory
01	Invalid function number	17	Not same device
02	File not found	18	No more files to be found
03	Path not found	19	Disk is write-protected
04	No more handles available	20	Unknown disk
05	Access denied	21	Drive is not ready
06	Invalid handle	22	Unknown command
07	Bad memory control blocks	23	Data error (CRC)
08	Insufficient memory	24	Bad request length
09	Invalid memory block address	25	Seek error
10	Invalid environment	26	Unknown media type
11	Invalid format	27	Sector not found
12	Invalid access code	28	Printer out of paper
13	Invalid data	29	Write fault
14	Not used	30	Read fault
15	Invalid drive specification	31	General failure

AH = 046H (70)
INT 021H (33)

Overwrite handle

Universal function

Make two dissimilar file handles point to the same file and position

Input
BX = existing file handle
CX = second file handle

Output
If function was successful:
CF = cleared
BX = original file handle
CX = duplicate of original file handle

If function was unsuccessful:
CF = set
AX = return code

Notes
Moving the file position of one of the duplicated handles causes the position of the other to be changed as well.

If the file handle in CX is already open, the file will be closed before duplication occurs.

Code	Standard Error	Code	Standard Error
00	Successful	16	Removing current directory
01	Invalid function number	17	Not same device
02	File not found	18	No more files to be found
03	Path not found	19	Disk is write-protected
04	No more handles available	20	Unknown disk
05	Access denied	21	Drive is not ready
06	Invalid handle	22	Unknown command
07	Bad memory control blocks	23	Data error (CRC)
08	Insufficient memory	24	Bad request length
09	Invalid memory block address	25	Seek error
10	Invalid environment	26	Unknown media type
11	Invalid format	27	Sector not found
12	Invalid access code	28	Printer out of paper
13	Invalid data	29	Write fault
14	Not used	30	Read fault
15	Invalid drive specification	31	General failure

AH = 047H (71)
INT 021H (33)

Get current directory
Universal function

Determine the path to the current directory for a particular disk drive

Input
    DL = drive ID
    DS:SI = pointer to data area

Output
If function was successful:
    CF = cleared
    DS:SI = pointer to pathname string

If function was unsuccessful:
    CF = set
    AX = return code

Notes
Drive IDs are numeric, following the drive letters (drive A: has a drive ID of 1, drive B:=2, drive C:=3, and so on). A drive ID of zero indicates that the default drive is to be used.

Be aware that some disk-related functions use drive ID 0 as drive A: in those cases when the concept of a default drive is not supported.

The returned pathname is relative to the root directory of the current disk. It does not contain a leading "\". Thus, if the current directory is the root directory, the pathname is zero length.

If this function fails, the return code is one of the standard error codes.

AH = 048H (72)
INT 021H (33)

Allocate memory
Universal function

Allocate a block of memory and return a pointer to that block

Input
BX = memory requested in paragraphs

Output
If function was successful:
CF = cleared
AX = segment address

If function was unsuccessful:
CF = set
AX = return code
BX = largest block size available

Notes
The base address of the allocated memory is 0000H. Thus, the complete address of the start of the buffer is AX:0000.

If the memory allocation fails, BX contains the largest block of memory available for allocation.

Code	Standard Error	Code	Standard Error
00	Successful	16	Removing current directory
01	Invalid function number	17	Not same device
02	File not found	18	No more files to be found
03	Path not found	19	Disk is write-protected
04	No more handles available	20	Unknown disk
05	Access denied	21	Drive is not ready
06	Invalid handle	22	Unknown command
07	Bad memory control blocks	23	Data error (CRC)
08	Insufficient memory	24	Bad request length
09	Invalid memory block address	25	Seek error
10	Invalid environment	26	Unknown media type
11	Invalid format	27	Sector not found
12	Invalid access code	28	Printer out of paper
13	Invalid data	29	Write fault
14	Not used	30	Read fault
15	Invalid drive specification	31	General failure

AH = 049H (73)   *Free allocated memory*
INT 021H (33)   *Universal function*

Release a block of memory to the free memory pool

Input
ES = segment block to return

Output

If function was successful:
CF = cleared

If function was unsuccessful:
CF = set
AX = return code

Notes

The memory block released must have been allocated by INT 21H function
48H *(allocate memory)*.

Code	Standard Error	Code	Standard Error
00	Successful	16	Removing current directory
01	Invalid function number	17	Not same device
02	File not found	18	No more files to be found
03	Path not found	19	Disk is write-protected
04	No more handles available	20	Unknown disk
05	Access denied	21	Drive is not ready
06	Invalid handle	22	Unknown command
07	Bad memory control blocks	23	Data error (CRC)
08	Insufficient memory	24	Bad request length
09	Invalid memory block address	25	Seek error
10	Invalid environment	26	Unknown media type
11	Invalid format	27	Sector not found
12	Invalid access code	28	Printer out of paper
13	Invalid data	29	Write fault
14	Not used	30	Read fault
15	Invalid drive specification	31	General failure

AH = 04AH (74) *Modify memory allocation*
INT 021H (33) *Universal function*

Change the size of an allocated block

Input
BX = requested size in paragraphs
ES = segment address of block

Output
If function was successful:
CF = cleared

If function was unsuccessful:
CF = set
AX = return code
BX = maximum possible size

Notes
The memory block modified must have been allocated by INT 21H function 48H *(allocate memory)*.

If the memory reallocation fails, BX contains the largest block of memory available for reallocation.

Code	Standard Error	Code	Standard Error
00	Successful	16	Removing current directory
01	Invalid function number	17	Not same device
02	File not found	18	No more files to be found
03	Path not found	19	Disk is write-protected
04	No more handles available	20	Unknown disk
05	Access denied	21	Drive is not ready
06	Invalid handle	22	Unknown command
07	Bad memory control blocks	23	Data error (CRC)
08	Insufficient memory	24	Bad request length
09	Invalid memory block address	25	Seek error
10	Invalid environment	26	Unknown media type
11	Invalid format	27	Sector not found
12	Invalid access code	28	Printer out of paper
13	Invalid data	29	Write fault
14	Not used	30	Read fault
15	Invalid drive specification	31	General failure

AH = 04BH (75)   *Execute program*
INT 021H (33)   *Universal function*

Load and execute a secondary program, returning control when that program ends

Input

    AL = subfunction code
    DS:DX = pointer to ASCIIZ string
    ES:BX = pointer to parameter block

Output

If function was successful:
    CF = cleared

If function was unsuccessful:
    CF = set
    AX = return code

Notes

This is an extremely powerful and complicated function. It is also one that is extremely difficult and dangerous to use from within a resident application. A complete explanation of this is beyond the scope of this summary. See the *IBM DOS Manual* for full details.

Code	Standard Error	Code	Standard Error
00	Successful	16	Removing current directory
01	Invalid function number	17	Not same device
02	File not found	18	No more files to be found
03	Path not found	19	Disk is write-protected
04	No more handles available	20	Unknown disk
05	Access denied	21	Drive is not ready
06	Invalid handle	22	Unknown command
07	Bad memory control blocks	23	Data error (CRC)
08	Insufficient memory	24	Bad request length
09	Invalid memory block address	25	Seek error
10	Invalid environment	26	Unknown media type
11	Invalid format	27	Sector not found
12	Invalid access code	28	Printer out of paper
13	Invalid data	29	Write fault
14	Not used	30	Read fault
15	Invalid drive specification	31	General failure

AH = 04CH (76)   *Terminate program*
INT 021H (33)   *Universal function*

Release control to DOS or a parent program, returning an exit code

Input

AL = return code

Output

None

Notes

This is the approved way for a DOS application to terminate. Advanced versions of DOS prefer that an application return an exit code.

DOS terminates the program, releases the memory used by that program, and then performs the following operations:

- Restores the termination-handler vector from 000AH in the program segment prefix

- Restores the CONTROL-C handler from 000EH in the program segment prefix

- Restores the critical-error handler from 0012H in the program segment prefix

- Flushes all pending file buffers

Finally, control is transferred to the termination-handler address, which then returns to DOS.

If this function fails, the return code is one of the standard error codes.

AH = 04DH (77)
INT 021H (33)

Get return code

Universal function

Determine the return code of a terminated child program

Input
None

Output
AX = return code

Notes
Use this function after an EXEC, to determine the return code of a subprogram.

The function is destructive, in that the return code cannot be read repeatedly.

Code	Standard Error	Code	Standard Error
00	Successful	16	Removing current directory
01	Invalid function number	17	Not same device
02	File not found	18	No more files to be found
03	Path not found	19	Disk is write-protected
04	No more handles available	20	Unknown disk
05	Access denied	21	Drive is not ready
06	Invalid handle	22	Unknown command
07	Bad memory control blocks	23	Data error (CRC)
08	Insufficient memory	24	Bad request length
09	Invalid memory block address	25	Seek error
10	Invalid environment	26	Unknown media type
11	Invalid format	27	Sector not found
12	Invalid access code	28	Printer out of paper
13	Invalid data	29	Write fault
14	Not used	30	Read fault
15	Invalid drive specification	31	General failure

AH = 04EH (78)
INT 021H (33)

Search for first match
Universal function

Find a file matching a search pattern in the specified directory

Input
CX = attribute to search on
DS:DX = pointer to ASCIIZ string

Output
AX = return code

Notes

File Attribute	Meaning
00H	Normal
01H	Read-Only
02H	Hidden
04H	System

This function must be called with a valid disk transfer area.

Code	Standard Error	Code	Standard Error
00	Successful	16	Removing current directory
01	Invalid function number	17	Not same device
02	File not found	18	No more files to be found
03	Path not found	19	Disk is write-protected
04	No more handles available	20	Unknown disk
05	Access denied	21	Drive is not ready
06	Invalid handle	22	Unknown command
07	Bad memory control blocks	23	Data error (CRC)
08	Insufficient memory	24	Bad request length
09	Invalid memory block address	25	Seek error
10	Invalid environment	26	Unknown media type
11	Invalid format	27	Sector not found
12	Invalid access code	28	Printer out of paper
13	Invalid data	29	Write fault
14	Not used	30	Read fault
15	Invalid drive specification	31	General failure

AH = 04FH (79)

INT 021H (33)

Search for next match
Universal function

Find the next matching filename in the specified directory

Input
DS:DX = information from first FIND call

Output
AX = return code

Notes
This function assumes that a successful call to INT 21H function 4EH *(search for first match)*.

Code	Standard Error	Code	Standard Error
00	Successful	16	Removing current directory
01	Invalid function number	17	Not same device
02	File not found	18	No more files to be found
03	Path not found	19	Disk is write-protected
04	No more handles available	20	Unknown disk
05	Access denied	21	Drive is not ready
06	Invalid handle	22	Unknown command
07	Bad memory control blocks	23	Data error (CRC)
08	Insufficient memory	24	Bad request length
09	Invalid memory block address	25	Seek error
10	Invalid environment	26	Unknown media type
11	Invalid format	27	Sector not found
12	Invalid access code	28	Printer out of paper
13	Invalid data	29	Write fault
14	Not used	30	Read fault
15	Invalid drive specification	31	General failure

050H (80)   *Not Used*
INT 021H (33)   *Universal function*

051H (81)   *Not Used*
INT 021H (33)   *Universal function*

052H (82)   *Not Used*
INT 021H (33)   *Universal function*

053H (83)   *Not Used*
INT 021H (33)   *Universal function*

AH = 054H (84)   *Get verify state*
INT 021H (33)   *Universal function*

Determine whether the system is performing read-after-write disk verification

Input
  None

Output
  AL = verify state (0 off; 1 on)

Notes
Verification happens by reading back the data just written, and comparing that result with the data that was *supposed* to have been written. Verification slows down access to the file system, but may increase reliability.

055H (85)

INT 021H (33)

Not Used

Universal function

AH = 056H (86)   *Rename file*
INT 021H (33)   *Universal function*

Change the name of a file, changing its location on the current disk if necessary

Input

DS:DX = pointer to ASCIIZ string (old name)
ES:DI = pointer to ASCIIZ string (new name)

Output

If function was successful:
    CF = cleared

If function was unsuccessful:
    CF = set
    AX = return code

Notes

Wildcard specifiers cannot be used in the old or the new names.

Code	Standard Error	Code	Standard Error
00	Successful	16	Removing current directory
01	Invalid function number	17	Not same device
02	File not found	18	No more files to be found
03	Path not found	19	Disk is write-protected
04	No more handles available	20	Unknown disk
05	Access denied	21	Drive is not ready
06	Invalid handle	22	Unknown command
07	Bad memory control blocks	23	Data error (CRC)
08	Insufficient memory	24	Bad request length
09	Invalid memory block address	25	Seek error
10	Invalid environment	26	Unknown media type
11	Invalid format	27	Sector not found
12	Invalid access code	28	Printer out of paper
13	Invalid data	29	Write fault
14	Not used	30	Read fault
15	Invalid drive specification	31	General failure

AH = 057H (87)
INT 021H (33)

File date and time

Universal function

Read or modify the timestamp on a file

Input

AL = 0 to get; 1 to set
BX = file handle if setting
CX = time
DX = date

Output

AX = return code
CX = time
DX = date

Notes

This function requires that the handle be opened by INT 21H function 3CH *(create file)* or INT 21H function 3DH *(open file)*

Bit pattern in CX	Meaning
FEDCBA9876543210	
DDDDDxxxxxxxxxxx	Hours (0-23)
xxxxxHHHHHHxxxxx	Minutes (0-59)
xxxxxxxxxxxSSSSS	2-second increments (0-29)

Bit pattern in DX	Meaning
FEDCBA9876543210	
YYYYYYYxxxxxxxxx	Year (relative to 1980)
xxxxxxxMMMMxxxxx	Month (0-12)
xxxxxxxxxxxDDDDD	Day (0-31)

INT 022H (34)   *Termination handler*

Address of the code that handles program exit

Input

None

Output

None

Notes

Never execute this interrupt directly.

The address stored here is copied to the program segment prefix of the currently executing program.

This code manages an orderly transition between the code that is currently running and that has requested termination and DOS or the previously running program that started the current program by the INT 21H function 4BH *(execute program)* function.

INT 023H (35)   CONTROL-C *handler*

Address of the code that handles a CONTROL-C interrupt

Input

None

Output

None

Notes

Never execute this interrupt directly.

The address stored here is copied to the program segment prefix of the currently executing program.

The code this vector points at manages the error condition that occurs when a CONTROL-C or a CONTROL-BREAK is typed.

INT 024H (36)   *Critical error handler*

Address of the code that handles hardware errors

Input

> *None*

Output

> *None*

Notes

Never execute this interrupt directly.

The address stored here is copied to the program segment prefix of the currently executing program.

This code manages the error condition that occurs because of a hardware error, such as a not-ready disk, or no paper in the printer. Its purpose is to provide a method for gracefully exiting or returning control to the program after the error has been corrected.

INT 025H (37) *Absolute disk read*

Reads a logical disk sector into a buffer

Input
AL = drive ID
CX = number of sectors to read
DX = starting logical sector number
DS:BX = segment:offset of disk transfer area

Output
If function was successful:
CF = cleared

If function was unsuccessful:
CF = set
AX = return code

Notes
Drive IDs are numeric, following the drive letters (drive A: has a drive ID of 0, drive B:=1, drive C:=2, and so on).

Be aware that some disk-related functions use drive ID 1 as drive A: with drive ID 0 indicating the default drive.

Error Code	Meaning
01H	Bad command
02H	Bad address mark
03H	Write-protect fault
04H	Sector not found
08H	DMA failure
10H	CRC failure
20H	Controller failure
40H	Seek failure
80H	Attachment failure

INT 025H (37)   *Absolute disk write*

Write a buffer to a logical disk sector

Input

AL = drive ID
CX = number of sectors to write
DX = starting logical sector number
DS:BX = segment:offset of disk transfer area

Output

If function was successful:
CF = cleared

If function was unsuccessful:
CF = set
AX = error code

Notes

Drive IDs are numeric, following the drive letters (drive A: has a drive ID of 0, drive B:=1, drive C:=2, and so on).

Be aware that some disk-related functions use drive ID 1 as drive A: with drive ID 0 indicating the default drive.

Error Code	Meaning
01H	Bad command
02H	Bad address mark
03H	Write-protect fault
04H	Sector not found
08H	DMA failure
10H	CRC failure
20H	Controller failure
40H	Seek failure
80H	Attachment failure

INT 027H (39)   *Terminate and stay resident*

Terminates the current program, returning control to DOS without releasing some or all of the memory allocated for that program

Input
DX = offset of last byte + 1 of memory to remain
CS = segment of memory to remain

Output
None

Notes
The heart of this book. It causes the current program to exit, without returning all of the memory used to the system pool.

The maximum amount of memory that can be retained with this call is 64 kilobytes.

This interrupt should be called only from .COM files. The load allocation of .EXE files must be explicitly managed by the programmer. .COM files are automatically constructed to load correctly.

Appendix D

Useful Books

A book like this one is not written in a vacuum. There are many books about DOS and IBM PCs on the market. This appendix lists the ones that were referred to in the creation of this book.

Probably the singularly most useful book was *Advanced MS-DOS* by Ray Duncan (Microsoft Press, 1986). This book contains many useful and interesting pieces of information and was invaluable in decoding some of the more cryptic aspects of the IBM PC. A must for every assembly-language programmer.

Another extremely useful book is the *Programmer's Guide to the IBM PC*, by Peter Norton (Microsoft Press, 1985). This book covers some issues that *Advanced MS-DOS* skips. Both books are more readable than the DOS manuals.

Sometimes, however, the DOS manuals are the only source of information. The *IBM-PC Technical Reference Manual* is available from IBM dealers. It is extremely cryptic and difficult to follow, but sometimes it is the only source of information on some important issues.

Finally, the *IBM Disk Operating System Manual* and the *IBM Macro Assembler Manual* are sure to be your constant companions during any attempt at writing assembly-language code. Both are included with their respective products.

Index